The Origin & Demise of Satan

Or The Beginning & End of Satan,
Devil, Serpent, Dragon or Evil

Jacob Poelman

Editor: Johanna Smelik

authorHOUSE®

AuthorHouse™
1663 Liberty Drive
Bloomington, IN 47403
www.authorhouse.com
Phone: 1-800-839-8640

First published by AuthorHouse   2/23/2010

ISBN: 978-1-4490-0297-8 (e)
ISBN: 978-1-4490-0295-4 (sc)
ISBN: 978-1-4490-0296-1 (hc)

Library of Congress Control Number: 2009910193

Printed in the United States of America
Bloomington, Indiana

This book is printed on acid-free paper.

Contents

INTRODUCTION

This book is based upon the expectation that the spiritual return (presence) of Jesus the Christ is to result in the elimination of sin and death during the thousand years of his Kingdom. Also, because Jesus the Christ paid the ransom for Adam and all his children, all born into this world are of Adam, as stated in 1 Corinthians:

> "For as in Adam all die, even so in Christ shall all be made alive." —1 Corinthians 15:22

That the return of Jesus the Christ is of the spirit, recognized by fast travel and a tremendous increase of knowledge in every field of human activity, pictured as the four winds of religious, social, financial and political powers, as prophesied in Revelation:

> "And after these things I saw four angels (messages) standing (calling out) on the four corners (support of social order) of the earth (society), holding the four winds (intensity of religious, financial, social, and political powers) of the earth (society), that the wind (influence) should not blow

(destroy) on the earth (society), nor on the sea (people), nor on any tree (person)." —Revelation 7:1

That the destruction of the world is not by literal fire, but that its destruction is symbolic of fiery troubling times, which gradually brings about removal of evil from the hearts of people through the increase of knowledge, which inspires demands for liberty, human rights, truth, justice, mercy, righteousness and the like. These increasing fruits of the spirit such as love, joy, peace, kindness, patience, and so forth reflect the spiritual presence in the hearts of people of Jesus the Christ, the spirit of the Lord at work as truth overcomes evil: love eliminates hate, knowledge replaces ignorance, and mercy alleviates poverty of mind and body.

The above statements echo Bible prophecy, which, translated from Hebrew and Greek, are not always clear to the average reader. Prophecy can transcend centuries of human activity, from the time of Adam and Eve to the end of the Kingdom of Jesus the Christ. Attentive Christians will discern that Bible prophecy harmonizes and corroborates all topics such as the Judgment Day, hell, the soul, the Lord's return, and Satan. Harmonious interpretation of prophecy then reveals God's justice and love for mankind, for "God is love." Therefore, a doctrine that claims billions of people face eternal torment when they never had the chance to hear of Jesus the Christ, the world's savior, or, having heard during the reign of evil, failed to understand the message, is false. The Apostle John wrote:

> *"He that loves not knows not God; for God is love."* —1 *John 4:8, KJV*

The Living Bible, Paraphrased says:

"But if a person isn't loving and kind, it shows he doesn't know God—for God is love."

Over the centuries, people in most nations have never had the opportunity to hear of salvation in Jesus the Christ; they did not hear of the Bible or that God is love, and therefore Christians might wonder why the Apostle John's statement does not harmonize with conventional beliefs of a Satan or eternal torment. So, the question to answer is: why would the Bible seem to project the idea to Christians that non-Christians face eternity suffering torment in a fiery hell? Or why does the Bible imply it is God's plan for mankind to have judgment under the reign of Jesus the Christ when unbelievers are already destined for eternal torment?

Another question: the Bible speaks often of the Kingdom of God coming upon earth, so why have the majority of Christians emphasized eternal heavenly existence for loved ones who have died, but ignored the times of restitution upon earth, when all in their graves are to be resurrected and judged, which, as the prophet Isaiah wrote, involves a trial period of approximately a hundred years for each?

> *"There shall be no more thence an infant of days, nor an old man that hath not filled his days: for the child shall die an hundred years old; but the sinner [being] an hundred years old shall be accursed." —Isaiah 65:20*

We can be assured that God's objective for humanity living upon earth has not changed; so what are the answers? Living in the times of the greatest increase of knowledge in human history, we are very fortunate that, as Christians, we can search for and understand the truth, which often conflicts with traditional concepts of doctrine and prophecy. The increase of knowledge leads to examination of man's doctrines, some of which are remnants of Christendom's Dark Ages that enforced ignorance and fear. But why is this happening? The answer appears to be that, during the Gospel Age, in order to retain or attain power over people or nations and to attract and control followers, religious leaders often did evil and misapplied Scripture to their advantage, and, in so doing, distorted and sullied the character of our Creator.

The doctrines of Judgment Day, hell, the immortal soul, the Lord's return, and Satan have one thing in common: all of these topics have suffered misinterpretation and misapplication as a result of fear, ignorance, superstition, power, and greed—all manifestations of evil in the hearts of men. Living in the Day of Enlightenment, the spirit of truth, righteousness, justice, and mercy, through the increase of knowledge, is bringing change upon earth during which God is in the process of judging Christendom and the nations as the Millennium, Thousand Years, Judgment Day, or Kingdom of Jesus the Christ progresses in righteousness in most people.

Many within Christendom do not perceive how the Kingdom of God is to materialize upon earth, or that God's Kingdom, under the stimuli of the spirit of righteousness, justice, love, and mercy, is progressively increasing daily, being reflected in the hearts of ever greater numbers of people (both religious and non-religious) who desire to live peacefully in a spirit of co-operation, justice, righteousness, and mercy, seeking that which is healthy and beneficial to all. In other words, the materializing of God's Kingdom does not require belief or acceptance of Jesus the Christ in its initial phase or its initial manifestation, but, in due time, to attain life eternal upon earth, it will require belief and acceptance by repentant minds motivated towards perfection in mind and body through knowledge of Jesus the Christ, the world's savior.

The Bible speaks of a grand and glorious future for those who love God, but the Bible also is emphatic that all the wicked will be destroyed. It is the objective of this book to show what this means for the reader and indeed for all the living, plus those who have lived upon this wonder-filled planet. In other words, prophecy directs us in the spirit of truth and context of reason to realize it is our responsibility to not allow feelings of lust, hate, jealousy, envy, and so forth to motivate our words and actions, and that we are at fault for the evil thoughts we conceive in our hearts and minds and then put into action. We are to put aside the traditional idea of Satan or Devil held by Christians in earlier ages (including translators), who, under the darkness of superstition and ignorance, interpreted the idioms or picture language of the prophets, our Lord, and the apostles to justify their fears and speculations that evil, which people conceive, is inspired by an "evil spirit being."

Today, in increasing ways, righteousness, justice, love, and mercy are making headway as people are learning to look for these qualities in self, others, and leaders. Also, increasing numbers of Christians, searching for truth, are whittling away at the errors and falsehoods that have burdened submissive believers over the centuries while powerful, zealous religious leaders, seminary-trained according to their belief system, continue to 'evangelize' their followers with Dark Age concepts while ignoring the revelation of truth that brings harmony to Scripture and prophecy.

In the public environment, we often see religious, political, medical, and commercial leaders failing the trust of the people, an indication that the Kingdom of Jesus the Christ does not dawn upon the earth without evil or lust persisting in the hearts of people who take advantage of others while ignoring justice, righteousness, and mercy. In contrast, we see Christians and adherents of most religions, even atheists, display unison in the spirit of righteousness and justice working together to make a better world.

The knowledge of what salvation entails is not commonly recognized, because tradition, creeds, rituals, entertainment, greed, and superstition form a greater attraction to people than the wonderful truth of God's plan through Jesus the Christ. Although many Christians find it difficult to accept non-traditional teachings, it can be spiritually beneficial to reason upon Scripture and history that challenges traditional concepts. Scriptures are to support the objective God has for all the families of the earth, past, present, and future.

This author encourages searching Scripture and history to provide harmonious answers as to who is responsible for evil based upon fact, reality, and truth while avoiding superstition, tradition, and erroneous belief. Today, the world, long under the influence of evil from the heart of man, is in the throes of massive change as the Gospel Age metamorphoses into the Kingdom of God. The hearts of many people, through the increase of knowledge, are progressively learning righteousness, justice, love, and truth. This education, through increasing knowledge, is assisted by the cutting edge of technology that helps reduce or eliminates fear, sorrow, guilt, greed, hate, and prejudice, etc., while learning righteousness, justice, mercy, liberty, peace, and love towards God and one another. The learning of righteousness is making its imprint upon the minds (or hearts) of increasing numbers of people; in comparison, recorded history (religious and secular) reveals how the limitation of knowledge (ignorance) in every aspect has brought harm and destruction.

The world of today is still suffering from the heavy dose of ignorance, fears, and prejudices carried over from past generations, but various sectors of societies (hundreds of beneficial organizations, financial, mental, medical, physical, and religious) have and are developing methods to combat the evils that plague mankind and to improve the well being of all. The darkness of evil conceived in the minds of men has brought nation against nation, religion against religion, and neighbor against neighbor, but conditions are changing as the inauguration of the Kingdom of Jesus the Christ takes place, the development of a ruling power over the earth of righteousness and justice. Signs of this are seen in that myths and traditions that promote spiritual emptiness are being questioned and rooted out—if you don't believe so, check out the Internet on any subject.

Bible prophecy may be interpreted differently in this book than what the reader is accustomed to. The interpretation of the prophecy of Isaiah may be an example, with words in parentheses to aid understanding.

> *"And in this mountain (government, kingdom) shall the LORD of hosts make unto all people (of every nation) a feast of fat things (abundant knowledge), a feast of wines (factual, doctrinal truths) on the lees (strong faith), of fat things full of marrow (life-giving knowledge), of wines on the lees well refined (truthful doctrine, consistent and harmonious)." —Isaiah 25:6*

Paraphrased from the 'Living Bible, we read:

> *"Here on Mount Zion in Jerusalem (God's Kingdom), the Lord of Hosts will spread a wondrous feast (abundant knowledge) for everyone around the world—a delicious (desirable) feast of good food (abundant, life-building truth), with clear, well-aged wine (undefiled doctrine) and choice beef (harmonious truths)."*

If you read something that you disagree with in this book, listen to your feelings to analyze their source, whether it is dislike, prejudice, anger, distrust, etc, that may surface. Can you determine where it comes from and how you can keep it under control? Surely, if the feeling is negative, an evil spirit being didn't cause it. Hopefully, what is offered in this lengthy introduction will inspire you to read the rest of the book in order to perceive the loving direction God provides to salvation. Do not allow your mind to be tied to tradition, but look for harmonious answers, both Scriptural and historical, that point to deliverance from sin and condemnation. Remember; God is love, not a God of vindictiveness or injustice; as Isaiah encouragingly wrote:

"They shall not hurt nor destroy in all my holy mountain: for the earth shall be full of the knowledge of the LORD, as the waters cover the sea." —Isaiah 11:9

This author has made every effort to present a harmonious perspective as to what the fulfillment of prophecy means for all who are living and who have lived upon this wonder-filled planet. In other words, prophecy directs us to truth in the context of reason, hope, and the justice of God's love; however, it is the individual's responsibility not to allow feelings of lust, hate, jealousy, envy, and so forth to motivate his or her words and actions, for we are responsible for the evil works conceived in our mind and acted upon. We are obligated to steer clear of the traditional idea that "evil spirit beings" initiate evil. It seems that believers in earlier ages, under the darkness of superstition, fear, and ignorance erringly interpreted symbolic words of the prophets, Jesus the Christ, and the apostles to justify their fears and superstitions that evil spirit beings are responsible for evil conceived in the heart's of men.

Today, in increasing ways, righteousness, justice, love, and mercy makes headway as people look to these qualities in self, in others, and from leaders. Also, greater numbers of Christians, searching for truth, are whittling away the errors and falsehoods that have burdened submissive believers over the centuries, who ignored revelations of truth that bring harmony to Scripture and prophesy. In the public environment, we see at times where religious, political, medical, and commercial leaders fail the trust of the people, an indication that the Kingdom of Jesus the Christ dawns upon the earth or that evil lingers in the mind's of some people, causing them to take advantage of others while ignoring justice, righteousness, and mercy.

The days are filled with challenges that often bring conflict within organizations and nations as citizens, in the spirit of liberty, truth, righteousness, justice, and mercy, endeavor to build a world society in which everyone will be respected and receive a fair share of the pie. We see leaders in various sectors of societies encouraging people to look for ways to lessen pollution, global warming, and crime. There is increasing cooperation in and among nations to control crime, provide for the needy, improve trade, and eliminate armaments and pollution. It is a time when the hearts of men in greater numbers recognize the need to reach out together so as to benefit everyone. These are signs that the commencement of God's Kingdom, in which the spirit of the Lord, working in the hearts of people, brings into existence the Kingdom of God.

An important point to keep in mind is that knowledge of what salvation entails is not commonly recognized because tradition, creeds, rituals, entertainment, greed, and superstition often have more attraction or justification to some people than the wonderful truth of God's plan of changing one's life by following Jesus the Christ. Although many Christians find it difficult to accept nontraditional teachings, some are willing to review and reason upon knowledge that challenges traditional concepts of Scripture that relate to restitution, resurrection, and judgment for the living and the dead. Hopefully, all readers of this book will develop a comforting perspective of why the changes in this world are to bring life without death, sickness, and evil in a society wherein dwells righteousness and justice.

Throughout this book, when the name 'Jesus' is used, it will be as 'Jesus the Christ'; the reason is that an angel or message to Joseph, in a dream in Matthew, said of Mary:

> *"And she shall bring forth a son, and you shall call his name JESUS." —Matthew 1:21*

"The name Jesus was given to our Lord, which in Hebrew means—'Help of Jehovah'" He is also referred to in the NT as the: *"Son of God; the Savior of men"*

Then in Matthew 16:16 we read:

> *"And Simon Peter answered and said, 'Thou art the Christ, the Son of the living God.'"*

The word 'Christ' is a title or epithet of Jesus, meaning 'Messiah' or 'to consecrate to office.' Messiah also means 'the anointed.' Thus, using the name and title "Jesus the Christ" helps the reader remember that our Lord's name has a separate meaning from his title or composition of his title. It is not something to start a new branch of Christianity over, but does offer the reader an understandable concept of what our Lord's name and title means; thus, we use the designation 'Jesus the Christ' as a reminder of its full meaning.

The names Satan, Devil, Serpent, and Dragon are capitalized, as they are names for evil as specified in the Book of Revelation, the prophecy from Jesus the Christ to John:

"And he laid hold on the Dragon, that old Serpent, which is the Devil, and Satan, and bound him a thousand years." —Revelation 20:2

Thanks be to God for His love and mercy to all mankind, which will be strongly revealed in due time, especially when the resurrection from the dead begins through His son: Jesus the Christ.

Jacob Poelman

INQUIRY CONCERNING EVIL

A preacher once said, "The Bible has undoubtedly endured greatest abuse and misunderstanding from rationalistic higher criticism and skepticism."

This may be so, but it also can happen that the Bible, investigated with rational criticism and skepticism, will bring forth revelation and inspiration. Over the centuries, critics and skeptics have experienced a changed life because the message of God's Word produced unexpected hope and trust within their hearts. Such inquiring minds have found the words of the prophets and apostles authentic and inspirational in that both writer and reader are motivated by God's spirit of justice, righteousness, love, and mercy. The apostle Peter understood this, saying:

> *"For no prophecy ever originated in human will, but men, under the influence of the Holy Spirit, spoke for God."* —2 Peter 1:21 (Gspd1)

It is my hope that in reading this book, you will allow its contents to be judged in a fair and reasonable manner, for the objective is to present a delightful perspective as to what the future holds for the world of mankind, both the living and the dead. Even skeptical minds, searching for answers to present life and future existence, can find the Bible inspirational, comforting, and a guide in the present, while offering strong hope and faith in the future, for it presents a logical and reasonable foundation for human existence in an all-encompassing scenario that not only covers man's creation and his experience with evil and death, but also the resurrection with restitution opportunity for life upon earth. Over a century ago, a well known pastor in his day offered a reasonable explanation for why God allowed evil, which has brought so much suffering and death. He wrote:

> "God first made his creatures acquainted with good, surrounding them with it in Eden; and afterward, as penalty for disobedience, he gave them a severe knowledge of evil. Expelled from Eden and deprived of fellowship with Him, God let them experience sickness, pain, and death, that they might thus forever know evil and the expediency and exceeding sinfulness of sin. By comparison of results they came to an appreciation and proper estimate of both 'And the Lord said: *Behold, the man is become as one of us, to know good and evil.*' ---Gen. 3:22 In this their posterity share, except that they first obtain their knowledge of evil, and cannot fully realize what good is until they experience it in the Millennium, as a result of their redemption by him who will then be their judge and King."

Some Christians have little desire to examine interpretations of Scripture if they are not in harmony with tradition. Hopefully, this book will help improve the reader's spiritual perception of Scriptural truths and increase overall knowledge of God's plan and purpose for this earth and humanity. A century ago, perception among Christians was unanimous that God allowed a powerful spirit being to become evil, who then enticed and converted other spirit beings into following the path of evil.

Thus, hordes of evil spirit beings were thought to exist to assist the powerful, evil spirit being called Satan to tempt people to sin. This long-held doctrine, based upon fear, will disappear under Kingdom conditions as the 'restitution of all things' continues to increase.

For now, the following question is to be addressed: Why would God create the human race with the ability to conceive good and evil, but also create an evil spirit being who conceives only evil to entice people into doing evil? In other words, is it necessary for an evil spirit being to tempt people into choosing evil if such emotions as lust, greed, anger, jealousy, envy, etc., triggered in the minds of people, give people the option to conceive evil or good? Why would it then be necessary to be plagued by enticements of an evil spirit being? Jeremiah reminds us that:

"The heart [is] deceitful above all [things], and desperately wicked: who can know it —Jeremiah 17:9

And the apostle James wrote:

"But every man (and woman) *is tempted, when he* (or she) *is drawn away of his* (or her) *own lust, and enticed."* —James 1:14

Isn't acting upon feelings of lust, hate, anger, envy, etc. a learned behavior? Otherwise, how is it that people are to learn righteousness? Also, why would God, in knowing the future, have a plan of salvation for humanity while supposedly sinful, "evil" angelic hosts are to be destroyed without a ransom or opportunity for salvation? Doesn't that concept indicate a double standard? God blesses us, if we have the interest, to perceive rational answers from the Bible to questions about God's wisdom, power, love, and justice.

There are many questions; for example, why do such names as Satan, Devil, Serpent, and Dragon produce frightening images in the minds of people? Has the Bible, in the context of man's fear, been misinterpreted to say that evil spirit beings exist to cause believers to do evil? Could it be that the human mind assumes or imagines that evil spirit beings exist in order to escape responsibility for sin? Why are books written to describe why and how evil spirit beings communicate with or cause harm to humans? Can an objective and rational investigation of Scripture bring forth enough evidence to convince unprejudiced, reasoning minds that fear of evil spirit beings over the centuries is psychological, mythical, and born of misinterpretation? Doesn't the Bible tell us it is God's purpose, through His son Jesus the Christ in his Kingdom, to bring blessings of restitution to humanity without fear of a Satan, Devil, Serpent, Dragon?

> *"And he laid hold on the dragon, that old serpent, which is the Devil, and Satan, and bound him a thousand years."*
> —Revelation 20:2

(Further explanation of this scripture is provided in this book.)

For many centuries, people have believed that temptation comes through the influence of evil spirit beings, even though the Bible and history of mankind overwhelmingly confirms that wicked thoughts and evil activity are conceived in the minds of people. The apostle Paul wrote:

> *"Now the works of the flesh are manifest, which are [these]; fornication, impurity, debauchery, idolatry, sorcery, enmities, quarrels, jealousies, resentments, altercations, factions, sects, envyings, inebrieties, revellings, and things similar to these: respecting which I tell you before, even as I previously told you, that they who practice such things*

shall not inherit God's Kingdom." —Galatians 5:19–21, Diaglott

(The Emphatic Diaglott; by Benjamin Wilson, an interlinear translation from Greek to English, is a word-for-word translation of the Vatican Manuscript #1209 and is well recognized among Bible students and scholars.)

In regards to works of the flesh, Paul also wrote:

> *"Let not sin therefore reign in your mortal body, that ye should obey it in the lusts thereof."*—Romans 6:12

This statement by the apostle points to evil as conceived and acted upon by people, not induced or inspired by evil spirit beings.

Paul also said:

> *"Study to show thyself approved unto God."* —2 Timothy 2:15

Wouldn't Paul's directive involve questioning the why and how of evil? The prophet Jeremiah wrote,

> *"I the LORD search the heart, [I] try the reins, even to give every man according to his ways, [and] according to the fruit of his doings."*—Jeremiah 17:1

God has created men and women with the ability to reason; to dream; to have visions and imagination; to do righteously; and to seek justice, love, and mercy. He allows them talents to be used for good, but He also created them with the ability to act upon such emotions as pride, anger, greed, fear, hate, ignorance, and superstition, which leads to choices between good and evil.

Thus, negative thoughts can lead to evil acts, a characteristic that has dominated the minds of many people; the Bible describes it as darkness in people.

Proverbs tells us:

> *"The way of the wicked [is] as darkness: they know not at what they stumble."* —Proverbs 4:19

Isaiah wrote:

> *"For, behold, the darkness shall cover the earth, and gross darkness the people."* —Isaiah 60:2

Thus, the word "darkness" depicts willfully wicked and ignorant thoughts that blank out the light of truth, justice, righteousness, and love. Under this darkness of wickedness and willful ignorance, descriptive names for evil were devised, such as Satan, Devil, Demon, Serpent, Dragon, and Lucifer—names invented by translators followed customary beliefs of the unknown and with fear-inspired superstitions that were projected as a persona or illusion of an evil spirit being who directs humans to think and act evil.

Interestingly, there's historical indication of how the principle of an "evil" spirit called a serpent, as first coming from Egyptian folklore, was accepted and brought along by the Hebrews in the Exodus, fortified under bondage in Babylon, became Satan and Devil, and was introduced into the Christian religion. Unfortunately, even today, after decades of enlightenment, to question the existence of a Satan and evil spirit beings meets strong resistance from traditional-minded Christians who forget or choose to ignore the fundamental reason why God has brought people into this world as told in Genesis:

"So God created man in his [own] image, in the image of God created he him; male and female created he them. And God blessed them, and God said unto them be fruitful, and multiply, and replenish the earth, and subdue it: and have dominion over the fish of the sea, and over the fowl of the air, and over every living thing that moves upon the earth."—Genesis 1:27–28

Then later in Jeremiah, centuries after evil was conceived and acted upon by Adam, we read:

"I the LORD search the heart, [I] try the reins, even to give every man according to his ways, [and] according to the fruit of his doings —Jeremiah 17:1

Today, signs abound that indicate that the increase of knowledge is changing an evil world into the Kingdom of Jesus the Christ. Though the activities of evil, wickedness, sin, immorality, injustice, etc. are headlined and focused upon, the spirit of justice and righteousness in the hearts of most people desire the end of evil, which has been predicted in a number of prophecies. One such prophecy is found in Psalms:

"Yea, all kings (heads of state) shall fall down (worship) before Him (God): all nations shall serve him. For He shall deliver the needy when he cries; the poor also, and [him] that hath no helper. He shall spare the poor and needy, and shall save the souls (lives) of the needy. He shall redeem their soul (life) from deceit and violence: and precious shall their blood be in his sight." —Psalms 72:11–14

This prophecy pictures the spirit of the Lord working in the hearts of people when they express compassion, justice, mercy, love, righteousness, truth, and the like. Since people are free, moral agents, they are able to choose between good and evil. However, over the centuries, evil, conceived and acted upon by humans, has been blamed on an evil spirit being. This belief has often induced people to exonerate themselves of personal responsibility for evil actions. But the increase of knowledge is changing this old belief. People now perceive in greater measure their responsibility for evil and blame their evil actions on poor choices rather than imaginary, evil spirit beings. Perceptive Christians are able to recognize that the increase of travel and of knowledge; prophesied by Daniel, is a major factor not only in eliminating the fear of Satan, but also in changing this world. The Prophet Daniel heard a voice say,

> *"But thou, O Daniel, shut up the words, and seal the book, [even] to the time of the end: many shall run to and fro, and knowledge shall be increased."*—Daniel 12:4

Thus, the tremendous increase of "running to and fro" (travel) and increase of knowledge throughout the world literally brings change to every culture. Consequently, increasing travel and knowledge are key aspects in people to learn to refrain from evil and to recognize the need for virtuous conditions in society. The Internet, satellites, television, radio, cell phones, mail, and publications are major inventions that not only communicate immorality, vice, and other evils, but also are instruments that conduct or are means of utilizing the virtues of righteousness, justice, love, truth, and mercy in the medical, religious, political, financial, or social context.

It is the growing exchange of information between people that escalates change and desire for good over evil, important criteria in the establishing of the Kingdom of God. The new restrictions by the US Congress regarding cigarette sales still allows people to make a choice in their health. Another example is that today's business and social system functions on trust; people trust one another to do what is expected or paid for. If trust evaporated from society, there would be total chaos. Banks would fail; governments would break down; people would stop relying on neighbors, financial gurus, doctors, and pastors. But, as knowledge increases, greater numbers of people find ways to trust, which often improves their lives and helps them avoid evil.

The rule of law and liberty operating through trust and cooperation can require years for this spirit or attitude to fully develop because people usually must feel convinced before they trust. The majority of people are still learning to trust their leaders thus, as knowledge increases, people learn how and who to trust, which reveals increasing, worldwide, pent-up desire and hope by many peace-seeking people for leadership in righteousness, truth, justice, and mercy. This comes about through knowledge and enlightenment of the spirit, which overcomes evil, Satan, Devil, Serpent, Dragon. There are exceptions to the rule, but as knowledge increases and communication grows, evil activity is facing unprecedented scrutiny under the spectrum of truth, righteousness, wisdom, justice, love, and mercy, which is the spirit of our Creator.

Over the centuries, these positive characteristics have been, and in many cases still are, overruled by the evils of greed, lust, hate, jealousy, envy, and the like. The black cloud of evil has been the major troubling, destructive dynamic throughout the world ever since Adam, but today we see increasing efforts for peace, justice, righteousness, love and mercy, of which Jesus the Christ, the apostles, and prophets prophesied, which is today, advancing in numerous societies. These virtuous efforts are intensifying and, in time, will purge from society the works of evil, for supporters and messengers of evil will learn and change or else disappear from society by their self-destructive attitudes.

9

Thus, gradually, a new world order is to materialize over the centuries (about nine hundred years), during which the Kingdom of our Lord is to increasingly cover the earth. This is seen in greater numbers of people looking for justice and righteousness from government and leaders. Knowledge and quick communication allow many movements for righteousness and justice to rise up, even as some people choose to destroy in order to attain power or control. This is still happening in some countries today. But, in God's due time, those choosing to continue in evil activity will build such a hardened character that it will be too difficult for them to overcome as the Kingdom grows. Thus, they will self-destruct, bringing upon their selves; the second death as the apostle John prophesied:

> *"But the fearful, and unbelieving, and the abominable, and murderers, and whoremongers, and sorcerers, and idolaters, and all liars, shall have their part in the lake (condemned) which burns with fire and brimstone (eternal destruction): which is the second death."* —Revelation 21:8

Or, as the apostle Paul wrote to the brethren at Ephesus:

> *"For this ye know, that no whoremonger, nor unclean person, nor covetous man, who is an idolater, hath any inheritance in the kingdom of Christ and of God."* —Ephesians 5:5

Today, we see changing religious, political, and business concepts and the spreading light of liberty, truth, righteousness, justice, and mercy. It's the process the Prophet Joel wrote of:

> *"And it shall come to pass afterward* (After the Gospel Age) *[that] I will pour out my spirit upon all flesh."* —Joel 2:28

God's spirit is being poured out; it started with the apostles and the faithful in Jesus the Christ during the Gospel Age, increases during his Kingdom. Another prophecy of Joel is also being fulfilled:

> *"I will also gather all nations (UN), and will bring them down into the valley of Jehoshaphat (decision), and will plead with them there for my people and [for] my heritage Israel, whom they have scattered among the nations, and parted my land."*   —Joel 3:2

Isaiah also wrote of today, as the Day of Judgment, in which the learning of righteousness changes the world:

> *"With my soul have I desired Thee in the night; yea, with my spirit within me will I seek Thee early: for <u>when Thy judgments [are] in the earth (societies)</u>, the inhabitants of the world <u>will learn righteousness</u>."*   —Isaiah 26:9

Over the centuries, the powerful effects of evil have brought extreme cruelty and destruction among humanity as religious leadership blamed man's wickedness on an imagined, evil spirit being. Religious leaders have staunchly claimed that a Satan instigates evil in the human mind. Today, some Christians still ignorantly insist that belief in a Satan is necessary for salvation even as they oppose investigation of this cunning doctrine. But this false and deceitful delusion of an evil spirit being called Satan, Devil, Serpent, and Dragon will vanish as knowledge increases and evil is overcome. This is the battle of Armageddon, a battle between good and evil, which tests individuals, institutions, and nations as the increase of knowledge pits truth against falsehood, love against hate, liberty against bondage, and liberality against greed. The Psalmist describes the battle:

> *"For the LORD knows the way of the righteous: but the way of the ungodly (evil or wickedness) shall perish."*
> —Psalms 1:6

The writer of Ecclesiastes said:

> *"For God shall bring every work into judgment, with every secret thing, whether [it be] good, or whether [it be] evil."* —Ecclesiastes 12:14

The apostle Peter advised:

> *"For he that will love life, and see good days, let him refrain his tongue from evil, and his lips that they speak no guile."* —1 Peter 3:10

The Prophet Ezekiel wrote:

> *"I will seek that which was lost, and bring again that which was driven away, and will bind up [that which was] broken, and will strengthen that which was sick: but I will destroy the fat (greedy) and the strong (powerful); I will feed them with judgment."* —Ezekiel 34:16

The apostle Paul warned:

> *"For we must all appear before the judgment seat of Christ (the Church or chosen are judged during the Gospel Age, the rest of mankind as the Kingdom materializes in power); that every one may receive the things [done] in [his] body (during restitution or Judgment Day) according to that he hath done (during the Judgment Day), whether [it be] good or bad."* —2 Corinthians 5:10

It is often said that the Bible is like a violin, as any tune can be played from it. This easily happens when Scripture, meant as pictorial, is viewed as literal, or vice versa. The reader is then at risk of developing a concept out of harmony with God's fundamental plan, which is promised in the following verses:

> *"And I will bless them that bless thee, and curse him that curses thee: and in thee (Abraham; Jews, and Arabs) shall all families (everyone born) of the earth be blessed."*— Genesis 12:3

In Psalms:

> *"And blessed [be] His glorious name for ever: and let the whole earth be filled [with] his glory; Amen, and Amen."*—Psalms 72:19

In Ecclesiastes:

> *"[One] generation passes away, and [another] generation comes: but the earth abides for ever."* —Ecclesiastes 1:4

Peter prophesied in Acts:

> *"Whom the heaven (religion) must receive until the times of restitution of all things, which God hath spoken by the mouth of all His holy prophets since the world began."* —Acts 3:21

And the apostle John in Revelation:

> *"And God shall wipe away all tears from their eyes; and there shall be no more death, neither sorrow, nor crying, neither shall there be any more pain: for the former (evil) things are passed away."* —Revelation 21:4

The above statements of the prophets and apostles must be kept in mind; otherwise the picture language of 2 Peter, quoted below, presents a scenario of the earth being destroyed by literal fire, which would change the objective of our Creator. Therefore, we are to look for harmonious explanations, which is done by understanding the idioms of the language or of the culture, which then helps us understand the intent and meaning of Scripture as used in the following prophecy (interpretation help is in bold and parentheses):

> *"But the day (Judgment) of the LORD will come as a thief in the night (unaware); in the which the heavens (evil in religion) shall pass away with a great noise (conflict), and the elements (creeds, doctrines, rituals, and evil) shall melt (dissolve) with fervent heat (controversy), the earth (evil society) also and the works (wickedness) that are therein shall be burned up (destroyed)."* —2 Peter 3:10

A literal interpretation of the above verse would not harmonize with previous scriptures or with the following two verses that speak of the earth being filled with knowledge of the Lord and people being judged in righteousness:

> *"For the earth (society) shall be filled with the knowledge of the glory of the LORD, as the waters cover the sea."* —Habakkuk 2:14

> *"But the LORD shall endure for ever: He hath prepared His throne for judgment. And He shall judge the world* **(society)** *in righteousness; He shall minister judgment to the people in uprightness. The LORD also will be a refuge for the oppressed, a refuge in times of trouble."* —Psalms 9:7–9

Emerging of the Kingdom

Prophecy is to be in harmony with other prophecy so as to present a unified vision of God's intent upon earth where societies are to function relative to His wisdom, justice, love, and power, the attributes that also guided our Lord Jesus the Christ in his mission of declaring the Good News and in giving his life as a ransom for all. The gift of his life, as a ransom for all, has opened the way for those who hear and are faithful in the Gospel Age, that is, the Church or faithful believers, and then the rest of mankind during restitution and resurrection, who learn of Jesus the Christ as their Savior, repent of their sins, seek righteousness and justice, and love their neighbor as themselves.

This has been the command of the Lord to his followers during the Gospel Age as they suffered adversity under the reign of evil, which tested their faithfulness. For the rest of mankind, it is during restitution and resurrection during the course of the approximate thousand-year spiritual reign of Jesus the Christ and his Church or those chosen from the Gospel Age. Many years are required for fair judgment as millions of people are raised in reverse generational order from the grave with opportunity to learn and progress up the highway of holiness, a process of a fair trial under an increasing rule of righteousness, justice, truth, love, mercy, patience and etc.

Kingdom conditions involve change from the Gospel Age, wherein Christians have generally suffered under the dominating forces of evil in its many forms. During the return or spiritual presence of Jesus the Christ and his Church, his administration of righteousness, justice, truth, mercy, compassion, love, etc. rises from the hearts of people as decades pass into centuries with righteousness and justice filling the earth. All people, including all those resurrected, are to have full opportunity to learn righteousness and to love their neighbor as themselves, or the second death will end their existence.

The past century having been engulfed in wickedness and evil, reached its peak as destructive forces of ignorance, superstition, fears, unemployment, violent crime, disease, wars, and lust became so widespread, more people were killed percentage-wise throughout the earth than ever before. But, change was affecting and altering societies when President William McKinley ran for reelection in 1900 with the successful campaign slogan "A Full Dinner Pail," conditions of that day were advanced beyond conditions of 1800 when Thomas Jefferson was elected, when evil methods were forced upon American natives through ignorance, lust, fear and greed. Those past scenarios were national, while the evil and destruction in the recent century was worldwide.

During the twentieth century, more people were killed in wars than in all previous centuries combined. However, today, conditions have changed for the better as knowledge increases, with most nations endeavoring to solve differences through negotiation rather than war. One reason is that today's religious, commercial, and financial interests demand it of politicians. Countries around the world are progressing in political and financial transformation with more citizens expecting higher education, improved food sources, financial and medical improvements, religious liberty, etc.; social changes not even visualized a hundred years ago.

Politics and religion in industrialized countries are being questioned and, in many cases, publicly criticized and often altered to satisfy demands of citizens for truth, righteousness, justice and prosperity. Nations, religions, and organizations opposing liberty and justice come under civil, political, and financial pressure from their citizens as other countries seek peaceful solutions. In religious circles, Catholicism is trying to juggle their tradition of Latin with English and Spanish. Women demand the right to preach from the pulpit. Homosexuality is claiming its rights as its adherents demand acceptance in society and in the churches. The doctrine of eternal torment for the wicked is fading from the pulpit, and the long-held doctrine that an evil spirit being is the source of evil that afflicts mankind is beginning to crack under the increasing light of reason and truth. The courts now operate under the rule that evil is conceived in the mind, rather than evil is suggested or influenced in the minds of people by evil spirit beings as claimed in the delusional witchcraft trial of 1692 in Boston.

As the Prophet Jeremiah wrote centuries ago:

> *"The heart [is] deceitful above all [things], and desperately wicked: who can know it?"* —Jeremiah 17:9.

The prophet wasn't speaking of a Satan, Devil, Serpent, or Dragon, but of evil being conceived in the heart of man.

Don't forget what Jesus the Christ said:

"A good man out of the good treasure of the heart brings forth good things: and an evil man out of the evil treasure brings forth evil things." —Matthew 12:35

The Lord also was not speaking of a Satan or a Devil. With the freedom to use numerous study aids, more Christians are finding that references to a traditional evil spirit being called Satan, Devil, Serpent, or Dragon conflicts with reason and Scripture, for they find out that the prophet Jeremiah was right when he said:

"The heart [is] deceitful above all [things], and desperately wicked: who can know it?" —Jeremiah 17:9

Do not the above statements of Jesus the Christ and the Prophet Jeremiah eliminate any need for existence of evil spirit beings? Do not the hearts of men generate more than enough evil without the necessity of an evil spirit being suggesting evil thoughts or initiating lust, anger, jealousy, hate, or other negative feelings? Isn't it time the long-held concept of evil spirits of the Bible is recognized as allegorical or figurative for evil? Wasn't the heart of man the source of evil even before Moses wrote what is known as the Pentateuch, the first five books of the Bible?

Isn't there overwhelming evidence that ever since Adam, evil has been conceived in the hearts of men under dark clouds of ignorance, superstition, lust, fear, anger, and jealousy? The truth gives us reason to understand why Moses made a pole with a brass serpent on it to counter the bite of a Serpent, for he allowed for the customs and beliefs of that time.

"And Moses made a serpent of brass, and put it upon a pole, and it came to pass, that if a serpent had bitten any man when he beheld the serpent of brass, he lived." —Numbers 21:9

The Bible was written by men instilled with the spirit of God—that is, of righteousness, justice, love, mercy, patience, wisdom, and truth—who saw society around them functioning under the evils of fear, ignorance suspicion, greed, hate, and bitterness. Those faithful prophets referred to the immoral condition of society as a darkness and gloominess governed by sin and wickedness, which, like a Serpent, activates in the individual suddenly, striking victims with poisonous fangs that are fatal. Thus, Moses used the serpent to represent in symbol how lust or evil is conceived in the mind and, in cunning fashion, ruins relationships, justifies evil activity, and destroys reputations. The author of Genesis, using the Serpent to represent evil or sin, wrote:

> *"Now the serpent was more subtle (sly) than any beast of the field."* —Genesis 3:

The Serpent or evil, being sly and deadly, is not only to be feared, but also to be looked upon as deadly. This statement of Moses is very helpful in that it ties the fear of the early Israelites of Serpents to the picture language used at that time. In other words, the characteristics of a Serpent are equated to lust, anger, hate, envy, or jealousy, which develops unexpectedly in the minds of people, these unwanted characteristics appear with out warning. Thus, Genesis 3:1 is better understood as follows:

> *"Now the serpent (lust of the mind) was more subtle (cunning) than any beast (animal) of the field."*

Looking at Moses' explanation of evil, we can better understand how Adam and Eve allowed lust (Serpent) to lead them into the evil of disobeying their Creator. They took of, or experienced, the fruit (product) of the tree of knowledge of good and evil. This interpretation helps us understand how the concept of Satan, Devil, Serpent, and Dragon developed and how the often-used pictorial language of the Bible is used. In a similar manner, the Bible refers to death as an enemy and the apostle Paul wrote that death is to be destroyed as the last enemy.

> *"The last enemy [that] shall be destroyed [is] (Adamic) death."* —1 Corinthians 15:26

Paul also wrote:

> *"For as in Adam all die, even so in Christ shall all be made alive* —1 Corinthians 15:22

Christians are to live by faith, but it is not to be a blind faith. If a person's heart is right with God, he or she will not be afraid to question sources to find the answer. Scripture, when rightly divided in the spirit of truth, will ignore tradition, ritual, custom, or institution. In scientific research, finding the truth is often accidental, which then provides knowledge that opens up the unknown or unforeseen. Thus, scientific and religious research can encourage a process that generates many of the blessings mankind enjoys during restitution. This can happen in the area of Scripture study. Truth in Jesus the Christ is not of tradition and ritual, but requires a steady, truthful effort that ignores or eliminates ignorance and fear. Such effort stimulates the mind to seek truth, righteousness, justice, mercy, love, and so forth in relationships, which as people progressively do so, helps to change attitudes and conditions into the Kingdom status required by our Creator during this millennium. The following statements with supporting Scripture illustrate this premise:

1. Recognition that people do not have souls, but are living souls who die and no longer exist but remain in the memory of God to be resurrected from death during the Kingdom of Jesus the Christ. As Scripture tells us:

"And the LORD God formed man [of] the dust of the ground, and breathed into his nostrils the breath of life; and man became a living soul (being)." —Genesis 2:7

"In the sweat of thy face shall you eat bread, till you return unto the ground; for out of it were you taken (made of): for dust you [are], and unto dust shall you return."—Genesis 3:19

"Wherefore, as by one man sin entered into the world, and death by sin; and so death passed upon all men, for that all have sinned."—Romans 5:12

"For since by man [came] death, by man [came] also the resurrection of the dead. For as in Adam all die, even so in Christ shall all be made alive, but every man in his own order: Christ the first-fruits (the Church); afterward they (the rest of mankind) that are Christ's (converts) at his coming (spiritual presence)." —1 Corinthians 15:21–23

"And so it is written, the first man Adam was made a living soul (being); the last Adam (Jesus the Christ) [was made] a quickening spirit —1 Corinthians 15:45

"Nevertheless, man [being] in honor abides not (no longer a living soul): he is like the beasts [that] perish."—Psalms 49:12

Neither men nor beasts have a soul, but are sentient beings— that is, living souls that die.

"For that which befalls the sons of men befalls beasts; even one thing befalls them: as the one dies, so dies the

other; yea, they have all one breath; so that a man hath no preeminence above a beast: for all [is] vanity. All go unto one place; all are of the dust, and all turn to dust again."
—Ecclesiastes 3:19–20

"And it shall come to pass, [that] every soul (person), which will not hear that prophet (learn and follow Jesus the Christ), shall be destroyed from among the people." —Acts 3:23

This tells us people do not have an immortal soul.

"Therefore will I divide him (Messiah) [a portion] with the great (those chosen to reign with him), and he (Messiah) shall divide the spoil with the strong (faithful); because he (Jesus the Messiah) hath poured out his soul (life) unto death: and he (Jesus the Christ) was numbered with the transgressors; and he (Jesus the Christ) bare the sin of many (all have sinned), and made intercession for the transgressors (all mankind)." —Isaiah 53:12

Jesus the Christ died a ransom for all and then resurrected a spirit. The first advent of Jesus the Christ was in the flesh to redeem man. His second advent is of the spirit upon earth, which through his spirit guides restoration of the hearts of people and blesses all who seek God in spirit and truth. Please consider the following scriptures:

*"Who gave himself a ransom for all, to be testified in due time." —*1 Timothy 2:6

"For even the Son of man came not to be ministered unto, but to minister, and to give his life a ransom for many." —Mark 10:45

"Christ hath redeemed us from the curse of the law, being made a curse for us: for it is written, cursed [is] every one that hangs on a tree."—Galatians 3:13

"I will ransom them from the power of the grave; I will redeem them from death: O death, I will be thy plagues; O grave, I will be thy destruction: repentance shall be hid from mine eyes." —Hosea 13:14

Jesus the Christ's return is not in the flesh, because as the following scriptures declare, he is no longer flesh or of human nature:

"My flesh I give for the life of the world." —John 6:51

"In the days of his flesh Jesus offered up prayers and supplications." —Hebrews 5:7

"The first man Adam was made a living soul (flesh); the last Adam (Jesus the Christ) was made a quickening spirit." —1 Corinthians 15:45

"Jesus (the Christ) was put to death in the flesh, but quickened (raised to spiritual life) in the spirit." —1 Peter 3:22

"Though we have known (Jesus the) Christ after the flesh, henceforth know we him no more." —2 Corinthians 5:16

"Who gave himself a ransom for all, to be testified in due time." —1 Timothy 2:6

"It does not yet appear what we shall be, but we know when he (Jesus the Christ) appears (spiritual presence), we (faithful Christians) shall be like him." —1 John 3:2

"And he that keeps His (God's) commandments dwells in Him, and He in him. And hereby we know that He abides in us, by the Spirit that He hath given us."—1 John 3:24

Again: the first advent of Jesus the Christ was in the flesh to redeem Adam & his seed. His second advent for (Judgment; Restitution; Thousand Years, or his Kingdom) is of the spirit; the dead are raised and the willing given life. All are blessed who seek God in spirit and truth.

The Lord's return or Second Advent is recognized by relatively few Christians, for, being of the spirit, his return "presence" is revealed by the gradual increase of righteousness, justice, and truth in the hearts of people throughout the world

"Neither shall they say, Lo here! Or, lo there! For, behold, the Kingdom of God is within you."—Luke 17:21

"Repent ye therefore, and be converted, that your sins may be blotted out, when the times of refreshing (restitution) shall come from the (spiritual) presence of the LORD."— Acts 3:19

"And then shall that (the) wicked be revealed, whom the LORD shall consume (destroy) with the spirit of his mouth (justice, righteousness, and truth), and shall destroy with the brightness (understanding) of his coming (presence)."—2 Thessalonians 2:8

"And they shall teach no more every man his neighbor, and every man his brother, saying, Know the LORD: for they shall all know me, from the least of them unto the greatest of them, said the LORD: for I will forgive

their iniquity, and I will remember their sin no more."—
Jeremiah 31:34

*"Behold, I come as a thief (the world is unaware the spirit of Jesus the Christ is growing in the hearts of many people). Blessed [is] he that watches, and keeps his garments (faith and trust in the Lord), lest he walk naked (evil values), and they see his shame."—*Revelation 16:15

"Where is the promise of his coming? For since the fathers fell asleep, all things continue as [they were] from the beginning of the creation (people not recognizing the Lord's return of the spirit)." —2 Peter 3:4

*"For as the new heavens (religion of righteousness and justice) and the new earth (righteous, peaceful, and caring society), which I will make (through His spirit), shall remain before me, said the LORD, so shall your seed and your name (Israel) remain and it shall come to pass, [that] from one new moon to another, and from one Sabbath to another, shall all flesh come to worship before me, said the LORD. "—*Isaiah66: 22

(un-repentant will have been destroyed with second death)

As mentioned, a fundamental sign of the Lord's return (presence) is that the righteous, just, and loving characteristics Jesus the Christ displayed are seen in the hearts of increasing numbers of people. The enormous increase of knowledge, communication and fast travel are primary signs that the restitution of all things began some time ago with people already cultivating fair and just laws in society. Thus, the spirit of the Lord grows as people seek truth, righteousness, justice, peace, and mercy in personal, financial, political, and religious activities, which lead to improved living conditions. Though some people at the present time do not declare Jesus the Christ as their Savior, many are developing a love and respect for their fellow man, which eventually can motivate them to acknowledge the overruling power of God's spirit of righteousness, justice, mercy, and love through Jesus the Christ, His son, mankind's Redeemer from the Adamic death penalty.

Under the trying, evil conditions of the Gospel Age, when ignorance, wickedness, and evil dominated the earth (societies), God has chosen those who are to reign with His son in the Kingdom. As the transformation from the Gospel Age into God's Kingdom occurs, restitution blessings raise living conditions as knowledge of the Lord and growth in His spirit increases throughout the world. In God's due time, the resurrection from the dead will begin, and as people are raised from the dead, they also will have opportunity to learn righteousness, justice, mercy, and love under a just administration. The following scriptures speak of this:

> *"Jesus said unto him, I am the way, the truth, and the life: no man comes unto the Father, but by me (the truth)."*—John 14:6

> *"Behold, he comes with clouds (trouble); and every eye shall see him (discern that justice, righteousness, and truth, as Jesus taught, brings life), and they [also] which pierced him: and all kindreds of the earth shall wail (changing conditions create fear as the reign of evil, Satan, Devil, Dragon, and Serpent gradually disappears) because of him (truth and love in Jesus the Christ). Even so, Amen."*—Revelation 1:7

> *"But thou, O Daniel, shut up the words, and seal the book, [even] to the time of the end (of the Gospel Age): many*

shall run to and fro, and knowledge shall be increased."
—Daniel 12:4

*"For as that lightning flashes (truth brilliant as light)
out of one part under heaven and shines to the other part
under heaven; so will the (spiritual presence) Son of man
be."* —Matthew 24:27 (Diaglott)

*"To the end (of the Gospel Age) he may establish your
hearts (the Church) un-blame-able in holiness before God,
even our Father, at the coming (presence) of our Lord Jesus
Christ with all his saints (chosen to be of the Church)."*
—1 Thessalonians 3:13

Geographical earth abides forever and will not be destroyed.
When a scripture seems contrary to this statement, it requires
re-interpretation so that it's meaning harmonizes with the
following verses:

*"For thus said the LORD that created the heavens; God
himself that formed the earth and made it; He hath
established it, He created it not in vain, He formed it to
be inhabited."*—Isaiah 45:18

*"[One] generation passes away, and [another] generation
comes: but the earth abides for ever."* —Ecclesiastes 1:4

The Kingdom of God grows as restitution blessings and
reconciliation bear fruit in the hearts of willing people:

*"And when he was demanded of the Pharisees, when the
Kingdom of God should come, he answered them and
said, The Kingdom of God comes not with observation:
Neither shall they say, Lo here! or lo there! For behold, the
Kingdom of God is within you."*—Luke 17:20–21

"Another parable put he forth unto them, saying, The Kingdom of Heaven is like to a grain of mustard seed."
—Matthew 13:31

Seeds of the Kingdom have been growing since the Lord's first advent when he gave his life as a ransom for all.

"Whom the heaven (religion) must receive until the times of restitution of all things, which God hath spoken by the mouth of all his holy prophets since the world began."
—Acts 3:21

"The LORD preserves all them that love Him: but all the wicked will He destroy."—Psalms 145:20

All are promised a resurrection, but many will not seek righteousness under the just and righteous conditions of the Kingdom. —Isaiah 65:20

"There shall be no more thence an infant of days, nor an old man that hath not filled his days: for the child shall die an hundred years old; but the sinner [being] an hundred years old shall be accursed (destroyed)."

The Living Bible, a Paraphrase, says:

"No longer will babies die when only a few days old; no longer will men be considered old at 100. Only sinners will die that young."

"Let favor be shown to the wicked (reprobate), [yet] he will not learn righteousness: in the land of uprightness (the Kingdom) he will deal unjustly, and will not behold the majesty of the LORD."   —Isaiah 26:10

Satan, Devil, Serpent, and Dragon are a concept, illusion, and invention of man to escape responsibility for conceiving and acting upon evil thoughts. Religion has given a persona to man's evil, which Jesus used to advantage—that way he avoided confusion and unnecessary opposition to his message. At appropriate times he voiced reality—as did the apostles and prophets—that people conceive evil, that it is not an evil spirit being that conceives evil, as the following scriptures testify:

> *"The* (human) *heart [is] deceitful above all [things], and desperately wicked: who can know it."* —Jeremiah 17:9

This picture language referring to evil *(Satan, Devil, Serpent, or Dragon)* has been misunderstood as literal: that an evil spirit being tempts people with evil thoughts. This interpretation ignores sin resulting from lust.

Jesus said:

> *For out of the heart proceed evil thoughts, murders, adulteries, fornications, thefts, false witness, blasphemies."*—Matthew 15:19

Peter wrote:

> *"Having eyes (lust) full of adultery, and that cannot cease from sin; beguiling unstable souls: an heart (mind) they have exercised with covetous practices; cursed children."*—2 Peter 2:14

James wrote:

> *"But every man is tempted, when he is drawn away of his own lust, and enticed. Then when lust hath (is) conceived,*

> *it brings forth sin: and sin, when it is finished, brings*
> *forth death."* —James 1:14–15

> *"For every one that does evil hates the light (truth),*
> *neither comes to the light (truth), lest his deeds should be*
> *reproved."*—John 3:20

> *"Then the devil (evil thought) took (visualized) him (self)*
> *up into the holy city, and set (visualized) him (self) on a*
> *pinnacle of the temple."* —Matthew 4:5

The thoughts of Jesus were about the method he should take that would demonstrate the glory of God through him. Having wrong or evil thoughts happens to everyone; it is dwelling upon evil thoughts and then acting upon them that is evil.

> *"And the LORD God said, Behold, the man is become as*
> *one of us, to know good and evil."* —Genesis 3:22

Jesus the Christ knew that a spectacular act would draw many, but it would not be in harmony with God's will. In Hebrews, we read:

> *"For we have not an high priest which cannot be touched*
> *with the feeling of our infirmities; but was in all points*
> *tempted like as [we are, yet] without sin."*—Hebrews
> 4:15

Thus, Jesus the Christ addressed temptation:

> *"Jesus said unto him (his evil thought) it is written again,*
> *you shall not tempt the LORD thy God."* —Matthew
> 4:5

Jesus the Christ avoided self-glorification, thus remaining faithful to his Heavenly Father

> *"And the great Dragon (evil) was cast out, that old Serpent (evil), called the Devil (evil) and Satan (evil), which deceives the whole world: he (evil) was cast out (opposed) into the earth (society), and his angels (evil messengers or supporters) were cast out (opposed) with him (evil)."*
> —Revelation 12:9

The apostle Paul also wrote allegorically.

> *"For we wrestle not against flesh and blood, but against principalities (evil organizations), against powers (evil teachings), against the rulers of the darkness of this world (teachers of error and superstition), against spiritual wickedness in high [places] (both religious and secular)."*
> —Ephesians 6:12

And John wrote:

> *"And he laid hold on the Dragon (evil), that old Serpent (evil), which is the Devil (evil), and Satan (evil), and bound him (evil) (during) a thousand years."*—Revelation 20:2

The <u>desire</u> to do evil will eventually be gone, for Isaiah wrote

> *"They shall not hurt nor destroy in all my holy mountain (government): for the earth (society) shall be full of the knowledge of the LORD, as the waters cover the sea."*
> —Isaiah 11:9

how the Devil Came into Existence

In the third chapter of Genesis it speaks of the Serpent as more subtle than any beast of the field. That Serpent was later called a devil; why would this be? Evidently Serpent and Devil have a similar meaning, but how did this come about? In Strong's Concordance, the meaning of Serpent (5175) is to hiss, whisper, or learn by experience. It implies conceiving of an idea. This is what occurred to Eve: she conceived and desired to learn the meaning of evil and enticed Adam to also learn; Moses, learning hieroglyphics under Egyptian schooling would probably draw pictures, to later be translated into Hebrew word 'serpent'.

Strong's (8163) from (8175) says the meaning of Devil is satyrs, hairy or shaggy, as of a goat. (8175) means fear, horribly afraid. The Hebrew word "*Sirrin*" and the Greek word "satyrs" mean the same thing, which is wild goats. It was imagined by the Greeks that the woods, especially after sundown, were filled with satyrs. Such imaginings are expressed in some cultures today; people still imagine a Devil with goat-like features as horns and tail. Another concept is the name "Belial," meaning "not prophet able," often applied to a Devil or to a Satan. At times the cultural language or the translator did not render harmonious statements. For example, in 2 Samuel we read:

> *"The anger of the LORD was kindled against Israel, and He moved David against them to say, go number Israel and Judah"*—2 Samuel 24:1

At that time in Israel God was thought to give punishments and to bless. Later, in 1 Chronicles we read the concept had developed where a Satan provoked David to number Israel. There we read:

> *"And "Satan stood up against Israel, and provoked David to number Israel.* —1 Chronicles 21:1

The Hebrew word for Satan means "adversary" or "opposer," which could apply to either a spirit being or a human.

In 1 Kings we read:

> *"And God stirred up [another] adversary to Israel."* —1 Kings 11:23

Israel was later influenced, when under captivity of Babylon to adopt their conqueror's concept of evil. There they found evil was of a Satan, but one without power to make a person do evil, but did tempt people to sin, thus an abstract Satan was the instigator of evil, while God brought good.

Later, when Israel was under control of the Persians, they heard more about the principles of good coming from God, but evil being of a Satan, an evil power that God created. Later, the Satan became the chief of evil angels and also the Serpent in the Garden of Eden. In Isaiah chapter 6:2, the Seraphim was included as a high-ranking evil spirit, but was considered an angel. In Numbers 21:6; the Hebrew word saraph is translated "fiery serpents." As mentioned before; the fiery serpents were biting the people, so Moses made a pole with a brass serpent at its top. Anyone bitten by a serpent would hurry to look at the brass serpent to be healed through faith. In Isaiah we read of Lucifer, which in Greek means light bringer. Servants waiting on the Babylonian King referred to him as Lucifer, a title meaning light bringer, applied later to a Satan.

> *"How art thou fallen from heaven, O Lucifer, son of the morning!; [how] art thou cut down to the ground, which didst weaken the nations! For thou (king of Babylon) hast said in your heart, I will ascend into heaven, I will exalt my throne above the stars of God: I will sit also upon the mount of the congregation, in the sides of the north: I will ascend above the heights of the clouds; I (the king) will be like the most High."*—Isaiah 14:12–14

The king eventually fell to captivity and death in the 'grave,' which is translated 'hell' in some translations. By the time John the Baptist came on the scene, the Jews looked upon a Satan as leader of the fallen angels whose pride made him think he could replace God. The Jews were firm in their belief that evil angels were kicked out of Heaven because they rebelled against God. When Cyrus conquered Babylon the teaching of Persian dualism was popular, which to Israel became an evil spirit being named Satan. The principles of good and evil were considered as having separate armies of good angels and evil angels. Satan as the chief of angels was removed with his evil angels from the heavenly realm to tempt people upon earth. Even then Satan was looked upon as still subject to God while he zealously tried to persuade as many converts into evil as possible on earth.

We should not accept this imaginative speculation, which required centuries for superstitious priests of Israel to figure out that an opponent of God was an evil spirit being who intended to control everyone on earth in opposition to God through machination of people's minds. This history of Israel's experience with disloyal priests insinuating that an evil spirit being, with millions of other evil spirit beings, must oppose God who are trying to thwart his plans for a paradise on earth for people, is finally being seen for what it is. In Isaiah we find the answer that reveals the truth.

The prophet wrote about the king of Babylon, but the priests ignored his accusation or the translators had their own ideas. Isaiah wrote:

> *"They that see thee shall narrowly look upon thee, [and] consider thee, [saying, Is] this the man that made the earth to tremble, that did shake kingdoms?"* —Isaiah 14:16

Isaiah was writing of the king of Babylon, but men have attributed his question to an evil spirit being, which they said is Lucifer, or Light Bringer, rather than to the king. Anyway, going on, in Isaiah 6:2 the Seraphim became part of the heavenly top angels, being referred to as Seraphim, Cherubim, Powers, Principalities, Virtues, and Thrones, but today the Seraphim is looked upon as an angel. The word *saraph* is Hebrew for 'to burn.' Interpreted *seraph* in English, it is used in Numbers 21:6 as referring to the poisonous bite of the serpents of the people. There it speaks of the LORD sending fiery serpents upon the people. Also, during the Assyrian rule, large tribes of nomads called Gog and Magog brought war and destruction across Asia for years and were also prophesied to terrorize the nations in the last day.

What we then see in Biblical history over the centuries is the concept of evil, conceived and acted upon by people, was being blamed on an evil spirit being, but today the increasing knowledge with instant communication and fast travel is fracturing that old belief system of an abstract, evil spirit being, a legend and myth that has been a forceful mythical figure throughout history. Evil or Satan every so often comes up against Scriptural truths that reveal evil is conceived by people, or as the writer of Ecclesiastes stated thousands of years ago:

"The heart of the sons of men is full of evil."—Ecclesiastes 9:3

People deceive themselves or are deceived by one another as to source of evil, which is called: Serpent, Satan, Devil, or Dragon as in Revelation 20:2. Scripture, history, religion, and secular sources use the four names for evil conceived in the hearts of people for an evil spirit being with millions of other evil spirit beings who were supposedly cast out of Heaven; they are thought to toil in leading people into evil and then eternal torment. In contrast, people who think Adam, Eve, and Eden are a myth can look at Israel, who has recorded its ancestors back to Adam. In addition, the apostle Paul, a highly learned, converted Pharisee, based salvation of the world, the hope of restitution, and resurrection for all upon the ransom of Adam and all his children by the Messiah; Jesus the Christ. If Adam had not existed, mankind would not be ransomed from the death penalty, as Paul wrote:

"For as in Adam all die, even so in Christ shall all be made alive." —1 Corinthians 15:22

Paraphrasing from 'Rossell Hope Robbins' Encyclopedia; The word 'devil,' meaning the personification of supreme evil, the foe of God, is from the Greek 'diabolos' but originally meant an accuser or traducer. In translating the Old Testament into Greek, the Egyptian Jews of the third century BC used the word 'diabolos' for the Hebrew 'Satan,' a spirit being whose function was to test the faithfulness of people to God. The spirit being was not evil but was considered evil because of its occupation. When this Greek Septuagint, the 'Old Testament,' was translated into Latin, '*diabolos*' became '*diabolus*' (early translation) or 'Satan' in the Standard Vulgate text, except in Psalms:

> "*Set thou a wicked man over him: and let Satan (evil) stand at his right hand.*"—Psalms 109:6

In the New Testament, the Greek word '*satanas*' meant something else, not a spirit being opposed to man (as in Job) but a spirit being opposed to God, as Jesus the Christ is quoted in his temptation in the desert "*Get thee hence, Satan (evil).*"—Matthew 9:10. '*Satanas*' meant the devil (evil) in the New Testament and Psalms 109:6, but in Revelation 12:9 '*satanas*' is translated: "*the great Dragon... that old Serpent, called the Devil, and Satan, which deceives the whole world: he was cast out into the into the earth* (society), *and his angels* (messengers) *with him*

The whole world has been deceived by man's allusion of an evil spirit being. Almost every religion has a place of power for an evil spirit being that does not exist; people have invented an invisible, evil spirit being, and people give honor and recognition to their own folly. "Earth" pictures society and "angels" often pictures messengers. The word "devil" (in Greek, "diabolos") is found about thirty-five times in the New Testament and means an accuser or slanderer, a calumniator or malignant falsifier, prominent characteristics or traits of evil in people. To comprehend how evil seeps into the human consciousness, the word "adversary" is used, meaning "opposing spirit," a spirit or attitude of evil as opposed to a spirit or attitude of truth, as our Lord said in the Gospel of John:

"But the hour comes, and now is, when the true worshippers shall worship the Father in spirit and in truth: for the Father seeks such to worship him." —John 4:23

In Acts, Paul said

... to turn them from darkness to light, and from the power of Satan (evil) unto God." —Acts 26:18

It is impossible for humans to describe in a comprehensible manner what spirit beings are or look like. Various names and descriptions are used, such as "ghost" or "apparition," but, in reality, people imagine a spirit being with a human form, sometimes with wings. A realistic way to understand a spirit being is the statement made by our Lord in the above scripture"

—true worshippers shall worship the Father in spirit and in truth."

Thus, spirit beings are indescribable, invisible spirit entities without form. In regard to Satan, the Diaglott uses "from the dominion of the adversary." Thus, Jesus was telling Paul he was to be a witness of him (Jesus) to turn the Jews and the Gentiles from ignorance to knowledge and from their sinful ways (evil thoughts and acts or adversarial thoughts and acts) unto God: (in righteousness).

The Hebrew 'Satan' as well as the New Testament Greek 'satanas' are translated 'Satan' in English. Later, the 'devil' was equated with 'demon,' although originally the words were distinct. The Greek 'demon' meant a 'guardian spirit' or 'source of inspiration.' But the Greek Septuagint used 'demon' for the Hebrew words meaning vengeful idols (*schedim*) or hairy satyrs (*seirim*).

The devil was legalized by the Council of Toledo in AD 447, but those early Christians did not always conceive of a devil in complete human form. They visualized the Devil as a human body having legs and feet like those of an ass, or as leopards, bears, horses, wolves, and scorpions. The lion was roaring and ready to attack, the bull tossing its horns, and a serpent writhing.

The Devils had their shape changed often, taking the forms of women, wild beasts, creeping things, gigantic bodies, and groups of soldiers. They often were said to smell filthy and foul. They took possession of humans and animals, some even living under the earth. Superstition and ignorance permeated beliefs that, under present enlightenment, would mark the person as mentally disturbed. But when there was no electricity and the darkness of night was lit sparingly with a torch or lantern, the minds of people were susceptible to illusion, hallucination, fear, and superstition. People were killed because they had warts, scars, or birthmarks on their bodies. They were often accused of having pacts with devils or being possessed by devils. Sometimes, mass hysteria affected wide areas of the population, where accused people were hanged or burned to death. Emotional and physical disabilities were of Satan, often ending in prison or death.

The Jews were exposed to the beliefs of the Zoroastrians; who believed in devils. From 538 BC until 330 BC, Zoroaster, the great Persian philosopher, taught that there were two principles: a principle of good, called Ormuzed, or light, and a principle of evil, called Ahriman, or darkness. The one was the cause of all the good in the world, the other the cause of all the evil. This dualistic doctrine strongly influenced the Hebrew mind. It was about that time that the book of Job was written with Satan making its appearance for the first time.

The oriental mind was accustomed to using symbolic and figurative language, which personalized the unfathomable powers that plagued the lives of Christians. It is from this picture language that we interpret the temptations of Jesus in the wilderness at the very beginning of his ministry. Jesus went silently and alone into the desert to ponder the purpose and direction that he was go. How should he use the power God gave him? He decided he would not use it for self, and he determined that he would not make stones into bread to eat, nor would he use any power to repel evil for personal benefit. Also, he would not to jump off the synagogue roof in order to attract a quick and easy following of believers.

These ideas came to his mind in the desert after forty days of fasting. In relating his experiences, it was perfectly natural for him to use current ideology and to phrase his narrative in symbolic language that related temptation as of Satan (evil). Therefore, we should not think that Jesus conversed with an evil spirit being as pictorially recorded in the fourth chapter of Matthew. The temptations of Jesus concerned the selfish use of God's power. All three temptations were concerned with the burning question of whether it would be right to take shortcuts to his goal in order to save time in bringing men into the kingdom of God.

The questions arose in Jesus' mind as he decided the way to conduct his mission; he did not have a conversation with a Satan. Jesus' use of picture language regarding the word *devil* was a natural accompaniment of his customary use of figurative language. He did not need a devil to account for an evil idea; he had free choice to not use evil in his mission, thus, his temptation by a 'devil' was in reference to what James said was "tempted by our lusts". Overcoming evil is a matter of choice. Loving God with all one's heart, mind, and strength and one's neighbor as self gives us control over lust and to do according to God's will.

how Belief in Satan has Changed

In the quest to understand how Satan originated, answers should be reasonable and consistent in interpretation. The harmonious theme of the Bible reveals that people conceive and instigate evil, that God has not created evil spirit beings to make or entice people to act evil. Even so, because some people are fully convinced that God created a Satan, an evil spirit being to afflict mankind, there may not be any amount of enlightening evidence, Scriptural or otherwise, that would convince such traditional believers to consider Satan (evil) as not a spirit being.

The Word of God tells us there will be full opportunity for understanding in the time of restitution, or Judgment Day, for people are to progressively learn during restitution blessings. Christians who long to understand the loving plan of God will find much comfort and answers in Charles T. Russell's *The Divine Plan of the Ages*. Although I find reason to differ on a few things he has written, he offers much information, spiritual aid, and many historical facts that give hope for the world during the Lord's spiritual return or presence, which is not a physical return.

It is common among many "religious" people to blame Satan or the Devil when something bad happens. This unseen, imagined foe becomes the scapegoat for evil or harmful acts conceived and committed by people who believe this invisible "being" instigates the evil that they choose to commit, and they often blame that mystical figure when things go wrong. Why does this phenomenon create such strong conviction in many religious people, and why do so many subject them selves to the illusion that an evil spirit being is lurking invisible nearby, ready to mess up their lives?

As often happens, firm believers in the Devil view statements that question the existence of a Satan as heretical doctrine. They feel secure with the images offered by traditional-thinking leaders backed by institutionalized authority that seemingly verifies the existence of the Devil or demons. Therefore, anyone questioning the existence of Satan or demons is on the wrong path, and to consider rational explanations as to the source of evil amounts to questioning their faith; however, the times do call for more light on the subject.

Mortimer F. Adler wrote in his book: *"The Angels and Us"* (p. 75)

> "The 'Theologian' says that no human being can act directly on the intellect of another, but only indirectly by affecting the latter's sense experience and imagination. Teaching is done through words, gestures, diagrams and imagination. Angels teach human beings in similar fashion; having power over bodies, they influence the operation of the human intellect by affecting the bodily organs of sense and imagination. Likewise, angels cannot directly determine acts of the human will. The inviolability of its freedom exempts it from such determination

either by angels or by human beings. But just as one human being can influence the will of another by efforts of persuasion, or by motivating it in one way or another through arousing emotions, so angels have even greater power to influence the will of individuals in these indirect ways."

Mr. Adler thought this assumption not worthy of acceptance. He also quotes Martin Luther as saying:

"The Devil is also near and about us, incessantly tracking our steps, to deprive us of our lives, our savings, health and salvation. But holy angels defend us from him, inasmuch as he is not able to work up such mischief as willingly as he would."

And John Calvin: "Since the Devil was created by God... this wickedness which we attribute to his nature is not from nature, but from corruption. They [evil spirits] were originally angels of God, but by degenerating have ruined themselves and become instruments of perdition to others."

Mr. Adler and I consider these teachings misleading. But to change conventional formal religious control in society, he wrote:

"The supernatural beliefs of theologians Martin Luther and John Calvin are in strong contrast to the writings of James Hitchcock entitled: 'What Is Secular Humanism?' His book covers the history of ideas that have brought even religious people to examine and reevaluate their own relationship to 'formal religion.' Throughout his book are constant references to ideas and efforts of individuals and groups opposed to or endeavoring to change conventional formal religious control in society.

Never once in his efforts to reveal the foundation and growth of secular humanism did he [Hitchcock] advocate that 'Satan' was the cause. He proposed that the movement of secular humanism, from the enlightenment period to his day, has been the ideas of persons embracing independence from formal religious thinking to independence of God. Not once was an evil spirit mentioned as the source of ideas of individuals. He wrote, 'Christians often fail to recognize that these ideas now provide the dominant model for man's view of himself and his world.' He pointed to evil and rebellion as the source and product of people, not an invisible, evil spirit being.

Gradually, liberals at the turn of the century came to believe that all religious formulations—scriptures, creeds, confessional statements and moral principles—were the products of a developing human consciousness, which changed history. They arrived periodically to expressions of truth, which seemed final and authoritative. Each time, they discovered these were inadequate and began the process again."

Mr. Adler concludes:

"Mr. Hitchcock's analysis is more realistic in contrast to Martin Luther and John Calvin's. Their assumption of right or wrong, saint or sinner limits perception of what the Bible actually embodies, since they generally assumed wickedness to be of Satan."

Like Mr. Adler, Steve Allen questioned the existence of the Devil. In his book entitled *Steve Allen on the Bible, Religion, & Morality*, he wrote:

"Whether the Devil exists or not, he provides a wonderfully effective service for one category of believers—those who, because of their unfortunate psychological makeup, appear to derive a good deal of satisfaction from feeling the emotions of hatred or guilt. Even as a young Catholic, when I was obliged to believe in the Devil, I was never able to figure out why he needed to exist at all, for I had come to realize that humans were more than capable of serious sinful behavior, so much so that they needed no encouragement from malign spirits.

Those who believe in the Devil also assume that he has been available, at all times, in all places, to tempt everyone who has ever lived. At the present moment, there are over five billion people on the planet earth. For all of them to be tempt able by the evil one, it must follow that he can be present in over five billion different locations at once and carry on as many monologues or dialogues at the same time. Concerning which one can say only that it is a remarkable assumption. That a God would have such power is simply a given, but there are supposed to be few if any godlike powers that are shared."

Steve Allen has additional comments on the Devil, but the above quotation illustrates his general viewpoint. There are other considerations that confront the Devil's existence or activity, or the ancient belief that an invisible, evil force is silently poised to cause a person to do evil, which is a contradiction to how the human mind works. The legal hypothesis is that a person who does evil to another does so of his or her own volition or will. The law will not accept a plea that a Devil suggests a person is to commit evil. The law holds that the evildoer or lawbreaker is responsible for his or her evil deed or he or she is mentally unstable.

Human beings as free moral agents and free will are out of the question if an invisible, evil spirit being is capable of exerting power over a person's will. This leaves us with a dilemma: if there is not a Devil or Satan instigating people to sin or do evil, what will we do with the Satan of the Bible that is supposed to have power to persuade, scare, and intimidate people? Actually, I do not know of any person claiming that Satan affects his or her thinking.

The answer to the Biblical Satan comes through the increase of knowledge, both secular and spiritual, which is bringing social change upon this earth, change that leads people (the willing, that is) to a glorious future without fear of a Satan. This vision comes into focus when we understand that the prophesied increase of knowledge creates progressive change in the hearts of people and is gradually transforming the evil world into the Kingdom of Jesus the Christ wherein dwells righteousness. The changes lead up to and beyond the resurrection, as restitution continues all during the approximately thousand years of Jesus the Christ's Kingdom. The Bible testifies that it is when the hearts of people seek righteousness and show love for one another that God's Kingdom is taking shape upon this earth.

The painful and at times alarming changes taking place throughout the world are gradually bringing awareness that expanding knowledge increases quality and length of life. Simultaneously, the spirit of love, mercy, humanitarian aid, kindness, and so forth with increasing knowledge are signs of restitution blessings promised by God through the prophets,

Jesus the Christ, and his apostles. Many prophesied changes have already occurred, and some prophecies are being fulfilled at the present time, while the fulfillment of other prophecies are still in the future. Those who watch can recognize, appreciate, and be comforted by the fact that the spirit of the Lord is growing in the hearts of many people, which is producing beneficial changes that are raising standards and living conditions into the new day, the Kingdom of Jesus the Christ.

The numerous blessings come under increasingly enlightened and righteous conditions of justice and equity, signs that the Kingdom of God, under Jesus the Christ, is being established amidst the clouds of trouble. Evaluating these encouraging signs of change in light of God's Word, we see the glorious day dawning in which fear-filled, irrational, and negative doctrines are abandoned, doctrines that have long clouded the vision of God's loving objective for the world and the establishment of His Kingdom upon earth.

As the apostle Paul prophesies in Hebrews:

> *"And this [word], yet once more, signifies the removing of those things that are shaken, as of things that are made, that those things which cannot be shaken may remain."*
> —Hebrews 12:27

Paul was saying that, as restitution progresses, doctrines, people's activity, governments, and institutions will be tested and shaken, and the troublous times will remove evil in societies, to leave only that which is beneficial to the Kingdom of God.

The Destiny of the Church

There are many changes to be made and problems to be solved as this turbulent world gradually transforms into a body of peaceful nations existing under the ruling spirit of righteousness, justice, peace, love, and mercy of Jesus the Christ's Kingdom. Erring doctrine is being uprooted, such as the popular, politically correct idea that, no matter what his or her religion, everyone upon death goes to heaven if he or she is good, but evildoers or those not approved are to face eternal torment. Many religious people underwrite the idea that it is loving and open-minded to consign people of all faiths to a heavenly reward, but there is no Scriptural support for this belief.

The message of Jesus and his apostles is clear: in following Jesus, Christians live their commitment to God in truth, righteousness, and love. Then, at the first resurrection, at the Lord's spiritual presence, having been judged and selected according to their faithfulness in following our Lord Jesus the Christ in the days of evil, those chosen are to receive a crown of life. Some scriptures point to this prospect as being meant for the Church, a "little flock" (Luke 12:32) while other scriptures indicate that different conditions apply for the rest of mankind. Scriptures pointing to the Church or the faithful and chosen are:

"Father, I will that they also, whom Thou hast given me, be with me where I am; that they may behold my glory, which Thou hast given me." —John 17:24

"For as many as are led by the Spirit of God, they are the sons of God." —Romans 8:14

"And if children, then heirs; heirs of God, and joint-heirs with Christ; if so be that we suffer with [him], that we may be also glorified together." —Romans 8:17

"And these all (the prophets), having obtained a good report through faith, <u>received not the promise</u>: God having provided <u>some better thing for us</u> (the Church), that they without us should not be made perfect." —Hebrews 11:39–40

"Blessed [be] the God and Father of our Lord Jesus Christ, which according to his abundant mercy hath begotten us again unto a lively hope by the resurrection of Jesus Christ from the dead. To an inheritance incorruptible, and undefiled, and that fades not away, reserved in heaven for you, who are kept by the power of God through faith unto salvation ready to be revealed in the last time (Kingdom)" —1 Peter 1:3–5

"And he that overcomes, and keeps my works unto the end, to him will I give power over the nations."—Revelation 2:26

"To him that overcomes will I grant to sit with me in my throne, even as I also overcame, and am set down with my Father in his throne."—Revelation 3:21

Scriptures that apply to the rest of mankind are:

"But they shall sit every man under his vine and under his fig tree (needs full-filled); and none shall make [them] afraid: for the mouth of the LORD of hosts hath spoken [it]." —Micah 4:4

"Before the LORD: for he comes, for he comes to judge the earth (society): he shall judge the world (societies) with righteousness, and the people with his truth." —Psalms 96:13

"As it is written in the book of the words of Esaias (Isaiah) the prophet, saying: "The voice of one crying in the wilderness, Prepare ye the way of the LORD, make his paths (teachings) straight. Every valley (social need) shall be filled, and every mountain (government) and hill (local government) shall be brought low (in submission); and the crooked (erring teachings) shall be made straight, and the rough ways (rules and rituals) [shall be] made smooth and all flesh (the willing) shall see the salvation of God."—Luke 3:4–6

"For as by one man's disobedience many were made sinners, so by the obedience of one shall many be made righteous."—Romans 5:19

"For as in Adam all die, even so in Christ shall all be made alive." —1 Corinthians 15:22

> *"And I will bless them that bless thee, and curse (destroy) him that curses thee: and in thee shall all families of the earth be blessed."* —Genesis 12:3

> *"And they shall not teach every man his neighbor, and every man his brother, saying, Know the LORD: for all shall know me, from the least to the greatest."* —Hebrews 8:11

Since there is no other way to attain life eternal but through Jesus the Christ, the world's savior, confusion will arise among some Christians and politicians who assume that unbelieving people or those of other religions should go to heaven upon death. The confusion clears away as the death of Jesus and his resurrection is seen to benefit everyone born upon this earth. The objective and implication of Jesus' death is a promise of immortality to those (the Church) who believe and follow Jesus during the Gospel Age when evil rules. But, for the world, the erring, confused belief of a destination of either heaven or hell will fade away (A binding of evil-Satan) as the world moves out of the darkness that for centuries has clouded the minds of men, from knowledge of life upon earth and to enjoy the blessings of restitution that brings life to willing hearts.

Isaiah tells us:

> *"For, behold, the darkness (ignorance) shall cover the earth (societies), and gross darkness (heavy ignorance) the people: but the LORD (spiritual presence) shall arise upon thee, and his glory shall be seen upon thee."* —Isaiah 60:2

The latter part of this prophecy refers to the nation of Israel and takes place at the time of the Lord's return (spiritual presence on earth). The great increase of knowledge during the Lord's return (presence) is producing blessings from God through a process that brings willing people (whosoever will) out of the darkness (ignorance) of which Isaiah wrote.

Those appreciating the Gospel or "Good News" of the Kingdom and seeking justice, mercy, truth, and righteousness manifest the spirit of the Lord and of his followers of the Gospel Age and are instrumental in the lifting of the darkness. They are as a light, displaying the love of Jesus to the world as Kingdom conditions unfold. Doctrine pertaining to the Kingdom, long preached from Christendom's pulpits, heavily tainted with fear and ignorance handed down from the Dark Ages, has given many Christians a distorted perception of life after death, but such ideas are gradually abandoned.

Eleanor Roosevelt once commented on why detrimental ideas (evil) are attractive to people. She said:

> "It is curious how much more interest can be evoked by a mixture of gossip, romance, and mystery than by facts."

In similar fashion, imagination and ignorance have long victimized the loving, merciful message of God's promises in Jesus the Christ for both Christians and the world. In religion, obedience to a Church system, creeds, and tradition has been more important than a search for truth, thus such thinking takes time to change, for example, in the early years of the Kingdom; leaders in religion, politics, commerce, and society appear prone to view people as haves and have-nots, or those who use their minds versus those who use their hands, or the upper-class as opposed to the lower-class. Under the rule of evil, countless societies have submitted to such rulers who have shown aspirations of grandeur.

For example, centuries ago, Plato wrote his Laws, an attempt at planning the just city. A critic later said:

> "Plato produced a blueprint for implanting beliefs and attitudes convenient to authority through the medium of suggestion by a strict and ruthless censorship. Also, the substitution of myths and emotional ceremonies for factual knowledge, the isolation of the citizen from the outside world, the creation of types with standardized reactions, and, as a final guarantee, by the sanctions of the police-state, to be invoked against all who cannot or will not conform."

Politicians and kings, along with many religious leaders, have often sought controlled conditions. Religious organizations have subjected their members to divisive structuring of the empowered over the non-empowered or the enlightened over the unenlightened. A classic example is the historic structure of the Roman Catholic Church, which followed this pattern by implanting beliefs, myths, ceremonies, and laws that has subjected its members to an empowered hierarchy. Today, this divisive type of structure is outdated and is breaking down because of increasing knowledge of Scripture, history, science, and human rights. Likewise, increasing knowledge is gradually eliminating the long-held concept of a Satan as the source of evil.

Doctor Albert Reville, in the 1870s, referred to this concept when he stated:

> "Nowhere does Jesus say that belief in the devil is one of the conditions of admission into the Kingdom of God. If the idea of the devil were a bare symbol, these conditions would remain literally the same: purity of heart, thirst for justice, love for God and man.

These are all of them, essentials which are entirely independent of the question whether a Satan exists or not."

Doctor Reville's viewpoint is that a Satan is unnecessary for any purpose—that if a Satan did or did not exist, conditions would be the same.

Prophecy tells of a time when the concept of an evil (Satan) spirit being will cease to be a scourge upon humanity. The prophet Isaiah, millennia ago, wrote:

> *"Come now, and <u>let us reason together</u>, said the LORD: though your sins be as scarlet, they shall be as white as snow; though they be red like crimson, they shall be as wool."*—Isaiah 1:18

Our Creator expects us, who claim to love Him, to reason together as we seek His will through righteousness, truth, peace, and love. Thus, in our search for answers, we are to reason with one another over questions such as the following:

Why would God require or need a Satan?

Are we living souls, or do we have a soul?

What is hell and where is it?

Are people predestined to heaven or hell?

Does evil come from lust (desire) of the mind?

Does a person conceive evil, or is evil incited in a person by an evil spirit being?

This is the objective of the Kingdom, to learn righteousness, to practice respect, love, kindness, and the like as people "reason together" in the spirit of our Lord. In the past, failure to reason together in the Lord's spirit resulted in the founding of numerous religious systems, with most of the systems teaching such doctrines as eternal torment under the supervision of a Devil and a heavenly reward for all those approved by a system's leadership. At times, doctrines have become controlling factors as leaders exploited members to the advantage of the religious system. Doctrine and tradition have played to the vanity, ignorance, and superstitions of followers by leaders who approve or disapprove the destination of the dead, whether it is heaven or hell.

Such prestigious positions of power and glory for religious leaders easily generated vanity and pride, which contradicts the humble and simple message Jesus the Christ and his apostles advocated and practiced. Likewise, those professing to follow Jesus the Christ but displaying pride in wealth or position have an attitude that is in sharp contrast with the advice and example that Jesus the Christ gave. It is not impossible (but very unlikely) for people with wealth to give all they have to the poor and follow Jesus the Christ. A person's commitment is also challenged by the Lord's spirit when he cautions not only to be careful about conduct, but also about goals in this present life. He said:

> *"Lay not up for yourselves treasures upon earth."*
> —Matthew 6:19

And:

> *"Jesus said unto him, If thou wilt be perfect, go [and] sell that thou hast, and give to the poor, and you shall have treasure in heaven: and come [and] follow me."*
> —Matthew 19:21   And last:

"Render unto Caesar the things that are Caesar's and unto God the things that are God's."—Matthew 22:21

In following the advice of Jesus the Christ, we are to gladly, not reluctantly, recognize our responsibility to differentiate between doing good or 'acting' good with selfish intent. Why then is it necessary that an evil spirit being evoke evil thoughts in our mind? How can we do the will of God if we are continually fighting off efforts of an evil spirit being that entices us with evil thoughts? And where do we get the idea that we are subject to evil spirit beings in the first place? Part of the problem is the manner in which we interpret the following Scriptures. For purposes of clarity, the scriptures attributing the source of evil to people are in *italic* print, while scriptures in **bold** print imply that an evil spirit being is the source of evil:

"And GOD saw that the wickedness of man [was] great in the earth, and [that] every imagination of the thoughts of his heart [was] only evil continually."—Genesis 6:5

"Now the serpent was more subtle than any beast of the field which the LORD God had made."
—Genesis 3:1

"Pride [goes] before destruction, and an haughty spirit before a fall." —Proverbs 16:18

"And the LORD said unto Satan, Behold, he [is] in thine hand; but save his life." —Job 2:6

"The heart [is] deceitful above all [things], and desperately wicked: who can know it? I the LORD search the heart, [I] try the reins, even to give every man according to his ways, [and] according to the fruit of his doings."
—Jeremiah 17: 9–10

"And he was there in the wilderness forty days, tempted of Satan." —Mark 1:13

"For out of the heart proceed evil thoughts, murders, adulteries, fornication, thefts, false witness, blasphemies."—Matthew 15:19

"And the LORD said unto Satan, Behold, all that he hath [is] in thy power; only upon himself put not forth thine hand. So Satan went forth from the presence of the LORD." —Job 1:12

"Take heed, brethren, lest there be in any of you an evil heart of unbelief, in departing from the living God."— Hebrews 3:12

"Then was Jesus led up of the Spirit into the wilderness to be tempted of the devil."—Matthew 4:1

… having eyes full of adultery, and that cannot cease from sin; beguiling unstable souls: an heart they have exercised with covetous practices; cursed children." —2 Peter 2:14

"But Peter said, Ananias, why hath Satan filled thine heart to lie to the Holy Spirit, and to keep back [part] of the price of the land?"—Acts 5:3

According to the verses in italic print, people are responsible for evil behavior. So why, in the bold print, is an evil spirit being responsible for man's fear, greed, jealousy, hate, lying, and so on? How can the Christian understand Scripture when it speaks of Satan, Devil, Serpent, Dragon, or evil spirit beings leading people into evil choices? Surely, God's purpose in allowing sin can be accomplished without evil spirit beings leading people astray. How are we to believe James when he wrote?

> *"Every man is tempted, when he is drawn away of his own lust, and enticed. Then when lust has conceived, it brings forth sin: and sin, when it is finished, brings forth death."* —James 1:14–15

James' statement is quite clear, yet it is easily ignored. He also wrote:

> *"A double minded man [is] unstable in all his ways."* —James 1:8

The Church, or those chosen from the Gospel Age, will have displayed a stable character and not double-mindedness. The spirit of Christians of the Gospel Age is to inspire willing hearts as restitution increases as people go up the highway of holiness even as the Adamic death penalty and sin vanishes upon earth. It is the spirit of love, justice, mercy, and righteousness of Jesus the Christ, growing in the hearts of people, that increasingly prepares societies for the beginning of the resurrection, all having fair opportunity to learn and change from ignorance and selfishness under the spiritual administration of Jesus the Christ and his Church in truth, love, justice, righteousness, and mercy, thus cleansing evil (Satan, Devil, Serpent, or Dragon) from the hearts of the willing. The reprobates or those insisting on continuing in sin or wickedness are destroyed by the second death

Spirit of Truth Binds Evil (Satan)

From Genesis to Revelation, God has provided picture language in His Word to describe conditions, predict events, and offer revelation as to man's past, present, and future. The authors often use figurative descriptions in reference to man's evil activity. For instance, John, in the book of Revelation, speaks of "that old Serpent," which is a reference to the same Serpent as in Genesis:

> "Now the serpent (evil) was more subtle than any beast of the field which the LORD God had made." —Genesis 3:1

The Lord, through his disciple John, clarifies this for us in Revelation, where the Serpent is also the Dragon, Devil, and Satan. John, in the spirit on the Lord's Day, was referring to evil in a figurative manner. He wrote:

> "And he laid hold on the dragon (evil), that old serpent (evil), which is the Devil (evil), and Satan (evil), and bound him (restrained evil during) a thousand years. And cast him (evil) into the bottomless pit (restriction), and

shut him up (restricted), and set a seal (promise) upon him (evil), that he (evil) should deceive the nations no more, till the (approximate) thousand years should be fulfilled: and after that he (evil) must be loosed a little season."
—Revelation 20:2–3

The pictorial language of the above verses describes evil choices and activity of people, not of an evil spirit being. Often, writers of the Bible presented visions using literal objects or conditions, which are sometimes zealously interpreted to be of a spirit realm or evil spirit being activity. This has made it convenient for the idea to take hold that evil spirit beings tempt people into choosing evil, while the idea of lust being conceived within people is disregarded. The concept of evil spirit beings hovering all around to interfere in the lives of people distorts reality in that it deceptively relieves people of responsibility for their evil choices or actions. The apostle Paul wrote:

"Where the spirit of the LORD is, there is liberty. —2 Corinthians 3:17

To some Christians, searching the background of the concept of evil or Satan is abuse of that liberty. But it is liberty in the Lord's spirit that has inspired this book. The objective is for us to come to an understanding of why and how evil was given its names, hoping that this knowledge would bring about a more informed perspective, as does truth about the ransom, or hell, the soul, the Lord's return (spiritual presence), the Trinity, Judgment Day, and so on. Why do Christians think researching the beginning and end of Satan or any of the above subjects as going too far if we are looking for truth? Wouldn't it be of help if we understand how and when the concept of how Satan, Devil, Serpent, and Dragon came into existence, as well as the manner in which this imaginary, elusive foe is to be bound? This surely has a part in the binding of this imagined enemy.

As we have learned in Jesus the Christ, our objective is to serve our God in the spirit of truth, righteousness, justice, love, mercy, patience, and so on; therefore, if the reader disagrees with information or ideas presented in this book and is of the Christian faith, remember, our Lord said we are still to love one another. Many, situations and opportunities abound in which the spirit of the Lord radiates from the hearts of people who share to aid those in need. This is of the Lord's spirit, and it is part of the binding of evil, Satan, Devil, Serpent, and Dragon. For centuries, Christians have looked for a literal binding, but how can a literal chain bind an evil spirit being? The binding suggests restriction and the pictorial answer to this pictorial dilemma is that the binding of Satan, Devil, Serpent, Dragon, or evil is accomplished by the spirit of the Lord accomplishing the binding with links of truth, righteousness, justice, love, mercy, and so forth. Each act of the above virtues is a link that helps bind evil, Satan, Dragon, Serpent, and Dragon.

Again, to remind us; the four names—Satan, Devil, Serpent, Dragon—mentioned by John are synonyms for evil and are clues to how Satan or evil is bound. Thus, as people endeavor during the time of restitution to develop a clean heart, they are to search the Scriptures, thirst for justice, and love our God and fellow men in Jesus the Christ. Thus, the binding of evil, Satan, Devil, Serpent, and Dragon takes place literally and symbolically; it is being accomplished through education of people in righteousness, justice, mercy, and love. It is learning and applying what is learned that reveals each person's character and faithfulness in implementing God's love, righteousness, justice, compassion, and mercy that leads to life. As Proverbs tells us

> *"Buy the truth, and sell [it] not; [also] wisdom, and instruction, and understanding."* —Proverbs 23:23

The words of Jesus the Christ in the Gospel of Mark tells us *"For from within, out of the heart of man, come evil thoughts."*—Mark 7:21

Jesus the Christ did not say that evil thoughts are of a Devil, but that they are from the heart of man. However, he did speak of a Satan in the abstract, as Matthew did (remember, it is a synonym of "evil"):

"And if Satan (evil) cast out Satan (evil), he (evil) is divided against himself (evil); how shall then his (evil) kingdom stand (remain)?"—Matthew 12:26

Is not the above interpretation what our Lord meant by "Satan casting out Satan"? As we have seen in previous verses, the Bible describes man as the source of evil, yet some scriptures seem to be emphatic that evil comes from an evil spirit being. To understand and harmonize these seemingly contradicting scriptures, it is important to remember the premise that evil originates in the hearts of men.

Ecclesiastes says:

"The heart of the sons of men is full of evil, and madness is in their heart while they live, and after that they go to the dead."—Ecclesiastes 9:3

The above scriptures harmonize with our Lord's words in Matthew:

"The good man out of the good treasure of the heart produces good, and the evil man out of his evil treasure produces evil, for out of the abundance of the heart the mouth speaks." —Matthew 12:35

Jesus the Christ was saying that good begets good and evil begets evil; thus the minds of people can produce both good and evil. Why, then would an evil spirit being be blamed? Other scriptures give strong support to the Lord's explanation; one is in Proverbs:

> *"My son, if sinners (not a Satan) entice thee; do not consent."* —Proverbs 1:10

In James we read:

> *"For where envying and strife [is], there [is] confusion and every evil work."*—James 3:16

Envy, strife, confusion, and evil are of people and the lusts of people, not of an evil spirit being; people are not blameless. It is clear that temptation and choice are of the individual, with enticement coming from lust in the mind, not from an invisible, evil spirit being.

As stated in 1 Kings:

> *"The King said moreover to Shimei, You know <u>all the wickedness which your heart is privy to,</u> that you did to David my father; therefore the LORD shall return thy wickedness upon your own head."*—1 Kings 2:44

The responsibility of behaving wickedly was Shimei's; an invisible, evil spirit being (Satan) cannot be blamed. By researching the history of the name Satan (Devil, Dragon, or Serpent) we are assured that people are the source of evil. The following explanations help us to understand.

1. The root meaning of the word "Satan" is "to persecute," as in persecuting self or others with evil thought or action.

2. According to Strong's Concordance, "Satan" means "adversary, accuser, opponent or arch-enemy of good." Is it not "adversarial" to a person's welfare when evil thoughts come into his or her mind? Thus, we are not to blame an invisible, evil spirit being for initiating evil in our mind.

3. The noun "Satan" is a synonym for "evil," Devil, Dragon, and Serpent. The word "evil," if used consistently in Scripture, would be much less confusing. For example, if the word "evil" is used rather than "Satan" in Luke, the emphasis would be placed on an act rather than on an evil spirit being:

*"I beheld Satan **(evil)** as lightning fall from Heaven **(religion)**."*—Luke 10:18

(The word 'religion' is used because people equate religion with spiritual or heavenly things; thus, Satan or evil is cast out of religion, similar to what Jesus said in Matthew:

"And if Satan (evil) cast out Satan (evil), Satan (evil) is divided against Satan (evil)." —Matthew 12:26

4. Since death and hell picture a condition, then "Satan" also pictures a condition. John the Revelator states that the Devil, Satan, Serpent, Dragon, evil, the beast, the false prophet, death, and hell (all symbolic terms) are cast into a lake of fire and brimstone, which is symbolic of eternal destruction as pictured in Revelation:

"And the Devil (Satan, Serpent, Dragon, or evil) that deceived them was cast into the lake of fire and brimstone (eternal destruction), where the beast (religious system) and the false prophet (duplicate systems) [are], and shall be tormented (sadly remembered) day and night for ever and ever." —Revelation 20:10

And further on in Revelation:

> *"And death (end) and hell (grave) were cast into the lake of fire (destroyed). This is the second death (end)."*
> —Revelation 20:14

The "lake of fire" is symbolic of destruction or the condition of death. "Brimstone" depicts complete destruction as brimstone added to fire increases heat. "Tormented" depicts sorrowful memories the living have of loved ones who have died the second death, which occurs because of refusal to seek righteousness, justice, and mercy during restitution and resurrection.

Remember what Peter said in Acts:

> *"And he shall send Jesus Christ, which before was preached unto you: Whom the heaven (religion) must receive until the times of restitution of all things, which God hath spoken by the mouth of all his holy prophets since the world began. For Moses truly said unto the fathers, A prophet (Jesus the Christ) shall the LORD your God raise up unto you of your brethren, like unto me; him shall ye hear in all things whatsoever he shall say unto you. And it shall come to pass, [that] every soul, which will not hear that prophet (truth in Jesus the Christ during restitution), shall be destroyed from among the people."*—Acts 3:20–23

> *And in Psalms: "The LORD preserves all them that love him: but all the wicked will he destroy" (during Restitution, Resurrection Judgment, Kingdom)* —Psalms 145:20

Billions of people, having never heard of Jesus the Christ until the resurrection, will hear as knowledge of the Lord increasingly covers the earth:

> *"They shall not hurt nor destroy in all my holy mountain (government): for the earth (societies) shall be full of the knowledge of the LORD, as the waters cover the sea."*
> —Isaiah 11:9

And from Romans:

> *"For it is written, [as] I live, said the LORD, every knee shall bow to me, and every tongue shall confess to God."*—Romans 14:11 (The wicked having been destroyed.)

5. God's justice demands equity. Because of sin, Adam died, thus requiring a ransom. Since all people are his descendants, all die because of the sentence inherited for his disobedience. However, because Jesus the Christ paid the ransom for Adam, all are included and promised a resurrection involving judgment that consists of learning righteousness and justice under supportive conditions:

    > *"Who gave himself a ransom for all, to be testified in due time."*—1 Timothy 2:6

    > *"For as in Adam all die, even so in Christ shall all (during restitution and resurrection) be made alive."* —1 Corinthians 15:22

6. In contrast; if 'fallen angels' were to exist, they would not have opportunity for restitution; since angels are considered individually created (not procreated—that is, not conceived like humans), each sinful angel would require an individual ransom. The concept of evil angels or evil spirit beings has many holes in it, and knowledge is its destruction. This takes care of the question: How is a person responsible for wickedness if an evil spirit being seduces or puts into

a person's mind the will or desire to do evil? The Bible is clear on where evil comes from, for we read:

"The wicked fall <u>by their own devices</u>. —Proverbs 11:19

"He that <u>pursues evil</u>, pursues it to his own death." —Proverbs 12:20

"Deceit is in the heart of <u>them that imagine evil</u>." —Luke 6:45

"An <u>evil man</u> out of the evil treasure of <u>his heart</u> brings forth that which <u>is evil</u>." —Matthew 12:35

7.   An evil spirit being does not cause or bring punishment or trouble upon people, for Isaiah wrote:

"I will punish the world <u>for their evil</u>, and the wicked <u>for their iniquity</u>." —Isaiah 13:11

From Jeremiah:

"<u>That nation will I punish</u>, said the LORD, <u>with the sword</u>, and <u>with the famine</u> and <u>with the pestilence</u>, <u>until I have consumed</u> (destroyed) *them by his hand."* —Jeremiah 27:8

From Lamentations:

"Thou (God) hast covered with anger, and persecuted us; Thou (God) has slain, Thou hast not pitied." —Lamentations 3:43

From Amos:

> *"You only have I known of all the families of the earth;*
> *therefore I will punish you <u>for all your iniquities</u>"*
> —Amos 3:2

From Paul's letter to Roman brethren:

> *"The wrath of God is revealed from Heaven <u>against all</u>*
> *<u>ungodliness and unrighteousness of men</u> who hold the*
> *truth in unrighteousness."*—Romans 1:18

1. Claiming that a Satan is responsible for a person's wickedness would give the person an excuse for doing evil and absolve him of personal responsibility—the devil made me do it!

2. "Man is a free moral agent with power or option to will evil or will good"

3. *"A man is drawn away of his own lusts.".*—James 1:14

4. *"The soul (mind) of the <u>wicked desires evil</u>."*—Proverbs 21:10

5. *"The wicked, through the pride of his countenance, will not seek after God: <u>God is not in all his thoughts</u>."* —Psalms 10:4

6. In Strong's Concordance, Satan is identified as the "arch-enemy of good, adversary, accuser, to lurk for. Root meaning: to persecute, hate, oppose self, to know good and evil."

7. Committing evil is an adversarial act. A person can accuse self through guilt or condemnation, or have conflict within in determining whether to do evil as we read:

    > *"Behold, the man has become like one of us, <u>knowing good</u>*
    > *<u>and evil</u>."*—Genesis 3:22

8. It has been said of Jesus:

He accepted evil that came upon him, absorbing it, rather than returning it. Peacemaking was uppermost in his whole way of life. He saw violence, both psychological and physical as the way of evil, while the way of God is in following righteousness and to:

> *"Love God with all thy heart and thy neighbor as oneself"*
> —Luke 10:27

9. This was the center of his life and of His message."

10. In Hebrews we read: *"Jesus was in all points tempted as we are, yet without sin."*—Hebrews 4:15

We are not tempted by an evil spirit being. Remember, James said:

> *"We are drawn away by our own lusts."* —James 1:14

11. In the temptation of Jesus in the wilderness, he realized the path of evil (Satan, Devil, Serpent, or Dragon) lay in using miracles for selfish reasons, such as if he turned stones into bread to satisfy his hunger. Similarly, to climb to the top pinnacle of the temple and cast him self down without sustaining injury was not the way to illustrate God's power. The people would quickly accept it as such, but it was not the way or objective prophesied for the Messiah for Moses said in Deuteronomy:

> *"Ye shall not tempt the LORD your God, as ye tempted [him] in Massah."* —Deuteronomy 6:1

And in Psalms we read:

> *"For he shall give his angels (prophetic messages) charge over thee, to keep (guide) thee in all thy ways. They*

(prophecy will declare) shall bear thee up in [their] (its) hands (power), lest thou dash thy foot against a stone (meaning: if you stumble before you finish)." —Psalms 91:11–12

During the Gospel Age, between our Lord's first advent and His second advent, evil or wicked people have led themselves and others into all kinds of trouble and sorrow, including death. Many, professing to be followers of Jesus the Christ, have been instigators of evil. The words of the apostle Paul were forgotten or ignored as "Christians" under the banner of Jesus the Christ conceived and carried out abuse upon other people in much wickedness.

In Romans, Paul wrote:

"Let not sin therefore reign in your mortal bodies, to make you obey their passions. Do not yield your members to sin as instruments of wickedness, but yield yourselves to God as men who have been brought from death to life."—Romans 6:12

The above statements tell us that Christians are not to yield to sin or be instruments of wickedness. Desire and passion are to be controlled and not allowed to develop into wickedness in either religious or secular settings. In the above verse, Paul is telling us that an evil spirit being does not instigate evil thoughts in a person, but that each person is tempted by evil thoughts generated by lust, fear, envy, jealousy, and the like. In blaming a Satan, the believer projects the impression that an imagined, evil spirit being is the cause of sin, but responsibility for the evil act is looked for in the transgressor.

Blaming a Satan or Devil for one's own lust is evil, also deceitful to self and God. Evil acts therefore are not to be blamed upon a Satan. David's sin with Bathsheba did not come about in one moment. He allowed the evil to be nourished with lustful thoughts and desires and then decided to act. So also the mind of any person, including the mind of a Christian, can conceive evil, lust, envy, jealousy, fear, and hate, which adversely affects self and others if acted upon. Thus, the evil that an individual speaks or acts upon is generated in the heart (mind).

Evil: A Choice

"For as he thinks in his heart, so [is] he." —Proverbs 23:7

Jesus used the symbolic or picture expression for evil by using Satan, Devil, Serpent, or Dragon.

I read long ago that: "Jesus spoke in an abstract sense without suggesting time and place? He did not refer to a Satan as the source of evil."

Paul also did not question belief in a Devil, for evil is its own adversary. Picturesque or symbolic words lend a colorful aspect to a subject or name. For instance, during the First World War, a statesman proclaimed the whole world to be "on fire" to convincingly describe the raging conflict among nations; he used a figurative word. In similar fashion, the apostle Peter wrote:

> *"Your adversary the devil (evil or lust within us), as a roaring lion, prowls about (anger, jealousy, prejudice,*

fear & etc.) looking for someone to devour." —1 Peter 5:8, NEB

Peter was using picture language and substituted the synonym "Devil" for evil. Evil is like a roaring lion, set off by fear, anger, jealousy, or hatred, and can devour (arouse the emotions) of those nearby. Hitler inflamed the minds of millions of people. He aroused anger, fear, and hatred in their minds against the Jews.

Peter continues in verse 9:

> *"To exercise self control, to be watchful"* (TCN Translation). *"Resist him* (it—i.e., evil, Satan, Devil, Dragon, or Serpent).

The apostle James wrote:

> *"Resist (think good thoughts) the devil (evil), and he (evil) will flee (disappear) from you, draw nigh to God (seek righteousness and justice) and He will draw nigh to you, wash your hands (do not sin), you sinners (Gdsp. Translation) You who are double-minded, see that your motives are pure."*—James 4:7–8, NEB

Replacing the name "Devil" with the synonym "evil" makes it clear that the statement of James to "wash your hands" is symbolic, meaning that you are to have nothing to do with evil, which is conceived in the mind, not inveigled into the mind by an evil spirit being.

The local paper (Grand Rapids Press) published an article about a symposium held in New Orleans at the American Psychiatric Association convention in 2001. The subject was "Evil Is in the Mind of the Beholder." The author of the article, Janet McConnaughey, wrote:

> "Evil' is not a word most psychiatrists like. But some are trying to find a way to measure it. Dr. Michael Welner, a forensic psychiatrist, asked more than 120 psychiatrists to help create a 'depravity scale, which could be used by the courts to judge criminals. He said: Every day, judges ask juries to decide whether crimes are heinous, atrocious, cruel, outrageous, wanton, vile or inhuman—aggravating factors that can increase sentences and even lead to the death penalty in some states. However, he added that 'the bulk of evil on a world scale is committed by ideologues and their followers.' Wars and persecutions, from the Spanish Inquisition to the fighting in Bosnia, show people are capable of 'bottomless cruelty to those outside the tribe, especially in times of hardship and hunger,' he said.
>
> Welner also discussed other research that has highlighted problems with trying to measure depravity in criminals, primarily that some traits associated with people who cannibalize, mutilate or torture their victims also can be found in people who don't commit such crimes.
>
> Dr. Cleo Van Velsen, a forensic psychiatrist from London, who was in the audience, said another challenge is determining why people commit acts that can be described as evil. 'We know they exist, but not why they are produced."

Thus, the judicial system seeks ways to operate in a unified manner, a process of improving society.

Evil in the Dark Ages

The beginning of the so-called Dark Ages lasted at least three centuries, beginning about AD 1200 to 1300. That time period developed into a diabolical, mentally sick, and fearful phase in human history. The worst part was, it was led by many of the clergy, mayors, lawyers, and rulers who, thought to be trustworthy, took advantage of their power over the people.

It is said that the world's greatest libraries contain millions of volumes on witchcraft from that time period. One of the largest and most complete of the libraries is at Cornell University. Its sources looked upon witchcraft as being in the area of theology, and how, at times, religious leaders, with the support of their congregations, encouraged the use of witchcraft. Witchcraft uncovers how the human descends beneath the worst of animals. During those dark and terrible years of the Dark Ages, Christians; were often led by superstitious leaders who blamed a Devil for anything strange and fearful. Scriptures that could bring charitable light to congregations were often ignored or kept quiet by repressive religious leaders.

The Bible, in Proverbs, while prophetic of Israel, can also apply to many "Christians" of the Gospel Age, for it says:

> *"They will call upon Me, but I will not answer. They will seek Me diligently but will not find Me, because they hated knowledge and did not choose the reverence of the LORD, they would have none of My counsel and despised My reproof, therefore, they shall eat the fruit of their way and be sated with their own devices. For the simple are killed by their turning away, the complacence of fools destroys them, but he who listens to Me will dwell secure and will be at ease without the dread of evil* **(Satan, Devil, Serpent, Dragon)**.*"*—Proverbs 1: 28–31

In 1 Corinthians the apostle Paul wrote:

> *"Now these things are warnings for us, <u>not to desire evil</u> as they did."*—1 Corinthians 10:6

Both Proverbs and Paul's words were and are often ignored. History reveals how religious and political leaders used religion to encourage ignorant and thoughtless people to desire evil and support violence and warfare. In contrast; our Lord acted and taught the opposite; we read in Hebrews where it speaks of the humanity of Jesus the Christ:

> *"Jesus was in all points tempted as we are, [yet] without sin."* —Hebrews 4:15

Isaiah prophesied of the Messiah (Jesus the Christ) in the wilderness:

> *"He shall eat curds and honey when he knows how to refuse the evil and choose the good."* —Isaiah 7:15

Jesus, at the age of twelve, <u>was learning</u> to "refuse the evil and choose the good" as told in Luke:

> *"And it came to pass, that after three days they found him in the temple, sitting in the midst of the doctors, both hearing them, and asking them questions."* —Luke 2:46

As followers of our Lord, we also are to learn by following his example in seeking the ways of wisdom, righteousness, and justice with Scripture as our guide. This is the most reliable manner in which to refuse evil and choose good. The implication of Isaiah's prophecy is that Immanuel (Jesus), as the Messiah and guided by God's holy (righteous, just, and loving) spirit, would be able to resist acting upon any evil thought that might come into his mind. Jesus did not dwell upon evil thoughts but rejected them, desiring every day to follow God's will of love, truth, mercy, righteousness, justice, and the like as the top priority in his ministry. Therefore, Jesus the Christ resisted all temptation of evil. The will to act upon righteous and just thoughts at all times has eluded people since Adam, except for our Lord.

It is not unusual that the practice of justice and righteousness loses its appeal for many people when faced with the temptation of glory, power, or riches, especially in a religious position. Evil is insidious; ever since Adam, there have been people in every generation, Jews or Christians, in positions of authority or power that have abused, deceived, or harmed others. History reveals that some Church leaders used their power to torment or kill other Christians for not following religious rules or tradition. That abuse of power occurred mostly in the Dark Ages. There have been other abuses of leadership since then, but not as overwhelming as in those dark years of superstition and fear.

The Bible, the light for Christians; was forcefully withheld from Christians by Church leaders and the state. By AD 1350, the Inquisition, under Pope John the Twenty-second, had burned over six hundred persons as heretics for practicing sorcery. The Inquisitors burned accused heretics, and then confiscated their property. Only when the courts stopped the confiscation of property did the accusations of witchcraft and persecution cease by both Church and state; it no longer was profitable. The evil heart of greed had dominated the heart of many under the cloak of religion.

Nothing about witchcraft and the Devil is more ominous than the suppression and destruction of man's right to think and ask questions. When leaders demand doctrine and tradition be held above investigation and truth, knowledge and liberty fall by the wayside. People then fail to progress intellectually and emotionally, as superstitious ideas become common. This is seen when Thomas Aquinas (a Catholic theologian), using popular theories sanctioned by Augustine (an earlier Catholic theologian), commented that, "devils had ability to transform men into animals." He then reasoned: "The Devil creates in the mind of a man an illusion and then from a body of air makes a second outward illusion to correspond to the mental illusion."

Such double talk was fostered on the people to the point where they saw a Satan around every corner. Evil thoughts and acts have dominated much of human existence. But today, progress is being made in that the veil of ignorance and superstition is being lifted. Discerning Christians recognize that evil is conceived in the mind of humans rather than inspired by an invisible, evil spirit being. The courts and news media give support to this fact in that those convicted of crimes are held responsible for their evil acts and their evil acts are not blamed on a Satan or Devil.

The writer of Ecclesiastes wrote many centuries ago:

> *"The heart of the sons <u>of men is full of evil,</u> and madness is in their heart while they live."*—Ecclesiastes 9:3

And, centuries before that statement, Moses wrote: *"The Lord God saw the wickedness of man was great in the earth."* —Genesis 6:5

In 1 Samuel we read: *"Wickedness proceeds from the wicked."* —1 Samuel 24:13

Again, in 1 Samuel we read: *"Nabal was churlish (rude, narrow-minded) and <u>evil in his doings.</u>"*—1 Samuel 25:3

Also in 1 Samuel:

> *"The <u>evil spirit from God</u> came upon Samuel"*—1 Samuel 18:10

Whether it is a mistranslation or a poor quote, the above statement (The evil spirit from God) is to harmonize with the rest of Scripture. It can help us comprehend what is meant when we recognize that the evil thoughts of Saul led to his evil act and that God allowed it. Even Jewish tradition supports this interpretation by acknowledging that sin and evil imaginings are part of every man. For example, in referring to those who do not grasp the Gospel, the apostle Paul in 2 Corinthians wrote:

> *"But if our gospel be hid, it is hid to them that are lost: In whom the god of this world (lusts, evil) hath blinded the minds of them which believe not"* —2 Corinthians 4:3–4

The apostle was speaking of people caring only for the present and not wanting to be bothered with the Good News in Jesus the Christ. The small "g" in "god" indicates that Paul referred to their thoughts focused only upon things or achievements of this world. Many Christians have interpreted this "god" to be an evil spirit being called Satan or Devil. As previously mentioned, "Devil" means "personification of supreme evil." The apostle was talking about the folly of trusting in things of this world that become as a god—i.e., the desire for possessions that consumes us.

The traditional concept of a Satan, Devil, Serpent, or Dragon often develops because of foreboding thoughts about conditions that a person cannot control. The human mind then begins blaming an imaginary Satan or Devil as the source of a problem. It is when feelings of helplessness create notions of uncontrolled evil at work that a person justifies the premise that an evil spirit being is the cause.

Today, in much of the world, we see dramatic advancements in mental and physical health along with greater equity and justice. These changes result from increasing knowledge, which are signs restitution blessings are at work, signs that the spirit of our Lord is at work or is present. This is a binding of Satan, Devil, Serpent, Dragon, or evil that entails centuries of progressive elimination of ignorance and superstition with social improvements through increasing knowledge in the willing of righteousness, justice, mercy, love, respect, and so on. It is the Lord's spirit operating in the hearts of people that gradually brings these changes in societies. Thus the Lord's spiritual presence is perceived by the abundance of righteousness, justice, truth, and mercy, which then tests and reveals what is good and what is evil within and around us.

A very important point to remember is that, in reading and interpreting Revelation especially, we are not dealing with the literal personage of the Lord but with the abstract or symbolic term of a condition, event, place, or entity. In other words, humans cannot see, touch, hear, or smell his presence. His presence is recognized by what transpires in the hearts of people. It is the legacy of righteousness, justice, truth, mercy, and love, the positive characteristics of our Lord, which his apostles and his followers live by and which, through God's spirit, are emulated and grow in the hearts of people. It entails a transformation of desire and motivation of the heart, the energy of the spirit, into tangible results. This becomes evident when people who do not know of God's saving grace through Jesus the Christ become loving and just, manifesting a spirit of righteousness and truth, and unknowingly become part of the gradual revealing of the Kingdom of Jesus the Christ upon earth.

In Revelation we read:

> *"And he laid hold on the dragon, that old serpent, which is the Devil, and Satan, and bound him* **(it about)** *a thousand years* **(evil is restrained during the Thousand Years)***."* —Revelation 20:2

However, we also read in 2 Peter: *"But, beloved, be not ignorant of this one thing, that one day [is] with the LORD as a thousand years, and a thousand years as one day."*—2 Peter 3:8

It appears Peter was saying that God does not apply an exact period of time of one thousand years from start to finish in which evil, Satan, Devil, Serpent, or Dragon is being bound, but, as one translation has it, evil, Satan, Devil, Serpent, or Dragon is being bound during an approximate thousand years.

If a specific time period were held to, the elimination of evil overnight would conflict with how God has dealt with change in the past. What is suggested, therefore, is that when restitution progresses far enough, those in the graves will be resurrected in reverse generational sequence and have the opportunity to learn righteousness during an approximate time period. The intensity of evil, Satan, Devil, Serpent, or Dragon will cease (evil's demise) as people make progress towards perfection. Likewise, at the end of the Kingdom, evil (Satan, Devil, Serpent, or Dragon) will be allowed for a short period of time in a final test for everyone professing faith and trust in Jesus the Christ. As John tells us in Revelation:

> *"And when the (approximate) thousand years are expired, Satan (evil, Devil, Serpent, or Dragon) shall be loosed out of his (its) prison (restriction) and shall go out (be allowed) to deceive the nations which are in the four quarters of the earth, Gog and Magog, to gather them together to battle: the number of whom [is] as the sand of the sea (millions of people resorting to evil). And they went up on the breadth of the earth, and compassed the camp of the saints about (attempt to establish rule of men, not of God) and the beloved city and fire (righteousness and destruction) came down from God out of heaven, and devoured them."* —Revelation 20:7–9

Through increasing knowledge during restitution it will also be revealed that there is one Almighty God, not a triune God, as we read in Genesis:

> *"The LORD appeared to Abram, and said unto him, I [am] the Almighty God; walk before me, and be thou perfect (righteous)."*—Genesis 17:1.

And in Deuteronomy *"Hear, O Israel: The LORD our God [is] one LORD."* —Deuteronomy 6:4

Moses did not advocate a triune god such as the heathen worshiped. There also is not an evil spirit being who is equal to or who is an opposing god to Jehovah God. The theological doctrine of dualism, i.e. that there are two eternal and opposing principles of good and evil, does not mean there are two opposing gods. It means that good and evil are values people act upon. It is not the invasion of the mind by an invisible, evil spirit being, though it has been assumed that way. As free moral agents, God has given us the ability and liberty to think and act according to the values of good or evil, prompted by praise, love, and peace or the opposite of selfishness, desire, lust, hate, and envy.

But, it's common in religious circles to profess that Satan or evil spirit beings cause evil along with insinuations of demon possession. Those claiming belief in a Devil ignore what they claim to believe, namely that an evil spirit being is hovering about them seeking to harm or mislead them even as they act upon their desires or lusts. The concept is as confusing as the concept of the trinity. Rational people recognize their responsibility for evil expressed by words and deeds, the result of feelings and emotions. The apostle Paul wrote of the Christian's responsibility for evil:

> *"And you he made alive (in Jesus the Christ), when you were dead through the trespasses and sins in which you once walked, <u>following the course of the world</u>, following the prince of the power of the air (passions of our flesh), the spirit (evil) that is <u>now at work</u> in the <u>following the desires of body and mind,</u> sons of disobedience. Among these <u>we all once lived in the passions</u> of our flesh,* —Ephesians 2:1—3; RSV.

Christians usually experience a mental struggle as truth (fact or revelation) confronts erring belief ingrained from childhood, for it is not simple for a person to change his or her belief system. To change from belief in the existence of an evil spirit being or Satan to unbelief in such a spirit being can be as great a struggle as changing one's belief that everyone has an immortal soul to the belief that everyone is a living soul, or to change from a belief in eternal torment to believing that a person, as a living soul, can face eternal destruction. Beliefs can change when one reasons in the spirit of truth, which ignores ritual and tradition thought to be sacred.

> In the Gospel of Matthew Jesus the Christ says: *"The good man produces good and the evil man produces evil."* —Matthew 12:35

The apostle Paul supports this in Romans:

> *"Let not sin reign in your bodies to make you obey their passions."* —Romans 6:12

Both Jesus the Christ and Paul were saying that each person has the power to either follow the way of righteousness or to act upon evil. It is the evil springing from within (fear, anger, lust, selfishness, and the like), which, if not controlled by one's mind, can result in harmful or sinful words and actions. The Christian is to be aware of this, as a relationship with the Heavenly Father depends upon faithfulness in thought and action in the spirit of truth.

Proverbs 23:7 tells us:

> *"For as he thinks in his heart, so [is] he."*

Evil acts are a product of evil thoughts. The Christian is to grow in self-control and awareness of potential evil from within, his or her faith and trust in God through Jesus the Christ is strengthened by learning to filter daily activities through a screen of thoughts and desire for justice, righteousness, love, mercy, and compassion. As James wrote:

> *"We are lured and enticed by our own desires."*—James 1:14

Awareness of potential evil is to be with us daily. To counter potential spiritual weakness, the apostle Paul cautions us in 1 Thessalonians to:

> *"Pray without ceasing"*—1 Thessalonians 5:17

This means to keep in mind the need to speak and practice righteousness and justice.

Past Decisions of Councils

In AD 367, after many years of debate, arguing, and even violence, councils of Christian leaders approved the sacred writings that make up what we now know as the Bible. Certain books and writings that were considered mythical, not relevant to spirituality, of doubtful authority, or not authentic were not included—thus the differences between the Roman Catholic-approved Bible and the Protestant Bible. The Apocrypha, for instance, was accepted by Roman Catholics but not by Protestants. Today, with present knowledge, interpretation of Scripture using the latest Bible translations will produce a variety of viewpoints. Religious history reveals the difficulty Christians have had in understanding sacred writings. An example is an interesting article titled: "Tartarus" that appeared in *The Bible Study Monthly* of January/February 1985, describing how the meaning of a word can change. The unidentified author wrote:

> "In the New Testament a little used word in connection with hell is 'tartarus.' The word refers to pits of nether gloom or gloomy caverns and comes from Greek mythology. The Greeks said that, far back in the early days of the world, there was a great

rebellion of the Titans. The sons of Uranus and his wife Gea rebelled against Zeus, the god of heaven. The conflict was fierce, but eventually the Titans were overthrown and cast down to Tartarus, which was then closed up with brazen gates, and there the rebels remain to this day.

Such stories of mythology enshrining some dim thought distorted recollection of events before the flood and, together with Greek ideas of immortality, began to effect the religious beliefs of the Jews years before the Lord's first advent. To some extent, the old belief in Sheol, where there was 'no knowledge, no device, nor work of any kind, and the thoughts of man perish' (Ecclesiastes 9:10 and Psalms 146:4) had become colored with ideas of future punishment. 'Tartarus' began to be accepted as a place where retribution would be meted out to the specially wicked. Meanings of the words Tartarus and Hades changed for many, but Jesus and the New Testament writers did not countenance the myths and stood foursquare for the traditional Sheol, a place of unconsciousness, of sleep, illumed with the certain hope of resurrection by virtue of Jesus, the Messiah."

Another unidentified *Bible Study Monthly* contributor, speaking of the time the Maccabees of Israel existed, stated:

"Little known to today's general public, a great number of writings of Jewish scribes existed in the days of Jesus. Some of the writings were looked upon as of the twelve patriarchs. The parchments were written between 137 BC and 107 BC. During that time, a Pharisee with a rare gift of writing secured publicity by using the names of the greatest men of ancient times and wrote what he thought each patriarch would have written. The twelve patriarchs were looked upon as intellectual giants, so the Pharisee would compose as the testament of each patriarch of Israel, from Reuben to Benjamin, a brief life story on each one's deathbed with all his children, grandchildren and great-grandchildren gathered about him.

Each story had moral guidance and if the patriarch fell into sin, he would tell of it and counsel everyone present not to err as he did. If he was virtuous, he would tell what rewards were his. There were remarkable expectations of the coming Messiah. These fabricated stories by an unknown writer, written as the thoughts of the patriarchs, were very prominent in the days of Jesus and the apostles, influencing their thought and diction as they spoke and wrote.

The Sermon on the Mount uses phrases from these testaments. Also, when the apostle Paul wrote from various locations, he freely borrowed from them. He may have even carried a copy of the testaments with him. From the testament of Levi, chapter 2:1–4, a part is quoted: 'Now, therefore know that the Lord shall execute judgment upon the sons of men, because when the rocks are being rent and the sun quenched and the waters dried up and the fire cowering and all creation troubled, and the invisible spirits melting away, and Hades takes spoils through the visitation of the Most High, men will be unbelieving and persist in their iniquity. On this account with punishment shall they be judged. Therefore the Most High hath heard thy prayer, to separate thee from iniquity and that thou should become to Him a son and a servant and a minister of His presence.'"

The writer of the article is of the opinion that the apostle Paul was quite familiar with this quote from Enoch, even though Enoch's writings are not included in the New Testament of the Protestant Bible. The article continued:

> "The Jews considered such writings (though not actually written by the twelve patriarchs) as sacred and worthy of following. It was not uncommon in the centuries before Christ for capable Jewish writers to shelter themselves behind other great names of the dead. They would imagine what Solomon or Enoch would say or sing on certain topics under given circumstances. The people considered it was not that writer but the words of their Solomon or Enoch uttering the prophecies. The book of Enoch, which is not accepted by many scholars as authentic, gives strong evidence of an unknown writer. For example, from the Secrets of Enoch 18:3–5: And they said unto me:

> These are the Grigori (soldiers of heaven) who with their prince (Satanail) rejected the Lord of Light, and after them are those who are held in great darkness in the second heaven and three of them went down to earth from the Lord's throne to the place Ermon and broke their vows on the shoulder of the hill Ermon and saw the daughters of men how good they are and took to themselves wives and befouled the earth with their deeds, who in all times of their age made lawlessness and mixing, and giants are born and marvelous big men and great enmity.

> And therefore God judged them with great judgment and they weep for their brethren and they will be punished on the Lord's day and I said to the Grigor:

I saw your brethren and their works and their great torments and I prayed for them, but the Lord has condemned them to be under the earth till Heaven and Earth shall end forever.

The Jews of the apostle Paul's day looked upon such writings as sacred and worthy of following though not written by the one whose name appeared at its heading. Also, the above portion from the 'Secrets of Enoch' illustrates how superstition and imagination were part of daily life at the time of our Lord's first advent."

There are other tidbits of history that can help us understand conditions affecting beliefs in that day. The Pharisees believed that a person's soul is immortal and that under the earth (in the grave) there will be rewards or punishments according to the way people have lived, whether virtuously or in evil. They believed evil souls will be detained in an everlasting prison ("Aionian Tartarus"; in Greek "aion" means "eternal"), but the virtuous shall have power to revive and live again. The historian Josephus endeavored to blend the Jewish belief in death and resurrection with the Greek idea of reward and punishment. This is another instance of revelations of God becoming entwined with worldly philosophies.

Our Lord and the apostles, to some degree, were aware of such myths in their day and sometimes used them to advantage, as the apostle Paul did on Mars' Hill in Athens. Peter's single allusion to Tartarus as the prison of fallen angels, a belief that was prevalent in that day, comes from the book of Enoch, a book that many Christians today do not accept as part of the inspired Word.

"Angel" Generally Means "Messenger"

"For if God spared not the angels (messengers, false prophets) that sinned, but cast [them] down to hell (grave), and delivered [them] into chains of darkness (ignorance), to be reserved unto judgment."—2 Peter 2:4

This verse from 2 Peter illustrates the colorful, figurative language of that day. The common interpretation is that spirit beings sinned and are kept in chains (restriction) of darkness, hell, nether gloom, or dungeons (as Goodspeed translates it) to await their doom. This raises the question: How can fallen angels (evil messengers) have the ability to suggest evil thoughts to people if they are in chains (bound) in darkness and therefore unable to contact people? Why would translators so often translate the Hebrew and Greek words for messenger with "angel"? Could it be that they were trying to apply a "spirit being" connotation to the context?

The word "messenger," depending upon the context, can refer to a deputy, angel, ambassador, king, priest, prophet, or teacher. If the reader visualizes only a spirit being when seeing the word "angel" when the context does not involve a spirit being, he or she will have distorted perception of the meaning of the text. Thus Peter's statement may be interpreted in three different ways:

1. That the sons of God were spirit beings materializing as men, took wives, and begot children who were giants, violent, ungodly, and wicked.

2. That the sons of God (priests, messengers, and prophets) were descendants of Seth who served God, but intermarried with women descended from Cain.

3. That the sons of God (priests, messengers, and prophets) were descendants of Seth, who in Noah's day were spiritual leaders or priests and lusted after and had relationships with the beautiful young women who served at the temple. The children born of these unrighteous unions, in turn, became strong in power and violent tyrants of great wickedness.

The third statement is preferable, as angels neither marry nor are given in marriage (i.e., they do not mate with humans) as stated by Jesus the Christ in the Gospel of Matthew:

> *"For in the resurrection they (people) neither marry, nor are given in marriage, but are as the angels of God in heaven."*—Matthew 22:30

Thus, except for very special occasions, God allows only limited contact between spirit beings and humans. We also find that followers of Jesus are often called "sons of God," and there is evidence that, before the flood, people who served God in the temple were referred to as sons of God. This designation relates to both the objective and faithfulness of the believers. The concept of fallen angels is a theory that seems to be written in stone with many Christians. But some Christians, after having thoroughly examined the subject, will consider the concept unacceptable. As is often the case, concepts or ideas are subject to a gauntlet of questions. A statement made by Pastor Charles T. Russell years ago provides excellent advice when it comes to accepting different ideas; he said:

> "We should learn to love and value truth for its own sake, to respect and honor it by owning and acknowledging it wherever we find it and by whomsoever presented. Accept truth wherever you find it, no matter what it contradicts and rely for ability to afterwards harmonize it with others upon the spirit of truth, which shall guide you into all truth as Jesus promised."

It has been said that truth is as we are or as we believe. Thus, it often happens after a religious leader has passed from the scene that devoted followers rally around that leader's writings and cease looking for further truth, especially any information that might question the founding leader's concepts or ideas. They may also fear asking questions about doctrine, as doing so would indicate unfaithfulness to the former leader's writings or lead to change that can be unsettling. In regard to unbelievers, the apostle Paul wrote in 2 Corinthians:

> *"The god of this world has blinded the minds of the unbelievers."* —2 Corinthians 4:4

Was Paul referring to an evil spirit being, a powerful opponent of God who has the power to subvert God's commands? Should not Paul's words harmonize with his previous statement to Christians in 2 Corinthians?

> *"But have renounced the hidden things of dishonesty, not walking in craftiness, nor handling the word of God*

deceitfully; but by manifestation of the truth commending ourselves to every man's conscience in the sight of God."—2 Corinthians 4:2

Paul was referring to the evil practice of some leaders to disgracefully use cunning ways in tampering with God's word, through which vacillating Christians are susceptible to evil machinations, as stated in Genesis:

"The <u>imagination of man's heart is evil</u> from his youth."
—Genesis 8:21

Also, in Ephesians, Paul wrote:

"That we [henceforth] be no more children, tossed to and fro, and carried about with every wind of doctrine, by the sleight <u>of men</u>, [and] cunning craftiness, whereby <u>they lie in wait to deceive</u>."—Ephesians 4:14

"The god of this world" in 2 Corinthians 4:4 refers not only to lust, sin, and wickedness, and the pride of people ignoring God's love through Jesus the Christ, but, through pride, have an unwillingness to see themselves as sinners. "The god of this world" also is not a reference to an evil spirit being that instigates evil. It is the lust of the heart or a hardness of heart, stirring the spirit of unbelief, which allows evil thoughts to lead to evil acts. Paul's words in Galatians reminds us:

"Be not deceived; God is not mocked: for <u>whatsoever a man sows</u>, that shall he also reap."—Galatians 6:7

In Genesis, we read about the source of evil:

"The LORD saw that the <u>wickedness of man was great</u> in the earth, and that every imagination of the thoughts

of his heart <u>was only evil continually</u>."   —Genesis 6:5

There is no blaming a Satan here. It is man's evil imagination and thoughts that, when acted upon, lead to sin. When thoughts are directed towards repentance, righteousness, love, and truth— Jesus being the great example of righteousness and truth—the individual can change and become a new person with a deeper awareness of his wicked and evil (Satan, Devil, Serpent, or Dragon) thoughts, which are unacceptable. In Hebrews we read:

> *"Take care, brethren, lest there be <u>in any of you an unbelieving heart</u>, leading you to fall away from the living God."*—Hebrews 3:12

The responsibility to maintain a believing heart rests with each individual. An invisible demon or a Satan does not put unbelief in the mind; rather, it is in allowing desire (or lust) in our minds to linger that tempts us into evil. When we focus our minds on practicing love, mercy, justice, truth, righteousness, and the like, we show evidence to others and to God of our belief and the love of God in our lives. Again in Hebrews we read:

> *"But strong meat belongs to them that are of full age, [even] those who by reason of use have their <u>senses exercised to discern both good and evil</u>."*—Hebrews 5:14

The apostle is telling us that we are to train our mental faculties to distinguish between righteousness and evil. This is verified in 2 Timothy:

> *"<u>Flee also youthful lusts</u>: but follow righteousness, faith, charity, peace, with them that call on the LORD out of a pure heart. But <u>foolish and unlearned questions avoid</u>,*

knowing that they do gender strife."—2 Timothy 2:22–23

But didn't Paul say in 2 Timothy:

"And [that] they may recover themselves out of the snare of the devil, (evil) who are taken captive by him (evil, Satan, Devil, Serpent, or Dragon) at his (evil, Satan, Devil, Serpent, or Dragon) will" —2 Timothy 2:26

This generates questions such as: How does an evil spirit being snare a person? How can the condition of being snared be recognized? How can the snared person be held responsible? Then, too, what does it mean to be a captive of 'the Devil'? How does this idea harmonize with other scriptures, such as Proverbs?

"Devise not evil against thy neighbor, seeing he dwells securely by thee."—Proverbs 3:29

"Devil," "him," and "his" in 2 Timothy 2:26 refer to a person's evil thoughts, not to an evil spirit being. If taken literally, how would an evil spirit being take a human captive? Does not "snare" refer to lusts of the flesh, as in jealousy, envy, desire, and so on? Do not evil thoughts become snares that involve evil (Satan, Devil, Serpent, or Dragon), which is manifested by a person's attitude and action? By the way, translators are divided over how to apply "him" and "his" in the phrase: *"taken captive by him at his will."* Some apply it to a Devil, while others apply it to God. The Diaglott, in its word-for-word English translation, uses "accuser" [enemy] rather than "devil." Isn't it when we know righteousness but choose evil that we allow our lusts to lead us into sin?

Proverbs cautions us to be careful in our choices:
*"Enter not into the path <u>of the wicked</u>, go not in the way
<u>of evil men</u>.* ---Proverbs 4:14

This instruction points to personal responsibility to make the
decision, before action, to control lust, hate, jealousy, envy,
pride, and so on. This would be why Paul reminded Timothy
in electing Church leaders:

> *"He (the elder) must not be a recent convert, or he may be
> puffed up with conceit and fall into the condemnation of
> the devil (evil, accuser); moreover he must be well thought
> of by outsiders or he may fall into reproach and the snare
> of the devil (accuser, Satan, Serpent, Dragon, or evil)"*
> —1 Timothy 3:6–7

Conceit surfaces when we allow evil and prideful thoughts or lust
to show in our actions and words. Electing a recent convert to
the position of leadership is harmful, as the person elected may
be tempted to display a superior or prideful attitude, bringing
condemnation and reproach, which would cast a shadow of evil
upon the Lord's name. An evil spirit being is not to be blamed
for the new convert's pride; the situation develops because the
congregation ignored the potential problem of a recent convert's
possible pride. Proverbs tells us:

> *"When pride comes, then comes shame: but with the lowly
> [is] wisdom."* —Proverbs 11:2

And James wrote:

> *"Each person is tempted when he (or she) is lured and
> enticed by his (or her) own desire (lust)."*—James 1:14

Thus, a recent convert, when elected elder or deacon, is subjected
to pride of superiority over fellow Christians

Jesus Tempted by Lust?

In Hebrews, we read of Jesus the Christ:

> *"For we have not a high priest who is unable to sympathize with our weaknesses, but one who in every respect has been tempted as we are, yet without sinning."*—Hebrews 4:15

Remember what James wrote:

> *"But every man is tempted, when he is drawn away of his own lust, and enticed."*—James 1:14

Jesus the Christ, aware of temptations, did not allow them to have any influence in his doing God's will. Through prayerful communication to his Heavenly Father he remained focused and maintained disciplined control at all times over his words and actions. It says in the Gospel of John:

> *"For I came down from Heaven, not to do my own will, but the will of Him who sent me."*—John 6:38

In the Gospel of Matthew we read of Jesus the Christ being led by the spirit of God into the wilderness (Matthew 4:1). The spirit of God was not a literal spirit being, but the desire, determination, and attitude of Jesus to do his Heavenly Father's will. His quest to serve God in spirit and truth required solitude and prayerful reflection upon Scripture, which would give him the insight to conduct himself in harmony with prophecy and in truth. After fasting forty days and nights according to Jewish Law, he became vulnerable to temptation. Nutritious food would be highly desired, and temptation built up to satisfy this need. To turn the stones into bread was tempting—wasn't he the Son of God with power according to prophecy? Did not the dreams and visions his mother experience—along with those of Joseph, the wise men, John the Baptist, Anna the Prophetess, Simeon, the shepherds, Elizabeth, Zechariah the priest, and the prophets of old confirm he would have the power to do so? Remembering what Moses told Israel in Deuteronomy, Jesus the Christ resisted the temptation to serve self:

> *"And He humbled you (Israel) and let you hunger and fed you with manna, which you did not know, nor did your fathers know, that He might make you know that man does not live by bread alone, but that man lives by everything that proceeds out of the mouth of the Lord.*
> —Deuteronomy 8:3

Applying the words of Moses to his own situation, Jesus the Christ overcame the temptation to use the power of God for personal gratification. He next considered the possibility of going to Jerusalem, to climb to the highest corner of the temple and jump off to illustrate that God's power would save him, for did not the Psalmist say:

> *"For He will give His angels (message of prophets) charge of you to guard you in all your ways, on their hands they*

will bare you up, lest you dash your foot against a stone."
—Psalms 91:10,11

Jesus the Christ countered this thought of temptation with the statement of Deuteronomy:

"You shall not put the Lord your God to the test."
—Deuteronomy 6:16

He determined that such a public display of illustrating God's protection over him was not God's will and put the temptation out of his mind. With the third temptation, Jesus imagined that, if he climbed to the peak of the highest mountain and looked out upon the kingdoms of this world, all those kingdoms and their splendor could be his through the power of God. Again Jesus resisted the evil thought and countered it with the words of Moses in Deuteronomy:

"You shall fear (have reverence for) the LORD your God, you shall serve Him and swear (vow) by His name."
—Deuteronomy 11:22

As the spirit of God through prophecy and prayer guided his thoughts, Jesus the Christ avoided what James later wrote as:

"Drawn away by his own lust and enticed."—James 1:14

Again, in Hebrews, referring to Jesus the Christ, it says: *"But was in all points tempted as we are."*—Hebrews 4:15

After being baptized by John in the Jordan River upon leaving Galilee (Matthew 3:13), Jesus the Christ, through the inspiration of God's Holy Spirit, proceeded into the wilderness. Matthew describes the experience of Jesus the Christ in the customary manner of his day by using the persona "Satan" as a metaphor for evil or "opposing thoughts," as Strong's Concordance informs us. We then understand how he was "tempted, as we are tempted." Keep in mind that Jesus spent forty days and nights in the wilderness; there, he fasted according to Jewish law, allowing basic food and limited water as he prayed and reviewed prophecies relating to his mission as the Christ or Messiah. Matthew's account limits his location to a specific area; he did not leave and travel to the temple in Jerusalem to be tempted, nor did he actually climb the highest mountain. Another detail to consider in the wilderness experience of Jesus is the comment of Matthew:

> *"Then the devil (evil thoughts) left him, and, behold, angels* (messengers) *came and ministered unto him."*
> ---Matthew 4:11

"Devil" refers to evil (Satan, Dragon, Serpent, or, as Strong's Concordance says, opposing thoughts) that tempted Jesus to overcome the evil of temptation to use the power of God for personal gain.

Why would the angels that came to him be spirit beings rather than messengers from John the Baptist? The latter suggestion is more reasonable, for Matthew wrote:

> *"Now when he (Jesus) heard (from John's messengers) that John had been arrested, he withdrew into Galilee."*—
> Matthew 4:12

Messengers from John evidently brought Jesus the Christ news of John's arrest and would also keep in contact to minister to him—that is, to bring water and basic food according to Jewish

Law required for fasting, along with parchments of the prophets during the forty days as told in Matthew:

> *"And when he had fasted forty days and forty nights, he was hungry afterwards."*—Matthew 4:2

This meant that Jesus was ready for some nutritious food. Thus, communication between Jesus the Christ and John the Baptist took place by means of messengers as they separately traveled the country as mentioned in Luke:

> *"When the men were come unto him, they said, <u>John the Baptist hath sent us</u> unto thee, saying, Art thou he that should come or look we for another?"* — Luke 7:20

Evidently, Jesus and John kept in contact by sending messengers to each other as they traveled in different areas.

Evil· an Act of Disobedience

The temptation to sin is described in a pictorial manner in the story of the Serpent and Eve in Genesis 3:1–5. Also, the conversation between God and Adam in vs. 9–12, between God and Eve in vs. 13, between God and the Serpent in vs. 14–15, between God and Eve again in vs. 16, and between God and Adam in vs. 17–19.

Before he sinned, Adam was warned against disobedience:

> *"God said to Adam: You may freely eat of every tree of the garden; but of the tree of the knowledge of good and evil you shall not eat, for in the day that you eat of it you shall die."*—Genesis 2:16–17

Adam was not to eat of the tree of the knowledge of good and evil. The word "tree" in Hebrew basically means "from its firmness" (Strong's Concordance 6086). This figurative use of "tree" also occurs in *Proverbs:" The fruit of the righteous is a tree (firmness) of life."*—Proverbs 11:30

And again in Proverbs: "Desire comes, it is a tree (firmness) of life." —Proverbs 13:12

Therefore, the figurative "tree" "from its firmness" of the knowledge of good and evil, to Adam and Eve, means to not yield to temptation, to not try the firmness of God's command by choosing to disobey, which is evil, which is the "fruit" Adam took of, thus violating God's command, the temptation is described by James:

"Then when lust hath conceived, it brings forth sin." —James 1:15

Eve chose to pursue her lust even though it meant disobeying God. After Adam chose to participate in the disobedience, sin affected their lives for the first time. Eve then said in Genesis 3:13:

"The Serpent (evil thought) beguiled me."

Eve was actually describing her experience of allowing her lust to control her actions. The evil, the insidious feeling (Satan, Serpent, Devil, or Dragon) of disobedience, became apparent to them after they chose to disobey.

In Genesis 3:1 we read:

"The serpent (Satan, Devil, Dragon, or evil) was more subtle (devious) than any beast of the field."

Strong gives the basic meaning of the word "subtle" as "cunning" or "crafty," the way of a serpent. This is a picture description of how evil can work in the thinking process. The question arises: Why would the Serpent be spoken of as "more subtle than any beast of the field"? The answer appears to be that the subtle thought (lust) was a new experience to Eve, and the thought of knowing both good and evil was beguiling to her. It compelled her to test God's "firmness" (tree) and satisfy her desire for knowledge of both good and evil. Another point is that, if the Serpent were a literal serpent, it would have to crawl and climb a tree, and the serpent's "seed" would also have to be literal, to be little serpents; furthermore, the account also says:

> *"Upon your belly you shall go, and dust you shall eat all the days of your life."*—Genesis 3:14

This picture language describes how low 'evil' (Serpent, Devil, Satan, or Dragon) is to be regarded; it is rebellious and destructive to our relationship with God. The Serpent symbolizes how evil comes from within us, and its seed is symbolic of how evil continues to negatively affect mankind through the hereditary (sin) factor from Adam, which ends in death. Thus, in this account, the writer in picture language speaks of the effects of evil and its final outcome.

> *"And the LORD God said unto the serpent (evil), because you (evil) have done this, you (evil) [are] cursed above all cattle, and above every beast of the field; upon your belly (low esteem) shall you go, and dust (destructiveness) shall you eat (be known for) all the days of your life (existence). And I will put enmity (fear) between you (evil) and the woman, and between your seed and her seed; it shall bruise (limit) your head (power), and you (evil) shall bruise (limit) his heel (activity)."*—Genesis 3:14–15

Thus, evil is referred to as a creature, which is cursed (condemned), crawls, eats dust, has enmity (is feared), has seed, has a bruised head, and bruises the heel of the woman's seed. The account, if perceived as literal, is not comprehensible, but when taken figuratively provides a general understanding of how sin began, its effect, and its ending. The picture of sin entering into the human thought process (such as with lust) can be seen in that devious thinking often results in feelings of guilt and fear. Thus:

> *"The serpent **(evil, Satan, Devil, or Dragon)** was more 'subtle' (devious) than any beast of the field."*—Genesis 3:1

Strong gives as the basic meaning of the word "beast" "to live" (#2416 & 2421). Thus "beast" in Genesis may be interpreted as an unexamined desire to live, or to live independently of God, and Eve became obsessed with this desire to live independently, avoiding responsibility to the will of God. This new feeling was a crafty and elusive craving that profoundly affected Eve. Her desire, unrestrained, clouded her judgment. Jesus, however, was fully aware of this human weakness and kept it at bay by prayer and evaluating his course of action daily in harmony with prophecy. The first five books of the Bible are generally accepted as written by Moses. In the first of the five books, Genesis, chapters 2 and 3, Moses used the word "Serpent" to identify evil. The name Satan is not used until 1 Chronicles:

> *"And Satan stood up against Israel, and provoked David to number Israel."* —1 Chronicles 21:1

Centuries later, as tradition developed to portray events in stories and symbolic terms, evil, as in Genesis 2 and 3, was still referred to as a Serpent, but in Revelation 12:15 the connotation is different. It says:

> *"The serpent cast out of his mouth water as a flood after the woman."*

As mentioned before, the Hebrew word "Serpent" (Strong, 5175) basically means "to whisper" or "to sense an idea." But the Greek "Serpent" (3789) has a different meaning: "sly, cunning, as of an artful malicious person." Therefore, when we accept "Serpent" (along with "Satan," "Dragon," and "Devil") as a reference to a literal, evil spirit being, then the references to a beast, false prophet, death, and hell in Revelation would also indicate literal beings or places (as mentioned before). But this does not make sense, for all are thrown into "the lake of fire," which is a symbolic term for a condition—that is, "destroyed", as told in two verses in Revelation:

> *"And the beast was taken, and with him the false prophet that wrought miracles before him, with which he deceived them (people) that had received the mark of the beast, and them that worshipped his image."*—Revelation 19:20

In picture language, both are cast alive into a lake of fire burning with brimstone (total destruction).

> *"And death and hell were cast into the lake of fire (destroyed). This is the second death."*—Revelation 20:14

We then understand that "Serpent" in Genesis 3:4 is an allegorical description of how evil thoughts were foremost in the mind of Eve. Although Adam and Eve were created with the ability to choose either good or evil, Eve, not having had previous experience with evil and not knowing how to deal with it, allowed temptation to rule in her mind. The fruit of the tree of knowledge of good and evil was not literal fruit, but symbolized the evil (Serpent, Dragon, Satan, or Devil) of disobedience, the choice of opposing God's firm command. As Jesus said:

> *"Even so every good tree (righteous and just character) brings forth good fruit; but a corrupt tree (wicked character) brings forth evil fruit."*—Matthew 7:17

Another example in which evil is given a persona as a spirit being is the name Satan in Zechariah. The prophet wrote:

> *"And he showed me Joshua the high priest standing before the angel (message) of the Lord, and Satan (evil) standing (temptation) at his right hand to resist him."*—Zechariah 3:1

Zechariah uses a metaphor that was common to the Babylonians, to Daniel and Ezekiel, a symbolic expression that evil (Satan, Devil, Serpent, or Dragon) had been done by Joshua, for in verse 4 it says that his iniquity (evil) was removed from him:

> *"And he answered and spoke unto those that stood before him, saying, take away the filthy (evil) garments from him. And unto him he said, Behold, I have caused thine iniquity (evil) to pass from thee."*—Zechariah 3:4

The iniquity (evil) is depicted by the term "filthy garments." The iniquity (evil) in this case is referred to as "Satan," while the evil of Eve's experience is referred to as "Serpent." In John 8:44, Jesus the Christ used: *"You are of your father the 'devil'.*

He applied this metaphor to the Pharisees because they displayed an evil attitude and intent. Since evil is common in the world, the apostle Paul would write in 2 Corinthians:

> *"The god (evil, Satan, Devil, Dragon, or Serpent) of this world hath blinded the minds of them that believe not."*
> —2 Corinthians 4:14

And the apostle James wrote:

> *"Bitter jealousy and selfish ambition is wisdom of this world and is earthly, unspiritual and devilish (evil, Satan, Dragon, or Serpent)."*—James 3:14

Both statements imply similar meaning but use different metaphors.

This attitude possessed the Pharisees as they allowed their lives to be ruled by the evils of hypocrisy, superiority, and jealousy. Thus, evil (Satan, Serpent, Dragon, or Devil) became the father (source) of their behavior. Another metaphor Jesus used is in John, where he said:

> *"For the ruler (evil, Satan, Devil, Serpent, or Dragon) of this world is coming, he (it) has no power over me."*
> —John 14:30

Since evil and wickedness are generated in the mind by allowing emotions of envy, anger, jealousy or lust to dominate, Jesus the Christ, knowing the evil that possessed the Pharisees in wanting to destroy him, did not allow evil emotions or thoughts of retaliation to have power over him but rather allowed the Pharisees' anger, jealousy, and hate to rule that he be put to death. The Goodspeed translation of John 16 indicates that Jesus the Christ did this to show the contrast between the righteousness of his motivation and the evil (Satan, Devil, Serpent, or Dragon) influencing mankind. He said:

> *"About uprightness, as shown by my going away to the Father, where you can no longer see me as shown by the condemnation of the evil genius of this world."* —John 16:10–11 (Gdsd.)

Put another way, Jesus was saying he was doing God's will and not the evil that controlled the minds of men.

In 1 Peter it says

> *"Be sober, be watchful, your adversary the devil* (evil) *prowls around like a roaring lion, seeking someone to devour.* —1 Peter 5:8

This is not meant literally, but is figurative language, for no one hears a roaring lion, nor is anyone literally being devoured. Peter is using the metaphor to picture evil as dwelling in the minds of the wicked, where it becomes the controlling factor that ignores righteousness or is blind to justice. In 1 Thessalonians the apostle Paul wrote:

> *"That is why we made up our minds to go see you—at least I, Paul, did more than once. But Satan (evil people) put difficulties in our way."*—1 Thessalonians 2:18

In using the phrase *"But Satan put difficulties in our way,"*

Paul was describing the implacable hatred manifested by the Thessalonians Jews in their persecution of Silas, Timothy, and Paul as recorded in Acts 17:5. The persecution strongly hindered their evangelistic efforts, eventually causing Paul to leave Thessalonica for Berea (Acts 17:10) and later Athens (Acts 17:15).

The apostle again uses the metaphor "Satan" for evil, as was commonly done that day. The evil (Satan, Devil, Serpent, or Dragon) was the opposition of the Jews at Thessalonica, the source of their troubles. In 2 Corinthians, the apostle uses the word "theos" (a divinity) for the "god of this world" (2 Corinthians 4:4). He is referring to the things men admire, such as honor, power, glory, and esteem above others. Verse 2 supports this interpretation:

> *"But we have renounced the hidden things of shame, refusing to adopt crafty ways or to tamper with God's message."*—2 Corinthians 4:2

In other words, the apostles were honest and just, avoiding any word or deed hinting of pride, jealousy, envy, and the like, that would appear evil (Satan, Devil, Dragon, and Serpent).

Belief Affects Interpretation

In studying Scripture, we easily interpret according to our personal convictions; thus, one reader can perceive the meaning of Scripture differently than another. Translators are also subject to this factor. This is a main reason for the existence of seminaries, so potential pastors can be taught along the lines of particular doctrines to interpret Scripture and Scriptural concepts "properly." For example, when the cause of an accident is considered, the Christian, Jew, or Muslim learns to say that, "it is God's will" or, depending on the nature of the accident, "the work of Satan." An unbeliever will be more prone to refer to the accident as bad luck or a wrong decision.

In reference to differences of perception, the *Harper's Study Bible* (p.1614) provides a footnote relating to a statement of Jesus the Christ in the Gospel of John:

"In the world you shall have tribulation."—John 16:33

The footnote on the page gives three orders (interpretations) of tribulation:

1. That which comes simply because we are alive and share in the fallen nature of the   human race (experiences like natural catastrophe, sickness, bereavement, and death).

2. Tribulations that (by God's permission) come to us from the malice of Satan because we have been delivered from his power and he strives to bring us back under bondage (1 Peter 5:8).

3. Tribulations that come more directly from the hand of God himself and are designed to purify or refine us (Job 23:10). These often overlap; thus God can and does use the afflictions in the first two categories to accomplish His work in us. Yet Christians should be careful to avoid attributing to God, or even Satan, that which they bring upon themselves. Afflictions resulting from our own folly we must face up to as our own, personal responsibility.

The second and third statements of this footnote are confusing. Such reasoning appears to be "authoritative" to the average reader, and if he is a believer, he may go through life trying to figure out the source of each tribulation as troubles come upon him. The writer of Job concluded the source of Job's affliction was his inability to perceive God's will, for he did eventually say:

> *"I have heard of thee by the hearing of the ear: but now my eyes see (can perceive) you."* —Job 42:5

Thus, for the Christian to figure out where tribulation is coming from (according to the last two statements) could bring a mental breakdown. The first statement is understandable and reasonable: affliction results from our actions or circumstances as members of sin-prone human race. Speaking of Job, strong evidence reveals the book of Job to be an allegory. The authorship and background information preceding the book of Job in the

Harper Study Bible states, "Sometimes [Job] is regarded as a parable or historical poem."

Reprint 1507 (a source for Bible students) considers the conversation between Satan and God in the book of Job to be allegorical. A few questions to be answered about the book of Job are:

1. Who wrote the book of Job?

2. Is the book of Job fiction or non-fiction?

3. Why would God conspire with Satan to tempt Job?

4. Job is depicted as a pious and sinless man. Why would he be punished (lose his children, home and wealth) if he did not sin? Does not the apostle Paul say in Galatians?

5. *"For whatever a man sows, that he will reap"?* (Galatians 6:7)

6. If this is not an allegory, how could Job be sinless? Was not Jesus the only sinless person?

Therefore, the book of Job is written as a moral story. The introduction to Job (*Harper Study Bible*) offers a helpful comment: "The book of Job evidently was written to seek out answers and questions concerning the reason for human suffering and why a loving God allows it." For us, understanding the story of Job as allegory brings it into harmony with the rest of the Bible. In Job, the name Satan is used metaphorically to depict evil or opposition to God. This appeared to be the custom of that day. Doesn't Job 42:11 say the Lord brought the evil upon Job?

Relative to present-day Christianity, the question is: What are we to believe in regard to tribulations and evil in this world? For example, the apostle Paul wrote of three occasions where certain Christians did evil and told the congregations what to do. In 1

Corinthians Paul speaks of an evil act where a man (a member of the congregation) was living with his father's wife (as man and wife), and the apostle advised that the man:

> *"Be delivered to Satan (or to leave them to the evil world)."*
> —1 Corinthians 5:1

In 1 Timothy the apostle wrote of two people and what he did:

> *"Whom I have delivered to Satan (to the evil world) that they may learn not to blaspheme."*—1 Timothy 1:20

In 2 Timothy, he wrote:

> *"Alexander the Coppersmith did me great harm, the Lord will reward him according to his works."*—2 Timothy 4:14

In verse 15, Alexander opposed Paul's message. It is not clear what Paul means in these three scriptures about individuals being punished for doing evil. For instance, how is one delivered to Satan? And why would God punish evildoers if an evil spirit being had power to cause them to sin? However, if the word "Satan" is understood to mean an evil activity or condition, the statements of Paul, along with the allegorical book of Job, may then be interpreted as alluding to the evil of opposition to the principles of God (righteousness and justice).

> Proverbs declares: *"A man's heart devises his way: but the LORD directs his steps."*—Proverbs 16:9

Also in Proverbs we read:

"The <u>foolishness of man perverts his way</u>: and his heart frets against the LORD." —Proverbs 19:3

There is no hint of an evil spirit being controlling a man's mind in these two statements. The persons who did evil, as mentioned by the apostle Paul, were themselves responsible for their evil deeds. No outside evil force seduced them to do evil (Satan, Devil, Serpent, or Dragon). Thus, being "delivered to Satan" would mean being "left to their evil choices."

An unidentified writer stated:

> "God has given man a truly wonderful brain to cope with all the problems of everyday life. But this brain has also two other marvelous functions. It provides a memory to bring back to the consciousness the things of the past, and an imagination, which can envisage the things of the future. The memory and the imagination, like most of our abilities, can be used for good or evil as did those living in the time of Noah, whose imagination was 'only evil continually' (Genesis 6:5). We also can dwell upon things of the past, which would depress or bring worry, or to look forward to real or fancied events, which might have a similar effect."

In 1 Corinthians, the apostle Paul, in reference to the wickedness of a person in the congregation, writes:

"Therefore put away from among yourselves that wicked person." —1 Corinthians 5:13

"Whom I have delivered to Satan (evil)." —1 Timothy 1:20

Do not both statements imply the same thing? Paul knew well the wisdom of Proverbs:

> "The *way of the wicked is like darkness*: they know not at what they stumble."—Proverbs 4:19

Paul then would mean: leave the wicked to their evil and do not worship with or associate with unrepentant evildoers. A helpful piece of information comes from Professor Wilson's translation (the Diaglott), where he uses the word "adversary" instead of "Satan."

Note: In Jewish history it was common for people to refer to evil or wickedness to be of 'the evil one'.

"Adversary" refers to the evil conceived in a person's mind that, when acted upon, becomes sin. Evil thoughts are adversarial to oneself. As Jesus said in Luke:

> "The good man out of the good treasure of his heart produces good, and the evil man, out of his evil treasure produces evil; for out of the abundance of the heart his mouth speaks."—Luke 6:45

Jesus clearly stated that the individual conceives or initiates evil. It does not come about by an evil spirit being placing evil thoughts in the mind. For example, in 1 Corinthians, the apostle writes of conjugal rights:

> "Do not refuse one another except perhaps by agreement for a season, that you may devote yourselves to prayer, but then come together again, lest Satan (evil, Devil, Serpent, or Dragon) tempt you through lack of self control."
> —1 Corinthians 11:3–4

Paul is warning that a Christian can be tempted, especially when having marital problems; through lack of self-control, to go outside the wedded relationship.

The admonition of James was:

> *"But every man is tempted, when he is drawn away of his own lust, and enticed."*—James 1:14

James is also clear that it is not an evil spirit being that lures or entices a person to take an evil course of action when marital problems arise.

James' warning is similar to Paul's counsel in 2 Corinthians:

> *"But I am afraid that as the serpent (evil, Satan, Devil, or Dragon) deceived Eve by his (its) cunning, (sly thoughts) from a sincere and pure devotion to Christ. For if someone comes and preaches another Jesus than the one we preached, or if you accept a different spirit than the one you received, or if you accept a different gospel from the one you accepted, you submit to it readily enough."*—2 Corinthians 11:3–4; RSV

The apostle Paul was pointing out the brethren's weakness to withstand the deceitfulness of false disciples was similar to Eve being tempted with an evil thought, which resulted in Adam's decision to disobey, which then destroyed their trusting relationship with God. As Adam and Eve were responsible for their disobedience, so also the brethren at Corinth were responsible for accepting a false disciple's preaching. Christians have a responsibility to follow what is just and right and to be aware of evil leadership.

The apostle used the metaphor of a serpent (an adversary) to describe the sly deceitfulness of evil thought that leads the mind from the path of righteousness and truth. A similar implication is found in Ephesians:

> *"Put on the whole armor of God, that you may be able to stand against the wiles of the devil (Satan, Serpent, Dragon, or evil thoughts)."*—Ephesians 6:11–13

The armor represents truth, righteousness, peace, love, and faith through knowledge in Jesus the Christ. Thus, the armor and the sword of the spirit (truth) are critical in opposing evil. If the evil (adversary, Devil, Satan, Dragon, Serpent, or opposing thoughts) of pride, greed, jealousy, hate, envy, and so on contaminate the mind; the virtuous armor of God is not being used, and the believer's faith suffers. This again raises the question: How can the human mind be possessed or afflicted by an evil spirit being and yet be held responsible? In the Bible, yes, even in the courts of this world, it is recognized that no person is held responsible for an act beyond that person's control. We some times see religious and political organizations look the other way when someone uses unethical means to attain control, the apostle Paul refers to them as:

> *"Principalities, powers, world rulers (politics) of this present darkness, spiritual hosts of wickedness in the heavenly (religious)* places."—Ephesians 6:12

Or, as another translation puts it:

> "Spiritual wickedness in high places of authority *(religion or politics)."*

In 2 Peter we read of spiritual rulers of darkness as: *"Heavens (evil in religion) that shall pass away with great noise (controversy)."*—2 Peter 3:10

In Colossians we read:

"Beware lest any man spoil you through philosophy and vain deceit, <u>after the tradition of men</u>, after the rudiments (methods) of the world, and not after (truth in) Christ." —Colossians 2:8

The Modern Language paraphrase helpfully states in Colossians:

"Disarming the rulers and authorities, he (Jesus the Christ) *publicly exposed them to disgrace as he triumphed over them by means of the cross."* —Colossians 2:15

The above scriptures contain pictorial language that is customarily assumed to refer to evil spirit beings. In that day it was often custom, in the process of providing information or the latest news, for the spokesperson to use pictorial language. Christians became accustomed to hearing parables, allegories, or metaphors describing governments, authority, and worldly conditions and situations. Likewise, they interpreted spiritual hosts, spiritual wickedness, heavens, principalities, and powers as pictorial expressions relating to religious, political leadership, and conditions. To comprehend that pictorial language, we need to understand the idioms of the culture and its manner of communication.

Tradition Versus the Mystery

It has been a usual trait in cultures to develop traditions, which often become a plague upon truth. Tradition and truth usually conflict, as tradition easily alters or distorts truth. Tradition can eliminate spontaneity and limit freedom of thought and communication. Jesus saw danger in tradition. In Matthew, in reply to the Pharisees' accusation that his disciples did not follow tradition, Jesus the Christ said:

> *"For the sake of your tradition you have made void the word of God."*—Matthew 15:6

And he quoted Isaiah:

> *"In vain do they worship Me: (God), teaching as doctrines the precepts (traditions) of men."*—Matthew 15:9

In John, in reply to the woman at the well who followed her ancestors in worship (tradition), Jesus said:

> *"God is spirit and those who worship Him must worship Him in spirit and in truth."*—John 4:24

Again, in Mark, Jesus tells the scribes and Pharisees that they were:

> *"Making void the Word of God of none effect through your tradition."*—Mark 7:13

Thus, Christendom has developed many factions of belief that enslave the believer's mind to rules, rituals, traditions, and even expectations of financial riches. In Colossians Paul warns of this, saying:

> *"Beware lest any man spoil you through philosophy and vain deceit, <u>after the tradition of men</u>, after the rudiments of the world and not after Christ."* —Colossians 2:8

Before saying the above, Paul had expressed his hope for the brethren:

> *"That their hearts may be encouraged as they are knit together in love, to have all riches of assured understanding, and the knowledge of God's mystery, of Christ; in whom are hid all the treasures of wisdom and knowledge."*— Colossians 2:2, RSV

The mystery Paul wrote of has not changed over the centuries. What has changed for the unwary is that there have been additions of rituals, customs, and spiritually unhealthy doctrine. The mystery of God does not involve any rituals such as lighting candles, making signs of the cross, or prayer beads. Such rituals may help a person feel better, but it casts a cloud over truth.

To the Colossian brethren, Paul described the glory of the mystery of God, saying:

"To whom God would make known what is the riches of this mystery among the gentiles; which is Christ in you, the hope of glory."—Colossians 1:27

He further explains this aspect of the mystery in Ephesians:

"That the Gentiles should be fellow heirs, and of the same body, and partakers of His promise in Christ by the gospel."—Ephesians 3:6

The Jews as a nation had failed to understand another part of the mystery as Paul explains in Romans:

"That <u>blindness in part is happened to Israel</u> <u>until the fullness of the Gentiles is complete</u> and so all Israel shall be saved."—Romans 11:25–26

The apostle describes to the Corinthian brethren another aspect of the mystery:

"I show you this mystery, we shall not all sleep (die), but we shall all be changed." —Corinthians 15:51

These promises are part of the mystery, which is in harmony with the "ransom doctrine" of 1 Corinthians, where we read:

"For as in Adam all die, so also in Christ shall all be made alive."—1 Corinthians 15:22

Paul's declaration reflect the words of Jesus in John:

"For God so loved the world that He gave His only begotten son, that whoever believes in him should not perish but have eternal life."—John 3:16

The harmony and wisdom of God's purpose and its mystery is seen through Jesus the Christ and revealed to his followers as they seek God's will in spirit and truth, but God's plan will easily elude those who are comfortable with tradition, custom, and rituals. Remember Paul's letter to Timothy:

> *"Study to show thyself approved unto God, a workman that need not be ashamed, rightly dividing the word of truth."* —2 Timothy 2:15

Thus, during the Gospel Age, the revealing of truth in Jesus the Christ identifies who are of the Church—a little flock, the chosen, that is, dedicated Christians who search and learn of the mystery (which is Christ in you) and who apply its qualities of love and truth in faithfulness in their lives as Jesus taught. It is in the Kingdom, during *"the restitution of all things"* (Acts 3:21), that the mystery is revealed to the world. The following scriptures speak of the mystery for hearing ears in the Gospel Age.

The apostle Paul wrote:

> *"And if you are Christ's, then you are Abraham's offspring* **(children)**, _heirs_ *according to the promise."* —Galatians 3:29

The apostle James told a crowd:

> *"Simeon (Peter) has related how God first visited the Gentiles, <u>to take out of them a people for His name</u>. And with this the words of the prophets agree, as it is written, After this I will return (spiritual presence), and I will set it up (the Kingdom), that the rest of men (the world) <u>may seek the Lord</u>, and all the Gentiles (Christians) who are called by My name."* —Acts 15:14–17

In 1 Thessalonians, Paul writes: "...and may the Lord make you increase and abound in love to one another and to all men, as we do to you, so that he may establish your hearts unblamable in holiness before our God and Father, at the coming (presence) of our Lord Jesus with all his saints." —1 Thessalonians 3:12–13

Jesus said in Luke:

"Fear not, little flock, for it is your Father's good pleasure to give you the kingdom."—Luke 12:32

And Paul wrote:

"Do you not know that the saints (faithful and chosen) shall judge the world?" —1 Corinthians 6:2

Paul also wrote:

"If we endure, we (faithful and chosen) shall also reign with him." —2 Timothy 2:12

John in Revelation said:

"Blessed and holy is he who shares in the first resurrection! Over such the second death has no power, but they shall be priests of God and of Christ, and they shall reign with him a thousand years."—Revelation 20:6

Below are other scriptures relating to the judgment of the world (general resurrection) and of those destroyed by the second death.

In Acts, Peter said:

> *"And it shall be that every soul (person) that does not listen to that prophet (Jesus the Christ during restitution) <u>shall be destroyed</u> from the people."* —Acts 3:23

From John, in Revelation:

> *"But as for the cowardly, the faithless, the polluted, as for murderers, fornicators, sorcerers, idolaters, and all liars, their lot shall be in the lake that burns with fire and brimstone (eternal destruction), which is the second death."* —Revelation 21:8

In Psalms:

> *"The LORD has made Himself known, He has executed judgment; <u>the wicked are snared in the work of their own hands</u>. The wicked shall depart to Sheol (the grave), and all the nations that forget God."* —Psalms 9:16–17

"Destroyed," "second death," and "Sheol" depict the death condition or non-existence that the wicked bring on themselves during Restitution in the Kingdom, while Christians who are tested, tried, and chosen in faithfulness, righteousness, truth, and love during the Gospel Age have their part in the first resurrection. Their spirit exhibited during the Gospel Age, are an encouragement to many going up the highway of holiness during the Kingdom of Jesus the Christ in the "restitution of all things" and as the second or general resurrection takes place.

As we read in Acts:

> *"And he shall send Jesus Christ, which before was preached unto you: Whom the heaven (religion) must receive until the times of restitution of all things, which God hath*

spoken by the mouth of all his holy prophets since the world began."—Acts 3:19–20

And Peter tells what happens to the world (evil in society) and heavens (evil in religions) that have existed:

"But the day of the LORD will come as a thief (not detected) in the night; in which the heavens (evil in religion) shall pass away with a great noise (controversy), and the elements (erring doctrine, rituals) shall melt with fervent heat (great trouble), the earth (evil society) also and the works (traditions, errors, and wickedness) that are therein shall be burned up (destroyed)."—2 Peter 3:10

In verse 13, he speaks of a new world (righteous and just society) that is to come:

"Never the less we, according to his promise, look for new heavens (religion of righteousness, truth, and love) and a new earth (just society), wherein dwells righteousness."
—2 Peter 3:13

In the Gospel of John we read the statement *"God so loved the world"* as not referring just to the literal world but to humanity. Jesus was saying that God loves mankind (not their sinful condition) and has made provision for their future. It is in the Gospel Age, during conditions of evil, that the call has gone out in the name of Jesus the Christ to worship God in spirit and truth in Jesus the Christ. Those who hear and are faithful are chosen by God to live and reign with His son Jesus the Christ in his Kingdom. Thus, the Gospel Age is a calling out for his name (his bride).

The Kingdom gradually materializes as restitution blessings increase; then, in God's due time, as righteousness, justice, and love have spread around the world, the general resurrection of mankind will take place. Those who learn and follow the path of holiness shall have eternal life upon earth, which becomes a paradise, the old world (evil in society) being burned up (consumed or destroyed) through fiery trouble. It is then that the prophecy of the prophet Habakkuk is fulfilled:

> *"For the earth (society) shall be filled with the knowledge of the glory of the LORD, as the waters cover the sea."*
> —Habakkuk 2:14

The world (social order before the flood and after the flood) existing under the reign of evil, Satan, Devil, Serpent, and Dragon are far different from "the world beginning to materialize." As the new world society grows under the spiritual guidance of Jesus and his Church (bride), there develops full opportunity for everyone to learn truth and righteousness. The first world existed from Adam to the flood, and the second world exists from the flood to Jesus the Christ's Kingdom of restitution. It is the Gospel Age that offers opportunity to follow Jesus the Christ in faithfulness during the time or reign of evil.

The Church, chosen by God, not by religious rules of men, consists of the faithful who hear, repent, and, appreciating the love of God through Jesus the Christ, separate themselves from the evil world (its unrighteous, deceitful, and evil ways) and faithfully follow Jesus the Christ in the spirit of righteousness, justice, and love under persecution and evil opposition. The apostle Paul wrote of those in his letter to the Church at Ephesus:

> *"According as he hath chosen us (who hear, repent, and faithfully follow the Lord) in him before the foundation of the world, that we should be holy and without blame before him in love."*—Ephesians 1:4

Christians, faithful unto death, are chosen and have the privilege to live and reign with Jesus the Christ in the New World, the 'Kingdom of God.'

Day of Increasing Knowledge

Living at the time of the end (transition of the Gospel Age into Kingdom conditions), we see righteousness and justice on the move in most cultures. High-population societies seem to make slower progress in righteousness overcoming evil, as Daniel prophesied. As Kingdom conditions grow, the initial stages of change are marked by revolts, crime, greed, and financial stress: for evil methods and ways are not given up without opposition from those who prefer evil ways. However, righteousness, justice, love, and mercy will continue to develop in the hearts of willing people to where the Kingdom of Jesus the Christ is recognized through the loving and compassionate character of people.

Wickedness is being replaced with righteousness and justice so that, when the resurrection from the dead commences, blessings of restitution have increased the length of lives, and most people have learned or are learning righteousness, those coming forth from the grave will see the world as paradise, a time the prophet Isaiah said will come:

> *"They shall not hurt nor destroy in all my holy mountain (government): for the earth (society) shall be full of the*

knowledge of the LORD, as the waters cover the sea."
—Isaiah 11:9

And as Jesus the Christ prophesied:

"Marvel not at this: for the hour is coming, in the which all that are in the graves shall hear his (Jesus the Christ) voice (as had Lazarus); And shall come forth they that have done good (tried and faithful during the Gospel Age); unto the resurrection of life (already judged); and they that have done evil (rest of mankind), unto the resurrection of judgment."—John 5:28

Again, some nations advance more quickly than others in the spirit of God, which is characterized by love, mercy, patience, kindness, and so forth. As increasing knowledge enlightens the hearts of millions, most people willingly abide by the spirit of truth, righteousness, justice, and love as they learn that:

"God [is] a Spirit: and they that worship Him must worship [Him] in spirit and in truth (not of a religious system)."—John 4:24

Willing minds learn to appreciate God's love and His plan in Jesus the Christ, a plan that promises a resurrection to life upon a peaceful earth filled with people who have learned to love Him, rather than repentant souls going to heaven and unrepentant souls to eternal torment at death. God's purpose has not changed from what He told Adam and Eve in Genesis; it is the hearts of people that change:

"And God blessed them, and God said unto them, be fruitful, and multiply, and replenish the earth, and subdue it: and have dominion over the fish of the sea,

and over the fowl of the air, and over every living thing that moves upon the earth."—Genesis 1:28

Or the promise He made to Abraham:

"And thy seed shall be as the dust of the earth, and thy seed (faithful believers) shall spread abroad to the west, and to the east, and to the north, and to the south: and in thee and in thy seed shall 'all' (everyone born upon earth) the families of the earth be blessed." —Genesis 28:14

The day we live in is called the "Information Age." Many Christians recognize that the worldwide increase of knowledge is bringing positive results. There are those who prefer the dark side and see only crime, conflict, and destruction ahead. However, recognition of social rights and justice for citizens are a couple of major changes as the desire for peace and liberty of the willing rises above the evil in the hearts of the unwilling throughout the earth. Although the evil of men affects every government and organization of every nation, the spirit of liberty, compassion, justice, and righteousness is gradually gaining victory in the battle between good and evil, the enormous Armageddon conflict.

The spirit of God of righteousness, justice, love, and mercy is being heard in increasing volume, and there are fundamental signs that the Kingdom of God is developing upon the earth according to Bible prophecy, as the following scriptures show:

"But the path of the just [is] as the shining light, that shines more and more unto the perfect day." —Proverbs 4:18

"For when Thy judgment (truths) [are] in the earth, the inhabitants of the world will learn righteousness." —Isaiah 26:9

"But seek ye first the kingdom of God, and his righteousness; and all these things shall be added unto you."—Matthew 6:33

"Neither shall they say, Lo here! Or, lo there! For, behold, the Kingdom of God is within you."—Luke 17:21

"All the ends of the world shall remember and turn unto the LORD: and all the kindred's of the nations shall worship before thee."—Psalms 22:27

Evil (Satan, Devil, Serpent, or Dragon) gradually becomes totally undesirable in the Kingdom. As righteousness and justice brings increasing change to conditions upon earth, the choice either to follow a beneficial and healthy lifestyle or to self-destruct by following the ways of evil and ignorance becomes more evident. There are numerous significant signs of the Kingdom's establishment—for instance, local and international efforts to eliminate obesity, starvation, smoking, and use of alcohol, plus many other movements. The negative conditions needing change are often the result of lifestyles that require knowledge and self-discipline to correct, often with loving help from others. A significant sign is that governments are making strong efforts to feed and house millions of people. Compared to a century ago, there are numerous agencies and organizations that also provide encouragement and assistance to the needy, while many individuals, having adequate resources, also help.

There are scores of fundamental problems, but individuals and nations are learning to solve them cooperatively. Thus, the spirit of the Lord grows in the hearts of people who also find answers to problems through a cooperative spirit of compassion, patience, mercy, righteousness, justice, and the like. Often the Bible is referred to in encouraging people to provide direction for each other, and we see much advertising to let people in need know in various ways that help is available. There are many methods for people to improve their lifestyles if they know how and where to go; thus, knowledge empowers and is the main blessing. In a similar, but spiritual, way, the Bible becomes the guiding light when those in need turn to it for direction and comfort. It does not waste words to point to the problem but always provides a solution, as from the following scriptures:

> *"The curse of the LORD [is] in the house of the wicked: but He blesses the habitation of the just."* —Proverbs 3:33

> *"For the drunkard and the glutton shall come to poverty: and drowsiness shall clothe [a man] with rags."* —Proverbs 23:21

> *"For they (truths) [are] life unto those that find them, and health to all their flesh."* —Proverbs 4:22

> *"Keep thy heart (mind) with all diligence; for out of it [are] the issues of life."* —Proverbs 4:23

From his youth, Jesus looked to the Proverbs for guidance. The Gospel of Luke and the Book of Hebrews both speak of his early desire to do God's will:

> *"And it came to pass, that after three days they found him in the temple, sitting in the midst of the doctors, both hearing them, and asking them questions."* —Luke 2:46

> *"Though he (Jesus the Christ) were a son, yet learned he obedience by the things which he suffered."*—Hebrews 5:8

Thus, Jesus the Christ learned from the Old Testament, from others, and from Scripture, attaining knowledge of and discussing the Heavenly Father's plan to be completed through the Messiah, which he recognized in himself. Determined in doing God's will, his courage fortified through prophesy and prayer, he patiently bore false accusations, taunts, and the terrible pain on the cross without desire to retaliate. The apostle Paul also grasped the meaning of prophesy to grow in the spirit of righteousness, justice, patience, love, and truth, which liberated his mind from the shackles of creeds, rituals, and traditions. He realized that God judges a person's heart and not the extent to which he follows rules, rituals, traditions, or law. As the apostle Paul wrote:

> *"Study to show thyself approved unto God, a workman that need not to be ashamed, rightly dividing the word of truth."*—2 Timothy 2:15

As most everyone realizes, it requires time and dedication to learn, with willingness to enlighten the mind, but it can bring freedom from creeds, rituals, and errant teachings. About a century ago, Pastor Charles Russell wrote how creeds limit the spirit saying:

> Few realize that from the time creed making began (About AD 325 for the Gospel Age), there was practically no Bible study for 1260 years. Few realize that during that time the creeds were riveted upon the minds of millions, shackling them to horrible errors, and blinding them to the Divine character of wisdom, justice, love, power. Few realize that since

the Reformation—since the Bible began to come back into the hands of the people—well-meaning but deluded reformers have been blinded and handicapped by the errors of the past, and, in turn, have served to keep the people in darkness. Few realize that real Bible study, such as was practiced in the early Church in the days of the apostles, has only now come back to Bible students.

It may also be added that the massive increase or explosion of knowledge in today's language brings virtual reality to the visions of Jesus the Christ, the apostles, and the prophets. The apostle Peter wrote:

> *"Nevertheless we, according to his promise, look for new heavens (truth in religion) and a new earth (just societies), wherein dwells righteousness.*—2 Peter 3:13

Relative to the apostle's words, the spirit of wisdom, truth, justice, righteousness, love, and mercy is primary in transformation of the evil world into a world wherein dwells righteousness. In Revelation, the apostle John describes in symbolism the process of God's Kingdom taking place upon earth:

> *"And the seventh angel (millennial message) sounded; and there were great voices (truth, righteousness, and justice) in heaven (religion), saying, the kingdoms of the world (rule under evil) has become [the kingdom](righteousness and justice) of our LORD, and of His Christ; and he shall reign for ever and ever."* —Revelation 11:15, RSV

The changes that move the world into God's Kingdom are taking place gradually. The kingdoms of this world are experiencing an overturning or a civil strife process that over time becomes the Kingdom of God in Jesus the Christ. Dark Age doctrines of Christendom and heathen religions still abound, and many Christian teachings still fail to resonate the glorious prospect of restitution and resurrection blessings, but the world is changing under the increase of knowledge, a main indication of the spiritual presence of Jesus the Christ. Sadly, many Christians do not discern this phenomenon of the world changing into the Kingdom of our Lord even as clouds of trouble bring to light the evil works of men to be judged, corrected, or destroyed. This is the work of the kingdom, the spirit of the Lord leading mankind in the vast changes required.

As restitution blessings increase, people learn to appreciate the differences in cultures. The prophet Haggai describes it as a shaking of nations. He wrote of the Lord revealing to him, saying:

> *"For thus said the LORD of hosts; Yet once, it [is] a little while, and I will shake the heavens (religions), and the earth (societies), and the sea (troubled masses), and the dry [land] (heathen); and I will shake all nations, and the desire of all nations shall come: and I will fill this house (Israel) with glory, said the LORD of hosts."*
> —Haggai 2:6,7

In the next few centuries, it is probable that every nation will proclaim, *"Blessed be the name of the Lord,"* especially when the resurrection from the grave begins. Then in reverse order, generations will come forth from the grave to learn of God's love in the spirit of righteousness and justice as the Kingdom of Jesus the Christ grows in power. It is a rule of iron in the sense that bribes, intimidation, deceit, prejudice, hate, and all things evil will be addressed and cooperatively corrected. In due time, all the willing shall live and know the Lord, from the least to the greatest, a time when most people will grasp the opportunity to attain life. As mentioned before, those who do not care, or who refuse to learn justice and righteousness and move up the highway of holiness, shall die a second death as warned in Revelation:

> *"He that hath an ear, let him hear <u>what the Spirit</u> said unto the churches; He that overcomes shall not be hurt of the second death."* —Revelation 2:11

As worldwide changes take place, the spirit of compassion and care continues to expand; sickness and disease is conquered even as necessary laws and social pressures counter the greed and wickedness of evildoers. Numerous beneficial organizations, created by caring people, help the needy throughout the world. There are significant signs that the injustices and greed of aggressive nations are being judged as the spirit of the Lord moves the hearts of people to demand righteousness and justice. This includes religious organizations that teach love for God and neighbor even as ethics and morals become more important than the threat of eternal torment, a fear-embedded teaching of the Dark Ages to frighten believers into faithfulness.

Today, this fearful doctrine is being questioned and abandoned through knowledge. Likewise, teachings of an evil spirit being called Satan, Devil, Serpent, and Dragon is beginning to have its "day of reckoning" as truth, questions, and reason encourage Christians to recognize that Satan, Devil, Serpent, and Dragon are metaphors for the evil that is from the hearts of men. It is interesting to note that the Bible does not require belief in the existence of a Satan or of evil spirit beings to attain salvation. For centuries, Christendom has echoed and expounded upon the existence of evil spirit beings while avoiding investigation of not only the background of Hell, but also of Satan.

Research now offers strong evidence that the teaching of evil spirit beings is based upon fear, superstition, and tradition, which are contradictions of the truth of God's love. These teachings are being questioned by spirit-led, inquisitive Christians, who recognize that as God's justice, wisdom, mercy, and love envelops the earth; the threat of a devil or evil spirit beings is being abandoned. Many people claim to be atheists, but the principles of God's righteousness, justice, love, and truth are taking root in the hearts of atheists and young people even as the evils of deceit, greed, and creeds continue to plague thoughtless Christians in the changing world. Thus, the need to harmonize Scripture with Scripture is important in understanding the refreshing panorama of God's plan, which eliminates evil from mankind.

It requires decades, possible centuries, for the love, righteousness, and justice required by God to eventually reflect from the hearts of all people. The Prophet Isaiah wrote:

> *"For precept [must be] upon precept, precept upon precept; line upon line, line upon line; here a little, [and] there a little."*—Isaiah 28:10

The prophet was referring to those who love the Lord while under the reign of evil, but his words can also apply to the Millennial Age of believers.

For example, in the nineteenth century, thousands of Christians from various branches of Christendom, hearing or reading of restitution and resurrection in God's coming Kingdom under the spiritual rule of Jesus the Christ and his Church, recognized that Scriptural truths had been ignored because of traditional doctrine.

They spent untold hours in discussion and study to gleam from Scripture the plan of God in Jesus the Christ. Independent of tradition and seminaries, they gratefully accepted God's plan of justice, love, and mercy. It was in following the prophets' advice in the search for truth in God's Word that the vision was pieced together as to what the prophet Habakkuk meant:

> *"The knowledge of the glory of the LORD will fill the earth as the waters cover the seas."*—Habakkuk 2:14

Generally, Christians have not visualized this scenario since the days of the apostles because man's gloom-and-doom doctrines have dominated attention or spiritual leaders did not understand or dared not to abandon traditional doctrine. But, searching Christians, studying prophecy and relevant scriptures as to how the Kingdom is to become a reality, found that popular doctrine was permeated with fear, superstition, and tradition, mainly from the Dark Ages. Christianity was in the clutches of ignorant and superstitious leadership during centuries of clouded doctrine that muddied the essence of the Word of God. Myths and fear had encouraged deceptive concepts to develop and become entrenched in the teachings of Christendom, such as an evil spirit being called Satan, Devil, Serpent, and Dragon supposedly instigating the evil in the world, while the vision of restitution—the days when evil is bound (replaced by truth)—was ignored.

But now the teachings of fear-filled imaginations are fleeing away from the light of truth and erring doctrinal myths. Today's inquisitive environment encourages the facts and truth on most all topics. The increase of knowledge and truth, experienced by both secular and religious people having access to history, language, and Scripture, is a major participant in this change. Christians reluctant to question the existence of a Satan, Devil, Serpent, and Dragon should keep in mind the fact previously stated, that the Bible does not imply or demand that belief in an evil spirit being called Satan is required for salvation.

Christians acquainted with the book *Tabernacle Shadows* will also find there is no place for a Satan or Devil in it. Comments are made about "the Adversary" on page 103, but it is an opinion, or interjection of thought. Also, the "Chart of the Ages" (inside back cover); has no place for a Satan, also called Devil, Serpent, or Dragon. However, it appears that the erring doctrine of an evil spirit being has survived through fear, superstition, or lack of research by Christians on the subject. The teaching has been as a thick fog hiding from view God's wisdom, righteousness, justice, mercy, and love. But by God's grace, increasing knowledge is destroying error, for it encourages all with hearing ears to look forward to the future when every willing heart will see God's love without the fear created by the myth of Satan, Devil, Serpent, and Dragon.

Love Eliminates Fear

The Bible tells us:

> *"There is no fear in love; but perfect love casts out fear: because fear has torment. He that fears is not made perfect in love."*—1 John 4:18

The apostle John brings out some important points:

1. There is no fear in love.

2. Perfect love casts out fear.

3. Fear is torment.

4. Fear and love do not co-exist in the heart.

Thus, fear of a spirit being called Satan has no part in God's love. To love and worship God in spirit and truth requires evaluation and comparing all Scripture relevant to subjects. Therefore, it is imperative that Christian's review the source of evil (Satan, Devil, Serpent, or Dragon) The subject needs to be examined in the light of history, facts, related Scripture, translations, and other factors that surround this fear-inducing concept created by man.

The question is asked: Why did Jesus the Christ and the apostles use the names Satan, Devil, Serpent, and Dragon for evil? The answer comes into focus when we look at Strong's *Exhaustive Concordance of the Bible*. It tells us both the Hebrew and Greek language have similar connotations for the words "evil" and "Satan." This gives reason to check out the when, how, and why "evil" had been given names as Satan, Devil, Serpent, and Dragon. In Latin, "evil" and "devil" have the same meaning. We then face the question, Did God allow evil to be called Satan, Devil, Serpent, and Dragon to hide His true plan for mankind? An excellent answer to this inquiry that is reasonable and in harmony with the Bible are of Charles T. Russell, I realize there are Christian's who dislike him because of prejudicial views. Some people will not speak to, or associate with people of other faith. Anyway, the following statement is reasonable and in harmony with Scripture and history. (words in parentheses are of this author):

> God not only foresaw that, having given man freedom of choice, he (man) would, through lack of full appreciation of sin and its results, accept it, but He also saw that, becoming acquainted with it, he (man) would still choose it, because that acquaintance would so impair his (man's) moral nature that evil would gradually become more agreeable and more desirable to him than good. Still, God designed to permit evil, because, having the remedy provided for man's release from its consequences, He saw that the result would be to lead him (man), through experience, to a full appreciation of 'the exceeding sinfulness of sin' and of the matchless brilliancy of virtue in contrast with it (sin)—thus teaching him the more to love and

honor his Creator, who is the source and fountain of all goodness, and forever to shun that which brought so much woe and misery.

Although the writer believed, according to knowledge held in his day, that an evil spirit being named Satan existed and was the instigator of sin along with other evil spirit beings, he presented a harmonious and reasonable explanation regarding God's purpose in permitting evil that is also in agreement with the words of the apostle James:

> *"But every man is tempted, when he is drawn away of his own lust, and enticed. Then when lust has conceived, it brings forth sin: and sin, when it is finished, brings forth death."*—James 1:14–15

How do we harmonize this statement of James with:

> *"And the LORD God said unto the woman, what [is] this [that] you have done? And the woman said, the serpent beguiled me, and I did eat. And the LORD God said unto the serpent, because you have done this, you [are] cursed above all cattle, and above every beast of the field; upon your belly shall you go, and dust shall you eat all the days of your life."*—Genesis 3:13–14

This account from Genesis is expressed in the picture language that was discussed earlier. The Bible was written for common, spirit-led people to read and understand, not just for theologians and preachers whose opinions are also subject to the following Scriptural directives of Proverbs and our Lord:

> *"Buy the truth, and sell [it] not; [also] wisdom, and instruction, and understanding."*—Proverbs 23:23

> And as Jesus the Christ said: "God [is] a Spirit: and <u>they</u> <u>that worship him must worship [him] in spirit and in</u> <u>truth</u>."—John 4:24

We are living in a time that involves a tremendous battle for the minds of men. Commercial establishments push the line to entice people to buy a certain product, but laws restrain them from most evil. Governments may push the line to limit truth; laws restrain leaders of organizations from advocating violence by supporters. Generations of people are experiencing the progressive movement of truth, justice, and righteousness that brings a better life. There are setbacks with social conflict, but as many societies are learning, peoples expectations are to be met, and differences to be handled in a righteous and just manner.

During the Gospel Age, the truth about the Kingdom of God upon earth was given a backseat to the error that, at death, the souls of most everyone goes on to heavenly bliss unless there is a general consensus that a person was too wicked, in which case his soul goes to eternal torment. In contrast, the increase of knowledge of Scripture prophecy, religious, and secular history indicates that the day of God's Kingdom is in its initial stage, in which learning of justice, righteousness, and love are main ingredients in the process that destroys the evils of hate, prejudice, jealousy, greed, and the like.

Again, compared to a few centuries ago, when religious views were more rigid, the religious concepts presented in this book are to be examined and discussed openly to see if they are in harmony with God's Word. This requires willing minds that endeavor to reflect God's love in righteousness, justice, truth, wisdom, and mercy as conditions change throughout the world. The increase of knowledge is stimulating awareness in serious-minded Christians of God's loving plan for mankind, wherein evil (Satan, Devil, Serpent, or Dragon) is gradually being pushed aside by the spirit of truth.

We live in the time when Christians experience greater freedom and have the means and opportunity to learn how evil is to fade from every heart that waits upon the Lord. Christians are able to see how the progressive change in religious and social attitude towards righteousness and justice is a fundamental sign of the Lord's return or spiritual presence spreading throughout the earth. There is a constant struggle for truth to overcome lies and deceit in the public forum, which encourages the publics desire for righteousness, justice and mercy. Many prophecies relating to the Lord's Second Advent (spiritual presence) point to the transforming of attitudes, which lead to the elimination of evil.

The prophecy in Psalms quoted below depicts trouble and destruction going on, with evil governments failing as people are enlightened and righteousness grows:

> *"The LORD reigns; let the earth (societies) rejoice; let the multitude of isles (nations) be glad [thereof]. Clouds (trouble) and darkness (ignorance) [are] round about him: <u>righteousness and judgment [are] the habitation of his throne</u>. A fire (destruction) goes before him, and burns (consumes) up his enemies (wickedness) round about. His lightening (truth) enlightens the world: the earth (society) saw, and trembled. The hills (governments) melted like wax (change) at the (spiritual) presence of the LORD, <u>at the (spiritual) presence</u> of the LORD of the whole earth. The heavens (religious powers) declare his righteousness, and all the (enlightened) people see his glory."*—Psalms 96:10–97:6

The Bible, translated from Hebrew and Greek, is not always clear to the average or at times even the well-educated Bible reader. For example, in the realm of prophecy, it often transcends centuries of human activity, making it essential to look for other prophetic Scripture to support specific topics such as: Judgment Day, Hell, from various branches of Christendom the Soul, the Lord's Return, or Satan (evil). The interpretation of prophecy needs to be consistent and in harmony with God's justice and love for mankind. Thus, a teaching of eternal torment is a contradiction to God's love when a Christian claims millions of people face eternal torment at death even if these people have never heard of salvation in Jesus. Thanks be to God, any torment is out of the question, for the Bible tells us:

> *"He that loves not knows not God; for God is love."* —1 John 4:8, KJV

The Living Bible, a paraphrase, not a translation, puts it this way:

> *"But if a person isn't loving and kind, it shows he doesn't know (understand) God—for God is love."*

God's love is always balanced with His justice and will continue to be so.

The Psalmist wrote:

> *"Justice and judgment [are] the habitation of thy throne: mercy and truth shall go before thy face."*—Psalms 89:14 and again in Psalms

> *"He shall judge the world in righteousness, He shall minister judgment to the people in uprightness."*—Psalms 9:8

There are many scriptures that indicate it has been God's plan to provide opportunity for every person born since Adam to have a fair judgment or trial period upon earth under the just and righteous spiritual reign of the world's Redeemer; Jesus the Christ. A few prominent prophecies supporting this claim are:

"For as in Adam all die, even so in Christ shall all be made alive." —1 Corinthians 15:22

"Marvel not at this: for the hour is coming, in the which all that are in the graves shall hear his voice and shall come forth; they that have done good (the chosen or the Church), unto the resurrection of life; and they that have done evil (the rest of mankind), unto the resurrection of judgment." —John 5:28–29/Psalms 89:14)

As mentioned, poor interpretation has also plagued concepts of the Judgment Day, Hell, Trinity, the Soul, the Lord's Return, and Satan. All of the subjects have suffered misinterpretation as a result of superstition, ignorance, lust, or fear. Today, because of the increase of knowledge, Christians searching for truth have whittled away many of the errors and falsehoods of previous centuries. In doing so, they have been following Paul's advice:

"Study to show thyself approved unto God, a workman that need not to be ashamed, rightly dividing the word of truth." —2 Timothy 2:15

Unfortunately, major doctrines of Christendom, having been filtered through the traditions of ignorance, lust, fears, and superstitions of the Dark Ages, still retain error and misinterpretation of important prophecy, which causes conflict with other prophecy as to reason, time, place, and purpose. But if the Christian searches and studies in the spirit of the Lord, he will see that the increase of knowledge is bringing mankind into

Kingdom conditions in which God's judgment of the nations takes place before the judgment of individuals on earth, which is the separation of the sheep (willing minds) and the goats (unwilling minds) on earth as pictured by Jesus the Christ in the following verse:

> *"And before him shall be gathered all nations: and he shall separate them one from another, as a shepherd divides [his] sheep from the goats."*—Matthew 25:32

Interpretation of the Bible should reflect God's wisdom, justice, love, and power, characteristics that governs all judgment in the Kingdom of our Lord Jesus the Christ. Some prophecies speak of people progressing up the highway of holiness in the Kingdom of our Lord, which is beginning to be seen in various ways today:

> *"And an highway (way of life) shall be there, and a way, and it shall be called the way of holiness (righteousness and justice); the unclean (reprobates) shall not pass over it; but it [shall be] for those: the wayfaring men, though fools, shall not err [therein]."*   —Isaiah 35:8

As mentioned, in God's due time, the resurrection is to begin and generations of people will come forth from the grave to have full opportunity to learn the truth of God's saving grace under the reign of righteousness and justice as promised by our Lord:

> *"Marvel not at this: for the hour is coming, in the which all that are in the graves shall hear his voice and shall come forth; they that have done good (the Church or body of Jesus the Christ, chosen from the Gospel Age), unto the resurrection of life; and they (the rest of mankind)*

that have done evil (have not known God), unto the resurrection of judgment."—John 5:28

Paul, in Acts 17:31, quotes a prophecy from Psalms, saying:

"He shall judge the world with righteousness and the people with His truth."—Psalms 96:13

In harmony with Paul's vision is the prophecy of John in Revelation:

"And I saw the dead, small and great, stand before God (resurrected); and the books (character individuals developed) were opened: and another book was opened (opportunity to change), which is [the book] of life (learning and trusting in God through Jesus the Christ): and the dead (unbelievers are also considered dead in sin) were judged out of those things, which were written in the books, <u>according to their works</u> (as they progress or do not progress in righteousness up the highway of holiness). And the sea (society, dead in sin) gave up the dead which were in it; and death and hell (the grave) delivered up the dead which were in them: and they were judged (given a trial period) every man according to their works (in doing righteously or doing evil)."   —Revelation 20:12–13

The promised Judgment Day gradually spreads throughout the world, recognized by the Lord's spirit of righteousness, justice, and truth emanating from the hearts, minds, or attitudes of people even as peace, health, housing, equity, and so forth under just laws increase. But those unwilling to learn to live justly and righteously, continuing in evil by abusing self and others, shall die a second death. Such people will be sadly remembered as reprobates unwilling to change. As Isaiah wrote:

> *"But with righteousness shall he judge the poor, and reprove with equity for the meek of the earth: and he shall smite the earth* (nations) *with the rod of his mouth* (truth), *and with the breath of his lips* (justice) *shall he slay the wicked."*—Isaiah 11:4

Another of Isaiah's prophesies:

> *"There shall be no more thence an infant of days, nor an old man that has not filled his days: for the child shall die an hundred years old; but the sinner [being] an hundred years old shall be accursed (die).* —Isaiah 65:20

The paraphrased version of the Living Bible helps us to understand:

> *"No longer will babies die when only a few days old; no longer will men be considered old at 100! Only sinners will die that young."*

As the Judgment Day grows throughout the earth, accompanied with restitution blessings, people will realize the improving conditions are signs of the Lord's return (presence) as Peter said:

> *"And He shall send Jesus Christ, which before was preached unto you: Whom the heaven* (religion) *must receive until the times of restitution of all things."*—Acts 3:20–21

The Psalmist wrote:

> *"The hills* (governments) *melted like wax at the presence* (spiritual return) *of the LORD, at the* (spiritual) *presence* (return) *of the LORD of the whole earth."*—Psalms 97:5, KJV

As mentioned before, the Lord's return *(presence)*, being of the spirit and not in the flesh, is manifested by the increase of learning and loving God and their neighbor as themselves from the hearts of people in righteousness, justice, mercy, and love, as Jesus commanded:

> *"You shall love the LORD thy God with all your heart, and with all your soul, and with all your mind, and with all your strength: this [is] the first commandment. And the second [is] like, [namely] this, you shall love your neighbor as yourself. There is none other commandment greater than these."* —Mark 12:30–31

A supporting quote from the Prophet Isaiah says:

> *"For when Thy judgments [are] in the earth, the inhabitants of the world will learn righteousness.* —Isaiah 26:9

Today, we see many positive changing conditions of the hearts of people throughout the world who are unaware that the changing conditions signal the Lord's return (spiritual presence) with promised restitution blessings. The increase of knowledge brings out the worst and the best in people in the removal of evil. Traditions, customs, and systems are being challenged in societies. Organizations of compassionate people offer their time and energy in kindness and care to those in need. The increasingly positive changes are a blessing to all even as evildoers who plague societies face a dwindling existence.

The world is still heavily handicapped with evil, as seen in the news media, movie industry, and commercial publications, but some businesses' existence depends upon increasing profit; thus at times they feel it necessary to give excess attention to evil activity because it sells and is profitable. However, the minds of most people are looking more and more for what is beneficial not only to self, but also to others. It is a day of learning and giving, of seeking righteousness, which in due time is to cover the earth. Jeremiah spoke of this need for change in the hearts of people when he wrote:

> *"The heart [is] deceitful above all [things], and desperately wicked: who can know it?"* —Jeremiah 17:9

Change is inevitable as the increase in knowledge and opportunity opens the way for the spirit of God to develop within people, no matter the hardship or turmoil, when they seek truth, love, and righteousness; rejoice in justice; and extend mercy. It is a transformation of hearts and of lives. In the meantime, the social, economic, religious, and political instabilities become problems, which tests the spirit of many as the Kingdom of our Lord grows to cover the earth. There have been and still will be times of despair, as the prophet Ezekiel writes:

> *"They shall cast their silver in the streets, and their gold shall be removed: their silver and their gold shall not be able to deliver them in the day* (time) *of the wrath of the LORD: they shall not satisfy their souls, neither fill their bowels: because it is the stumbling-block of their iniquity."*—Ezekiel 7:19

The wrath of God began with the Adamic death penalty. It strikes all of mankind and has been the main curse down through the ages, accompanied with disease, harsh weather, droughts, wars, and so on, often a prelude to death. But the prophet Isaiah saw the day when deserts will blossom:

> *"The wilderness and the solitary place shall be glad for them; and the desert shall rejoice, and blossom as the rose."*—Isaiah 35:1

A prophecy often quoted from pulpits but not easy to accept for listening ears in a literal fashion is where Isaiah prophesied:

> *The wolf and the lamb shall feed together, and the lion shall eat straw like the bullock: and dust [shall be] the serpent's meat. They shall not hurt nor destroy in all my holy mountain* (government), *said the LORD.*—Isaiah 65:25

The prophet was picturing peaceful conditions of God's Kingdom upon earth, a time coming when the hearts of every willing person will love and want to practice peace, righteousness, justice, mercy, patience, and so forth.

Isaiah offered many prophecies of coming restoration, some that the prophet Micah repeated. Today, programs and laws are instituted for the benefit of all; necessary laws are created to control wickedness as nations advance two steps forward, one-step backward, decade after decade in knowledge and responsibility. The prophet Micah prophesied these transitional conditions from the Gospel Age into the Kingdom of Jesus the Christ, saying:

> *"And he (through the spirit) shall judge among many people, and rebuke strong nations afar off; and they shall beat their swords into plowshares, and their spears into pruning hooks: nation shall not lift up a sword against nation, neither shall they learn war any more."* —Micah 4:3

Absorbed with the troubles in this world, many Christians fail to see the signs of worldwide advancement in human relations, including increasing attention to helping the poor and educating willing minds. Thus, the spirit of the Lord works in the hearts of people, calling attention to peace, aid, love, ecology, and respect for others regardless of religious, ethnic, or political conditions; this is changing an evil world into the Kingdom of God under Jesus the Christ and his Church, which Christians have prayed for over the centuries:

> *"Thy Kingdom come, Thy will be done on earth."*— Matthew 6:10

Signs are all about us that indicate billions of prayers ("Thy Kingdom come, Thy will be done on earth as it is done in Heaven") are being answered. Though the Middle East is in a self-destructive mode today in religious conflict fueled by the forces of ignorance, greed, and power against liberty, justice, righteousness, and love, many other parts of the world are showing evidence of seeking peaceful means, because public pressure calls for everyone to receive his or her share in prosperity that increasingly blossoms throughout the world.

There are areas making little progress tackling problems, but the spirit of the Lord of righteousness, peace, justice, compassion, and truth will affect them in time, for the Lord's spirit is increasingly applied to solutions of needs and disagreements in many countries. Such means are becoming more determined in fairness and just progress—indications of the spiritual presence of the Lord.

The Bible speaks often about how the Kingdom of God is to develop upon earth. The following scriptures are only a few that relate to how the spirit of God operated in the Old Testament, how it led the Lord Jesus the Christ in his mission, how it guided the apostles and the Church (the faithful) in spirit and truth during the Gospel Age, and last, how it guides the world during restitution when all who seek righteousness and justice attain life during the Lord's spiritual presence in His Kingdom.

Thus, change comes through the spirit of God in the lives of the willing.

> *"Neither shall they say, Lo here! or, lo there! for, behold, the kingdom of God is within you.* —Luke 17:21

> *"Then he answered and spoke unto me, saying, This [is] the word of the LORD unto Zerubbabel, saying, Not by might, nor by power, but by my spirit, saith the LORD of hosts."*—Zechariah 4:6

> *"But rather seek ye the kingdom of God; and all these things shall be added unto you."*—Luke 12:31

> *"It is the spirit that quickens; the flesh profits nothing: the words* (truth) *that I speak unto you, [they] are spirit, and [they] are life."*—Luke 12:31

Unfortunately, many people, including many Christians, do not perceive the Kingdom of Jesus the Christ developing upon earth. They see only crime, war, and a future of an Armageddon-type destruction, but positive changes are taking place. Remember, Jesus answered the Pharisees' question as to when the Kingdom would come:

> *"The Kingdom of God comes not with observation: Neither shall they say, Lo here! Or, lo there! For, behold, the Kingdom of God is within you."* —Luke 17:21

Or, as the Living Bible puts it:

> *"One day the Pharisees asked Jesus, "When will the Kingdom of God begin?" Jesus replied, "The Kingdom of God isn't ushered in with visible signs. You won't be able*

> *to say 'It has begun here in this place or there in that part of the country,' for the <u>Kingdom of God is within you</u>."*

Jesus was speaking of the spirit of God in the hearts of people that would reveal the Kingdom of God rising out of the ashes of an evil-led world. If scientific predictions of the icecap melting come about, millions of square miles of coastal land will flood, and every country will be affected by the migration and resettlement of millions of people. The heart of man will be tried to the utmost in sharing and compassion as the coasts of multiple nations experience flooding conditions. But, even in the face of many kinds of trouble, the blessings will continue to increase as they did amidst wars and calamities during the past century.

The knowledge of the Lord is growing to cover the earth to the point where righteousness and justice will overtake and eliminate evil from the hearts of all the living. The prophet Amos wrote of this happening:

> *"Behold, the days come, said the LORD, that the plowman (the truth in Jesus the Christ) shall overtake the reaper (evil and Adamic death), and the treader of grapes him (spirit-begotten) that sows seed; and the mountains (governments) shall drop sweet wine (truth and justice), and all the hills (opposition) shall melt."* —Amos 9:13

In every country, justice, righteousness, and truth are desired of public officials and leaders in commerce and religion. The modern ability to exchange information between people is opening up opportunity for improvement and creates prospects of better conditions from country to country. Needs must be constantly addressed by leaders in every field to meet public demands. The prophet Isaiah wrote:

"Thus said the LORD, Keep ye judgment, and do justice: for My salvation [is] near to come, and My righteousness to be revealed."—Isaiah 56:1

"And it shall come to pass in the last days (end of the Gospel Age and beginning of the Kingdom), *[that] the mountain* (government) *of the LORD'S house* (righteousness and justice) *shall be established in the top of the mountains* (governments), *and shall be exalted above the hills* (political and religious organizations); *and all nations* shall flow unto it *(in righteousness and justice)."*—Isaiah 2:2

As the Kingdom of Jesus the Christ is established upon earth through the spirit of God, the transition is reflected in many hearts, which show love for one another even as evil appears to dominate from time to time. The many interpretations and projections in this book often differ from traditional interpretations of prophecy, but this is to provide understanding of the scope of God's plan for mankind, a plan that points to the resurrection of the dead that is to take place upon earth.

The resurrection is not a joining together of an immortal soul with a new body but is rather a bringing back to life, by the power of God from His memory, of sentient beings with the mind and characteristics developed in their previous lives of all the people who have lived and died upon earth. The apostle Paul, in 1 Corinthians, writes of different types of bodies: earthly bodies and heavenly bodies. Those faithful are chosen in Jesus the Christ during the Gospel Age and are resurrected in the spirit:

"And as we have borne the image of the earthy, we shall also bear the image of the heavenly."—1 Corinthians 15:49

This is the promise of Jesus the Christ. It may sound impossible to men, but it is not impossible with God. That the existence of people upon earth evolved by chance through evolution is far less believable than that all life upon earth, in its time, is by design and purpose through the creative, overruling power of God. Therefore, as Christians, we are not to forget the apostle Paul's assurance of our Creator's promise through the ransom sacrifice of our Redeemer:

"...there shall be a resurrection of the dead, both of the just and unjust." —Acts 24:15

Increasing Kingdom Conditions

Living during the end of the Gospel Age, we see the initial stage of transition into Kingdom or Millennial conditions. Righteousness and justice are becoming more prominent, a process of improvement which requires decades. Ironically, in many cases, it can be Christians referring to themselves as conservative who oppose policies that benefit the needy or for those not of the same politics. Fear and prejudice often hide behind patriotism; thus those failing to do as the apostle Paul advised in 2 Corinthians are apt to find their characters unchangeable or reprobate and thus unfit for eternal life:

> *"Examine yourselves, whether ye be in the faith; prove your own selves. Know ye not your own selves, how that Jesus Christ is in you, except ye be reprobates.* —2 Corinthians 13:5

A reprobate fails to see the need for change in order to be a righteous and just person. As world conditions proceed on God's schedule, the day is coming when the excuses of reprobates will go unheeded, for when is no progress in a person improving his or her character, he or she will be considered a reprobate. The prophet Zephaniah wrote of the opportunity for all, beginning with the nations in the Day of Judgment (a thousand years, Millennium, Kingdom) to learn to serve the Lord with one-consent or spirit:

> *"Therefore wait ye upon me, said the LORD, until the day that I rise up to the prey: for my determination [is] to gather the nations, that I may assemble the kingdoms, to pour upon them mine indignation, [even] all my fierce anger: for all the earth* (society) *shall be devoured with the fire* (destructive trouble) *of my jealousy. For then will I turn to the people a pure language* (truth and justice), *that they may all call upon the name of the LORD, to serve him with one consent."*—Zephaniah 3:8–9

Jeremiah prophesied:

> *"A noise shall come [even] to the ends of the earth; for the LORD hath a controversy with the nations, He will plead with all flesh; <u>He will give them [that are] wicked to the sword</u>, said the LORD."*—Jeremiah 25:31

The twentieth century was the high point in the gathering of nations, and is still happening: societies recognize the need for communication and cooperation among leaders. The Kingdom of Jesus the Christ of righteousness, justice, and love is to develop in power to where sin and Adamic death will gradually cease, with the blessings of restitution affecting every nation as seen today in many ways, such as improving living conditions and longer life.

This all comes into existence in troubling times, but the increase of knowledge is producing great prospects for the future. For example, in the realm of cell research, the November 2008 edition of *Life Extension Magazine* contains a detailed article by author

Julius Goepp, MD, that tells of an interview with a Dr. West (along with recent news from Harvard researchers) indicating that it appears scientists can unlock the inner workings of our cells and "mass produce" virtually any cell or tissue type in the human body in a youthful state.

An interesting assessment of the day we live in is that God is allowing all the changes taking place upon earth to appear to be natural phenomena, which leaves the minds of people to discern His will at work without detecting a literal or physical application. So His will is recognized in the changes, but is seen only by Christian's looking.

There are enormous advances in every aspect of human progress, including readily accessible tissue and organ transplants the obliteration of genetic disorders; the end of chronic, age-related diseases; and life without death. These discoveries are not of evil; they are results of progress in an enlightened day that God is allowing. Someday mankind will enjoy. life without the threat of Adamic death. Death is not to be a part of life for those who love God. It may sound strange the increasing charity of the hearts and minds of people, is to coincide with an increasing youthfulness of the flesh. The prophets wrote of this promised miraculous prospect, and the world's Redeemer Jesus the Christ, referred to that day in the Gospel of John:

> *"Marvel not at this: for the hour is coming, in the which all that are in the graves shall hear his voice."*—John 5:28

The Prophet Joel wrote:

> *"And it shall come to pass afterward, (Gospel Age) [that] I will pour out my spirit upon all flesh; and your sons and*

your daughters shall prophesy, your old men shall dream dreams, your young men shall see visions."—Joel 2:28

Peter also quoted this prophecy, but he related the start of the spirit of God being poured out to Pentecost, meaning that Christians, begotten of the spirit during the Gospel Age and found faithful, are chosen as the body of Jesus the Christ to reign with him in the spirit.

In the book of Job, it is implied that, after God provides a ransom for all and restitution takes place, along with the resurrection as Jesus promised; people attaining life will experience the joy of their flesh returning to its youthfulness.

"His (people's) *flesh shall be fresher than a child's: he shall return to the days of his youth."*—Job 33:25

And Isaiah prophesied:

"And the glory of the LORD shall be revealed, and all flesh shall see [it] together: for the mouth of the LORD hath spoken [it]."—Isaiah 40:5

Isaiah also said:

"And it shall come to pass, [that] from one new moon to another, and from one Sabbath to another, shall all flesh come to worship before me, said the LORD." —Isaiah 66:23

And the prophet Ezekiel:

"And I will give them one heart (Israel first), *and I will put a new spirit within you; and I will take the stony*

heart out of their flesh, and will give them an heart of flesh." —Ezekiel 11:19

In Luke:

"And <u>all flesh shall see the salvation of God</u>." —Luke 3:6

Knowledge is enlightening the hearts of many people seeking means and aid for self and others through a healthier lifestyle mentally, morally, physically, spiritually, and financially. Methods and ways to improve life are discussed daily on TV, Internet, radio, and in the printed media. On the topic of religion, there is unprecedented opportunity for earnest minds to understand prophecy and the counsel of our Lord Jesus the Christ regarding righteousness and justice. Everyone is to benefit over time as restitution blessings increase and righteousness and truth affect people's lives. Most people do not realize that the tremendous increase of knowledge, which brings change all around, was prophesied centuries ago.

The prophet Zephaniah saw the day approaching, and his words have given much encouragement to those who wait for the Lord:

> *"Seek ye the LORD, all ye meek of the earth, which have wrought His judgment; seek righteousness, seek meekness: it may be ye shall be hid in the day of the LORD'S anger (Adamic death, the evil days)."* —Zephaniah 2:3

Prophecy tells us that the condemnation of death, inherited from Adam, applies during the days of the Lord's anger. Prophecy also portrays the day when God's anger ceases and the willing are blessed with peace, love, justice, prosperity, and life. For example, the apostle Paul wrote of the end of that day when:

> *"And they shall not teach every man his neighbor, and every man his brother, saying, Know the Lord: for all shall know me, from the least to the greatest."*—Hebrews 8:11

The apostle Paul saw that the wonderful truths of God's purpose in Jesus the Christ entails life upon a peaceful earth filled with people restored to perfection and a trustful relationship with God, rather than people looking to a heaven or eternal torment destination at death. He understood that the command God gave Adam and Eve was to multiply and fill the earth, and that the day would come when that command would be completed:

> *"And God blessed them, and God said unto them, be fruitful, and multiply, and replenish the earth, and subdue it: and have dominion over the fish of the sea, and over the fowl of the air, and over every living thing that moves upon the earth."*—Genesis 1:28

We can see that day drawing near, but for now, evil is still a strong force upon earth, with many under its influence and holding many in its grasp.

Paul wrote of this to Christians:

> *"Wherein in time past ye walked according to the course of this world, according to the prince (evil) of the power of the air, the spirit (evil) that now (still) works in the children of disobedience.* —Ephesians 2:2

The great increase of knowledge is touching every part of the world in this Information Age. Christians looking for the Lord's return can connect the dots of secular and religious history with prophecy, enabling them to recognize that worldwide increase in knowledge brings positive change and improvement.

Thus, righteousness and justice replacing greed, lust, jealousy, suspicion, ignorance, hate, and abuse of power, are results of the spirit of the Lord increasing under liberty of democracy, where righteousness, justice, love, mercy, kindness, joy, peace, gentleness, goodness, faith, etc. can blossom in every person desiring life. Social rights and justice are increasing along with the desire for peace and righteousness in almost every country upon the earth.

It is a spiritual and social struggle in every society to eliminate evil that is conceived in the hearts of people, infiltrating governments and organizations everywhere. People working for liberty, justice, and righteousness do not visualize an overnight change, realizing it is a gradual process, an Armageddon battle between good and evil, in which good is eventually to prevail over all evil. As the decades pass by, the spirit of God develops in the hearts of greater numbers of people, gradually revealing the Kingdom of God to those watching for it according to the prophecy of Isaiah:

> *"For when Thy judgment (righteous, justice and truths) [are] in the earth, the inhabitants of the world will learn righteousness."* —Isaiah 26:

The Judgment Day, approximately a thousand years long, is becoming more evident as most people chose to live within the parameters of righteousness and justice rather than follow the ways of evil; many people look for righteousness and justice that leads to security and quality life, avoiding evil, which leads to trouble and destruction. As the Kingdom of our Lord Jesus the Christ becomes more prominent, the commandment given Israel will increasingly echo in the hearts of people of every nation:

> *"You shall love the LORD thy God with all your heart,*
> *and with all thy soul, and with all thy might."*—
> Deuteronomy 6:5

Willing people, applying this commandment in their lives, find it brings peace and satisfaction with diminishing problems, as opposed to the results of evil, which is full of trouble. Worldwide changes are taking place, the spirit of compassion and care is increasing and major discoveries in medicine are conquering sickness and disease, which opens the way to further blessings of physical and spiritual improvement with love and respect for others. Length of life is increasing; law and social pressures are countering greed and the evil of wickedness.

Numerous organizations, created by caring people, help the needy around the world. These are only a few of the significant signs that evil is being judged and impeded by the spirit of the Lord in the hearts of people. As mentioned before, the prophet Zechariah wrote of how God accomplishes His will by His spirit in the hearts of people, a phenomenon that is increasing upon earth:

> *"Then he answered and spoke unto me, saying, this [is]*
> *the word of the LORD unto Zerubbabel, saying, Not by*
> *might, nor by power, but by my spirit, said the LORD of*
> *hosts."* —Zechariah 4:6

At the present time, many positive changes are revealing the spirit of the Lord working in the hearts of many people. Some may call it being a Christian or being civilized, but, whatever it is called, in nation after nation, people are learning of their rights and expecting justice. Thus, worldwide pressure brings change in laws and methods to correct evil conditions. The changes develop in social, political, financial, and religious organizations being judged through troubles that leave behind old methods and concepts. In religions, the teaching of eternal torment and other doctrines of fear embedded from the Dark Ages are being questioned. Presently, the teaching of an evil spirit being called Satan, Devil, Serpent, and Dragon as metaphors for evil is facing scrutiny. Some Christians recognize the Bible does not require belief in existence of a Satan or of evil spirit beings to attain salvation.

For centuries, fear in Christendom has supported the concept that evil is of a spirit being called Satan who torments people in a place called hell, but now this and other doctrines built upon fear, superstition, and tradition that hide the truth of God's love are being examined, with fear eliminated by spirit led inquisitive Christians becoming aware that God's justice, wisdom, and love is progressively enveloping the earth to benefit and bless everyone with hearing ears.

Thus, the principles of God's righteousness, justice, and truth take root in the hearts of more and more people even as the evils of fear and greed continue to plague a changing world. When Scripture is harmonized with Scripture, the enlightening panorama of God's loving plan is seen to be taking place on this earth as the prophet foretold:

> *"Knowledge of the glory of the LORD will fill the earth as the waters cover the seas."*—Habakkuk 2:14

For decades, radio, TV, the printing presses, and now the Internet have been and are major factors in changing an evil world through enlightenment and attention to righteousness and justice, even as they also are factors in contributing to evil. For centuries, fear, superstition, and tradition have clouded doctrine and blackened the essence of the Word of God with myths that have created deceptive doctrine proclaiming an evil spirit being called Satan, Devil, Serpent, and Dragon as the instigator of evil in the hearts of men that, it has been taught, sends an immortal soul to a terrible place of eternal torment.

It is the day that this misconception is abandoned, as people realize a spirit being cannot be the source of evil while, at the same time, the heart of man is also the source of evil. Jesus the Christ said:

> *"A good man out of the good treasure of the heart brings forth good things: and an evil man out of the evil treasure brings forth evil things."*—Matthew 12:35

And as the prophet Jeremiah wrote:

> *"The heart [is] deceitful above all [things], and desperately wicked: who can know it?"*—Jeremiah 17:9

It is out of fear that people have believed religious leaders' interpretation of Scripture that they are deceived by an evil spirit being that instigates evil thoughts in their hearts rather than acknowledging that they themselves conceive evil in their hearts and choose to act upon it. Through the centuries, people have shifted blame for lust, unrighteousness, greed, jealousy, and so forth upon a mythical figure and perpetuated the concept of evil spirit beings for that purpose. The increase of knowledge, however, is eliminating such myths and evil concepts through the dynamics of truth, righteousness, and justice, God's fundamental tools in restitution blessings.

Today, there is a general recognition that individuals are responsible for conceiving and acting upon evil thoughts, which is a controllable factor within individuals. Thus, reality tells us evil can and will eventually be bound by the recognition and application of righteousness, justice, love, and mercy. A helpful aspect is that the news media offers plenty of information and advice on how to improve self and to help others; however, people, having the ability to change, must want to change, learn to think, and do righteously and justly with and for one another.

This is what the Kingdom is all about, of increasing acknowledge, seeing those who need aid of all types, and responding to that need. This has not been emphasized in the Christian faith, as it should have been during the Gospel Age. Also, the truth about the Kingdom of God materializing upon earth was given a back seat to the concept that, at death, the believer's soul goes to heavenly bliss or, if wicked, to eternal torment. This has confused the general theme of the Bible, which points to times of restitution and resurrection as fundamental in the Kingdom of righteousness, justice, and love to develop and flourish throughout the earth. It speaks of generations of the dead being resurrected from the grave into a righteous and just society, wherein the teachings of a Satan and eternal torment do not exist and fear will not distress the mind.

In regards to this teaching of error, it is reasonable to look for the teachings of a Satan and eternal torment to disappear before the resurrection begins because increasing knowledge brings about an unraveling of the belief structure of a Satan or Devil. Hopefully this book, *The Origin and Demise of Satan*, will be a source to eliminate such false doctrines of men so that when evil is conceived in the minds of people there is no necessity for evil spirit beings. As people learn and grow in truth, their words and actions are to reflect God's love, righteousness, justice, wisdom, and mercy in order to have life.

A well known scripture that expresses the love of God is the promise told by our Lord and Savior; Jesus the Christ:

"For God so loved the world, that He gave His only begotten Son, that whosoever believes in him should not perish (die), but have everlasting life."—John 3:16

Our Lord Jesus the Christ gave his life as a ransom for Adam and all his seed, thus all, being children of Adam, are covered by the ransom price and promised a resurrection from the grave. But first, during the Gospel Age, is the calling out for his name, as Jesus said in Matthew:

"For many are called, but few [are] chosen."—Matthew 22:14

Therefore, many have been called, but it is those faithful in spirit and truth under the reign of evil who are chosen to live and reign with our Redeemer, Jesus the Christ, in his Kingdom. The Kingdom work is the restoration of mankind to what was lost through Adam's sin, which before he sinned, was a trusting and loving relationship with his Creator, a life without sin and death upon earth. This is the work of the Kingdom, a restoration process to all who travel up the highway of holiness. The initial stage of restoration is taking place upon earth in present centuries. There is a great deal of prophetic evidence that the day Jesus told his followers to pray for, of which Scripture has consistently prophesied, is taking place on earth today.

Remember prophecy of Psalms:

"The Lord reigns; let the earth rejoice; let the multitude of isles (nations) be glad [thereof]. Clouds (trouble) and darkness (ignorance) [are] round about him (spiritual presence): righteousness and judgment [are] the habitation of his throne. A fire (destruction) goes before him, and burns (consumes) up his enemies (the wicked) round about. His lightning (truth) enlightens

the world: the earth (society) *saw, and trembled. The hills* (governments) *melted like wax* (are changed) *at the* (spiritual) *presence of the LORD, at the* (spiritual) *presence of the Lord of the whole earth. The heavens* (religion) *declare his righteousness, and all the* (watching) *people see his glory."*—Psalms 97:1–6

A realistic perception as to the source of evil helps us understand the changes going on in societies around the world. According to the above Bible prophecy, the world and countries are experiencing the troubling transition from the Gospel Age to the Millennial or Judgment Age, the New World, the Kingdom of Jesus the Christ. This concept, proposed over a century ago, is prophesied of as the second coming (presence) of our Lord Jesus the Christ.

Our Lord's return (presence) is therefore recognized by the increasing spiritual enlightenment in word and deed—the "fruits of the spirit"—as most people endeavor to respect what God has created and to live and love righteousness in the name of Jesus the Christ. Today, we find the majority of people hope and want conditions that are conducive to a healthy society. Though evil still pervades society, we observe that most people look for conditions in which righteousness, justice, prosperity, and peace prevail. The following scriptures speak of how such conditions become reality:

"Neither shall they say, Lo here! Or, lo there! For, behold, the Kingdom of God is within you (the mind)."—Luke 17:21

"And the nations of them which are saved shall walk in the light of it (God's Kingdom)*: and the kings* (leaders) *of the earth bring their glory and honor into it* (through

righteousness and justice, the spirit and truth which manifest God's Kingdom)."—Revelation 21:24

"Behold, I come quickly, and my reward (of life) *is with me." And the inspired John replies, "Even so, come, Lord Jesus."*—Revelation 22:12–20

"And the Spirit and the bride (the little flock or faithful, chosen by the Lord from the Gospel Age) *say, come. And let him that hears say, come. And let him that is thirsty* (for truth and justice) *come. And whosoever will, let him take the water of life* (truth in Jesus the Christ) *freely* (as restitution blessings lead the world into the Kingdom of Jesus the Christ)."—Revelation 22:17

We may ask, are not righteousness and justice encouraged in major religions, and isn't that a process of learning? After all, there has been positive change in most religions towards reason, justice, and tolerance for others even though they all have their radical activists. The following statements, made over a century ago helps us focus on an answer that is scriptural and harmonious in our understanding of our Lord's return (or presence).

"Some Christians forget the Master's special warning to his little flock: *'Take heed to your selves lest that day come upon you unawares, for as a snare shall it come on all them [not taking heed] that dwell on the face of the whole earth'* (Luke 21:34–35). Again, we may rest assured that when; *All kindreds of the earth shall wail because of him' when they see him coming.* ---Revelation 1:7 no reference is made to the conversion of sinners. Do all men wail because of the conversion of sinners? On the contrary, if this passage refers, as almost all admit, to Christ's presence on earth, it teaches that all on earth will not love his appearing, as they certainly would do if all were converted.

Some Christians expect an actual coming and presence of the Lord but set the time of the event a long way off, claiming that through the efforts of the Church in its present condition the world must be converted, and thus the Millennial Age be introduced. That when the world has been converted, and Satan bound, and the knowledge of the Lord caused to fill the whole earth, and when the nations learn war no more, then the work of the Church in her present condition will be ended; and that when she has accomplished this great and difficult task, the Lord will come to wind up earthly affairs, reward believers and condemn sinners.

Some scriptures, taken disconnectedly, seem to favor the latter statement; but when God's Word and plan are viewed as a whole, the Scriptures favor the opposite view, viz.: That Christ comes before the conversion of the world, and reigns for the purpose of converting the world; that the Church is tried during the Gospel Age, and that the reward promised the over comers is that after being glorified they shall share with the Lord Jesus in his reign, which is God's appointed means of blessing the world and allowing the knowledge of the Lord to come to every creature." Such are the Lord's special promises:

'To him that overcomes will I grant to sit with me in my throne' ---*Revelation 3:21*

'And they lived and reigned with Christ (about) *a thousand years'*—Revelation 20:4

According to this concept, which is reasonable and Scriptural, our Lord's return (spiritual presence) can be recognized by the increasing manifestation of "fruits of the spirit" in word and deed by growing numbers of people, many professing his name and living accordingly, which, as all will admit, is an advancement out of the dark ignorance that has permeated societies over past centuries. This mind/body-altering effect is prompted by increasing knowledge, in which truth, justice, righteousness, mercy, peace, and the like are prominent forces growing in the hearts and health of people who have a hearing ear. Thus, the sword (truth) of the spirit is stirring hearts and minds in overcoming the evils of ignorance, hate, injustice, jealousy, suspicion, and so on. It is the time, spoken of by the apostle Peter, in which a flowering climate of "restitution of all things" is leading mankind out of darkness (ignorance), of which Peter prophesied:

> *"Whom* (Jesus the Christ) *the heaven* (religion) *must receive until the times of restitution of all things* (presently happening), *which God hath spoken by the mouth of all his holy prophets since the world began."*—Acts 3:21

Why Evil is Called Satan

Looking at some interesting historical information as to how the abstract concept of evil developed into a persona called Satan, we find before the time of Jesus the Christ; the Nation of Israel heard of and adopted a different understanding of evil while in bondage to Persia. They liked the idea of the two principles of good and evil seen as opposites that could be connected to both God and an evil spirit being called Satan and Serpent that tempted Eve in the garden.

Paraphrasing from 'Asimov's Guide to the Bible" Pg. 538 +, we hear:

> There were nine classifications of beings between God and man, angels the lowest, then archangels, Principalities, Powers, Virtues, Dominations, Thrones, Cherubim and Seraphim, mentioned in Isaiah 6. Today; 'seraphim' another word for 'angel.' The name; Lucifer, comes from a different source. In Isaiah we read: Isaiah 14:12–15 read: *'How art thou fallen from Heaven, O Lucifer, Son of the Morning... For thou hast said in thine heart, I will ascend into*

heaven… Yet I will be like the Most High… Yet thou shalt be brought down to Hell.

The name 'Lucifer' came from the Babylonian King's pride, the custom being, to use metaphors to the king. 'Morning Star' referred to his appearance being welcome as the morning star at dawn. (Their lives depended on it.) The verses in Isaiah concerning Lucifer pictured the king's fall from absolute power to captivity and death as the morning star falling to hell (the grave). By New Testament times, became Lucifer, the leader of the 'fallen angels', and hurled out of heaven and into hell.

The Greeks saw Venus as the evening star 'Hesperos' and the Morning Star 'Phosphorus.' Hesperos means 'West,' the evening star in the West. The morning star is Phosphorus, or 'Light Bringer,' or 'Daystar to become, 'Lucifer' or Light Bringer; Helel in Hebrew, Phosphorus in Greek, and Lucifer in Latin. Thus 'Lucifer' comes from the custom of using metaphors for the Babylonian King.

The verses in Isaiah concerning Lucifer, relate to the king's fall from strong power to captivity and death, a description of the fall of the morning star to hell or the grave. Later these verses had a different meaning. The Jews developed the myth that Satan had been the leader of the so-called fallen angels who rebelled against God with the name Lucifer applied to Satan, of whom it was said; he thought in his pride that he would replace God; however, but, he and other rebels were kicked out of Heaven.

Evil, conceived and exhibited by humans, began to be blamed upon an abstract, evil spirit being. Today, increasing knowledge with instant communication and, with that, the tremendous increase in travel, are having a big part in fracturing the old belief system while providing exceptional insight into this legend or myth that pervades Bible history. This brief review of Israel's belief system, provides a realistic trail of how evil is blamed on a mythical figure, rather than from the minds of people, and why the author of Ecclesiastes would write:

"The heart of the sons of men is full of evil."—Ecclesiastes 9:3

But, Daniel writing of his vision, heard a voice say:

"But thou, O Daniel, shut up the words, and seal the book, [even] to the time of the end: many shall run to and fro, and knowledge shall be increased." —Daniel 12:4

The tremendous increase of running to and fro and increasing knowledge throughout the world are key dynamics in the eventual elimination of evil through cooperative interest and the exchange of ideas in truth, righteousness, justice, and mercy, which gradually generate positive conditions in the "four winds" of Revelation 7:1,

"And after these things I saw four angels (messages) *standing on the four corners of the earth, holding the four winds of the earth, that the wind should not blow on the earth, nor on the sea, nor on any tree.*

The four winds are interpreted as the financial, political, social, and religious conflicts that affect all the world. This can be seen when the USA and other countries apply political and financial pressure to persuade certain nations to eliminate injustice. Even China, it has been reported, requested an African nation to improve their public image on human rights in order for China to trade with it. As these changes occur throughout the world, the Lord is completing, or may already have completed, his choice of the last of his Church (little flock, his body):

> *"And then shall he* (Jesus the Christ) *send his angels*
> (messages)*, and shall gather together his elect* (little
> flock, the Church) *from the four winds (financial,*
> *political, social, and religious sectors), from the uttermost*
> *part of the earth* (societies) *to the uttermost part of heaven*
> (religion)*."*—Mark 13:27

Throughout the world, evil activity increasingly faces scrutiny under the spectrum of truth, righteousness, wisdom, justice, love, mercy, and the like. Ever since Eden, these beneficial characteristics have been subjected to the evil ruling powers of greed, lust, hate, jealousy, envy, and so on, but we now see the positive aspects of righteousness, justice, love, and mercy rising above the clouds of evil. Human and animal rights are gaining priority in the public domain. Ecology and health standards are being assessed so as to benefit the public. Those who do not follow the laws, when caught, are subjected to incarceration or financial penalties. Capital punishment and torture are increasingly opposed in most nations.

There is still plenty of evil throughout societies or in the hearts of people, but there is definite movement towards tolerance, peace, security, employment, and mental and physical health with improving lifestyles and medical facilities, all signs of the Kingdom. Though many Christians think that, upon the Lord's return, people will be given a perfect body instantly, that expectation would be contrary to Scripture relating to how God dealt with nations and people in the past, except for a few special incidents. Jesus the Christ said, as recorded in Luke:

> *"For there is nothing covered, that shall not be revealed;*
> *neither hid, that shall not be known."* —Luke 12:2

The Lord's words indicate a process in which truth works in the hearts of people of encouragement that each person is to evaluate his or her words and actions, thus learning that in time, righteousness and justice brings life. A significant sign of the Lord's spiritual presence is that the public, in increasing numbers of countries are served by a vigilant news media, which reports righteousness and justice as well as unrighteousness and injustice. Freedom of the news media, in many cases, leads the way to human rights and much better living conditions above what previously existed under the dark clouds of ignorance and evil that still infects the minds of many, though to a lesser degree; Evil has been the ("prince and power of the air") throughout the world. As the apostle Paul wrote:

"Wherein in time past ye walked according to the course of this world, according to the prince (evil) *of the power of the air, the spirit* (of evil) *that now works in the children of disobedience."*—Ephesians 2:2

However, increasing knowledge opens and spreads the desire for peace, justice, righteousness, love, and mercy. This phenomenon is growing to lead the way in destroying the works of evil, including pollution and war. The thinking of the public is often opened to constructive change when a calamity or destructive event happens; these changes then reduce possibility of a similar event, which then draws the world further into the Kingdom of God upon earth wherein dwells righteousness and justice. The Internet, satellites, television, radio, cell phones, mail, and publications are products of the increase of knowledge that communicated the news of America electing an African-American for president. Such change stirs most people for the better as the world looks for America to lead the way in bringing change as our Creator has planned it.

Again, in Daniel, we read:

> *"And at that time shall Michael* (Jesus the Christ) *stand up* (return, a spiritual presence), *the great prince which stands for the children of thy people: and there shall be a time of trouble, such as never was since there was a nation [even] to that same time: and at that time thy people* (Israel) *shall be delivered, every one that shall be found written in the book* (of life). *And many of them* (mankind) *that sleep* (are dead) *in the dust of the earth* (the dead) *shall awake* (resurrected to a trial period), *some to everlasting life, and some to shame [and] everlasting contempt* (second death)."—Daniel 12:1–2

There is a worldwide, pent-up desire and hope for righteousness, justice, prosperity, and peace, qualities that are growing under the relentless increase of knowledge and enlightenment. The world is experiencing the initial centuries (through troublesome and harsh changes) of the approximately thousand years of Jesus the Christ's Kingdom, in which sprouts the fruits of the spirit, which spread to eventually overcome Satan, Devil, Serpent, Dragon, Lucifer, or any other name by which evil is called. Religious, political and economic concepts, and ethics are increasingly judged, corrected, or punished under the swelling spirit of freedom, truth, righteousness, justice, and mercy. It is a learning process that troubles society, but is destructive to evildoers, for the increase towards righteousness and justice is altering societies daily. The prophet Joel prophesied that this day would come:

> *"And it shall come to pass afterward (Pentecost), [that] I will pour out my spirit upon all flesh."*—Joel 2:28

Isaiah wrote of this day as a time period of judgments and of learning righteousness:

"With my soul have I desired thee in the night; yea, with my spirit within me will I seek thee early: for <u>when thy judgments [are] in the earth, the inhabitants of the world will learn righteousness.</u>"—Isaiah 26:9

Over the centuries, the powerful forces of evil from the minds of men have brought extreme cruelty and destruction to and among humanity. During those long, dark centuries, the blame for man's wickedness was directed at an imagined, evil spirit being, staunchly believed to instigate evil in human thought. Even today, some Christians contend that belief in an evil spirit being called Satan is necessary for salvation even as they oppose investigation of this devious fantasy. As mentioned, this false and deceitful idea of an evil spirit being called Satan, Devil, Serpent, and Dragon will vanish as knowledge increases. The battle of Armageddon is a battle between good and evil that tests individuals, institutions, and nations. It involves knowledge replacing ignorance, truth for falsehood, love over hate, liberty opposing bondage, and liberality replacing greed. The apostle Paul wrote of how evil is removed from societies:

"And this [word] (truth), *Yet once more, signifies the removing of those things that are shaken, as of things that are made, that those things which cannot be shaken may remain. —*Hebrews 12:27

As John wrote in Revelation:

"And after these things I saw four angels standing on the four corners of the earth, holding the four winds of the earth, that the wind should not blow on the earth, nor on the sea, nor on any tree.

The following scriptures harmoniously portray the struggle between good and evil that begins in the Gospel Age and ends during the Kingdom:

> *"For the LORD knows the way of the righteous: but the way of the ungodly shall perish."*—Psalms 1:6

> *"For God shall bring every work into judgment, with every secret thing, whether [it be] good, or whether [it be] evil."*—Ecclesiastes 12:14

> *"For he that will love life, and see good days, let him refrain his tongue from evil, and his lips that they speak no guile."*—1 Peter 3:10

> *"They that plow* (do) *iniquity, and sow* (benefit from) *wickedness, reap the same."*—Job 4:8

> *"I will seek that which was lost, and bring again that which was driven away, and will bind up [that which was] broken, and will strengthen that which was sick: but I will destroy the fat (greedy) and the strong (powerful); I will feed them with judgment.* —Ezekiel 34:16

> *"For we must all appear before the judgment seat of Christ (both the Church and the rest of mankind); that every one may receive the things [done] in [his] body, according to that he hath done, whether [it be] good or bad."*—2 Corinthians 5:1

TRANSITION INTO THE KINGDOM

During the stages of the Kingdom of God upon earth, righteousness grows and evil loses its hold upon the hearts of most people with a general, increasing expectation that everyone is to share in earth's bounties rather than a relatively few controlling the wealth. Kindness is becoming common as the spirit of righteousness, justice, truth, caring, love, and goodness enriches those who seek life and learn to do good and abhor evil. The Lord's spirit, working in the hearts of those desiring to live righteously, reflects the attitude that brings them into the new world, "where-in dwells righteousness." The following prophecies are only a few of the many that speak of these enlightening and changing conditions:

> *"They shall not hurt nor destroy in all my holy mountain* (the Kingdom)*: for <u>the earth</u>* (societies) *<u>shall be full of the knowledge of the LORD, as the waters cover the sea."</u>*
> —Isaiah 11:9

> *"Behold my servant* (Jesus the Christ)*, whom I uphold; mine elect, [in whom] my soul delights; I have put my spirit upon him: he* (his spiritual presence) *shall bring*

forth judgment (during the Kingdom) *to the Gentiles* (or the world)."—Isaiah 42:1

"And it shall come to pass in the last days (during the Gospel Age, beginning at Pentecost, the calling out for his name, then into the Kingdom or Millennial Age when the knowledge of the Lord covers the earth), *said God, I will pour out of my Spirit* (truth, righteousness, justice, and love) *upon all flesh."*—Acts 2:17

Nevertheless we, according to his promise, look for new heavens (no evil in religion) *and a new earth* (no evil in Societies), *wherein dwells righteousness.* —2 Peter 3:13

"And I heard a great voice (message) *out of heaven* (righteous religion) *saying, Behold, the tabernacle of God [is] with men, and he will dwell with them, and they shall be his people, and God himself shall be with them, [and be] their God. And God shall wipe away all tears from their eyes; and there shall be no more death, neither sorrow, nor crying, neither shall there be any more pain: for the former things are passed away."*—Revelation 21:3–4

People will learn that an imaginary, evil spirit being, which supposedly entices them, is not the source of evil, but that evil is conceived and acted upon in the minds of people. This factor will be more obvious as increasing knowledge brings greater awareness of civil and animal rights along with ecological recognition of righteousness, justice, truth, love, mercy, patience, and the like. These values are to prevail in the hearts of willing people even as the evils of selfishness, lying, greed, hate, superstition, and violence fade into the past. Those who seek life will understand God's love for this world through Jesus the Christ. They will learn to live righteously and shun evil of any fashion.

Knowledge calls out for freedom and understanding, the opposite of bondage and ignorance, which have chained the minds of believers to erring doctrines and empty rituals that have been misleading and controlling. The growth in righteousness and truth results in the abandonment of doctrinal error and empty rituals in religion. Such change is gradually taking place in the religious systems today. Canons or decrees requiring financial payment as penance, not working on Sunday, eating fish on Friday, and the use of Latin in church services are some of the rules and rituals being abandoned in enlightened societies. Many Christians recognize that the Church is not an imposing structure to meet in, but rather that it consists of believers with hopes, aspirations, and conduct that reflects the love, truth, righteousness, and justice of God through the world's savior, Jesus the Christ.

Truth, righteousness, and justice are beginning to affect the Muslim religion as its people hear of liberty and justice in the call for freedom of choice in women wearing the burka and religious figures controlling the political system. As the Gospel Age transforms into the Kingdom of Jesus the Christ, divisiveness between Christian organizations, and even other religions will fade away as an umbrella of truth, justice, righteousness, and mercy spreads the realization that it is these values, intertwined with the salvation message of Jesus the Christ, that brings life to those who practice them faithfully. As the prophet Jeremiah prophesied:

> *"I, the LORD, search the heart, [I] try the reins, even to give every man according to his ways, [and] according to the fruit of his doings."*—Jeremiah 17:10

Over time, evil (Satan, Devil, Serpent, or Dragon), in both the religious and secular sectors of societies, will vanish and make way for the virtues of truth, justice, righteousness, mercy, and love, a growing process in compliant hearts, as people make progress away from the dark clouds of ignorance, superstition, and lies ingrained in many religious and secular systems. The apostle Peter wrote of powers that exist under the cloak of evil, where the practice of evil methods and lies gain power in adherence, requiring a transformation led by the spirit of truth, righteousness, justice, and love.

In pictorial language, Peter wrote:

> *"But the heavens* (religion*) and the earth* (society), *which now, by the same word are kept in store, reserved unto fire* (destruction) *against the Day of Judgment* (Thousand Years, Jesus the Christ's Kingdom, the Millennium) *and perdition* (destruction) *of ungodly men."*—2 Peter 3:7

Along the same lines, he continues:

> *"Nevertheless we, according to his promise, look for new heavens* (religion free of evil) *and a new earth* (society free of evil), *wherein dwells righteousness."*—2 Peter 3:13

Throughout the Gospel Age, Christians have struggled with the fear-filled doctrine of eternal torment, which is a contradiction of God's righteousness, justice, and love. This erring doctrine, once heavily promoted by religious leaders, still hangs on with relentless tenacity in the more traditional religious sectors. Many Christians do not comprehend that the ominous threat of eternal torment distorts the love of God and clouds the future with fear. Interestingly, as the cobwebs of erring teachings are swept away, signs of our Lord's return (presence) become more evident to the watchers. It is the brightness (increase of knowledge) of the Lord's return (spiritual presence) that is destructive to doctrines founded upon fear. Thus, the following listed dogma; fade away as knowledge and truth increase:

1. That God created a powerful spirit being named Lucifer—also referred to as Satan, Devil, Serpent, Dragon, or Leviathan—that became evil, with the main purpose of tempting humans to do evil.

2. That each person has an immortal soul that goes to a heavenly existence upon death, and that immortal evil souls will spend eternity in eternal torment.

3. That the Judgment Day consists of speedy pronouncements that souls will spend eternity either in heaven or in hell, a place of eternal torment.

4. That the "evil spirit being" (Satan, Devil, Serpent, or Dragon) and his demons exist to tempt people into sin and then oversee the torment of their immortal souls.

5. That God has "predestined" certain people to go to heaven, while the rest go to eternal torment.

6. That Jesus the Christ's return will be in the flesh and that he is to sit on a literal throne in Jerusalem to judge immortal souls in resurrected bodies.

7. That this earth is to be destroyed by literal fire.

8. That Jesus is God the Father and the Holy Spirit (three-in-one or Triune God).

9. That, to have salvation, the doctrine of a Triune God must be believed.

When believers' thoughts are shrouded in erroneous ideas such as the above, they cannot help but be fearful of future judgment. But God communicates through His spirit, as seen with the prophets and apostles. They perceived God's true objectives in dreams and visions. In Daniel, we read:

"And Daniel had understanding in all visions and dreams."—Daniel 1:17

And John the Revelator: *"I was in the Spirit on the LORD'S day"* —Revelation 1:10.

Thus, the prophets and apostles, through faith and in the spirit of justice, righteousness, and truth, discerned that God had created the earth, which is to be filled with people willing to live according to God's values and to love Him. They will see that God's character is one of righteousness, wisdom, justice, love, and mercy, which is revealed through the life, death and resurrection of the Messiah, mankind's Redeemer, Jesus the Christ. The prophets, in the spirit, foresaw that the qualities of God's character were to be manifested in the Messiah, Jesus the Christ, and to be learned and lived accordingly by his followers. Thus, God through His son: Jesus the Christ chose specific individuals from the nation of Israel to reveal His will and purpose.

It was through His spirit, that God communicated to the patriarchs, prophets, Jesus the Christ, apostles, and faithful Christians the understanding of His will. Therefore, it is the spirit of God—that is, truth, justice, righteousness, wisdom, love, and mercy—that motivates the hearts of those who seek Him and who learn about, trust, and love Him, as the following scriptures tell us:

"For the prophecy came not in old time by the will of man: but holy men of God spoke [as they were] moved by the Holy Spirit."—2 Peter 1:21

"And he hath filled him (Bezaleel, the son of Uri) *with the spirit of God, in wisdom, in understanding, and in knowledge, and in all manner of workmanship."*— Exodus 35:31

"The Spirit of the LORD spoke by me, and his word [was] in my tongue." —2 Samuel 23:2

"But [there is] a spirit in man, and the inspiration of the Almighty that gives them understanding."—Job 32:8

"And the child (John) grew, and waxed (developed) strong in spirit, and was in the deserts till the day of his showing (revealing) unto Israel." —Luke 1:80

"[Even] the Spirit of truth; whom the world cannot receive."—John 14:17

"I was in the Spirit on the LORD'S day, and heard behind me a great voice (revelation), *as of a trumpet"* —Revelation 1:10

The apostle Paul did not only write to the Church in how to develop in God's spirit; he also indicated how the spirit of God is to lead the hearts of willing people in God's Kingdom:

"Finally, brethren, whatsoever things are true, what-so-ever things [are] honest, whatsoever things [are] just, what-so-ever things [are] pure, whatsoever things [are] lovely, whatsoever things [are] of good report; if [there

be] any virtue, and if [there be] any praise, think on these things." —Philippians 4:8

Priests, preachers, and teachers who fail to keep this foremost in their minds, fail their students. Leaders who sexually assault children, allowing their lust to dominate their thoughts and actions, betray their trust. It isn't an evil spirit being that entices them to act evil; it is their will, led by desire or lust for things that appear pleasurable, but are destructive. An evil spirit being did not inveigle their minds to act with evil intent; the person allowed their own lust to take over.

Some people project an appearance of normalcy but, in reality, fail themselves and others, allowing lust to control their minds. They have not learned to follow the apostle Paul's advice, which is fundamental to spiritual thought, attitude, and action. The mind of the Christian learns to function in a passion for truth, righteousness, justice, purity, love, goodness, virtue, and praise. These qualities reflect the character of God and Jesus the Christ, qualities that guide the faithful to salvation. Thus, through a loving, righteous spirit, holding fast to faith in Jesus the Christ and through self-discipline in thoughts and actions, the Church (the little flock) has prepared itself for God's purpose of restitution and judgment of the world.

John the Baptist, quoting the prophecy of Isaiah, pictures people as having the opportunity to learn and live in the Kingdom:

"As it is written in the book of Easiest (Isaiah) *the prophet, saying, The voice of one crying in the wilderness, Prepare ye the way of the Lord, make his paths* (teachings) *straight. Every valley* (social needs) *shall be filled. And every mountain and hill* (national and local government) *shall be brought low* (humble in service)*; and the crooked* (erring doctrines) *shall be made straight* (righteousness

and justice will rule), *and the rough ways [shall be] made smooth* (knowledge and aid will be available). *And all flesh shall* (have opportunity to) *see* (recognize) *the salvation of God.*"—Isaiah 40:3–5/Luke 3:4–6

The day John the Baptist was referring to is the Thousand Years of restitution of all things, the transformation to Kingdom conditions that is presently taking place, which is the objective of our Lord's return *(spiritual presence)*.

As Peter said:

> *"And He shall send Jesus Christ, which before was preached unto you: Whom the heaven* (religion) *must receive until the times of restitution* (the Kingdom) *of all things, which God hath spoken by the mouth of all his holy prophets since the world began."* —Acts 3:20–21

The apostle Paul gives that same assurance in his first letter to Timothy:

> *"For this [is] good and acceptable in the sight of God our Savior, who will have all men to be saved, and to come unto the knowledge of the truth."*—1 Timothy 2: 3–4

This prophecy, as do other prophecies, reveals the Day of Restitution as a learning process. As restitution progresses, everyone, although many are in the grave, is promised resurrection in Jesus the Christ, a process which covers a thousand years. Some Christians expect a sudden, miraculous transformation at the end of the Gospel Age, an instant change in the behavior of people, perfect weather patterns, an overnight utopia as Jesus the Christ circles the earth on a cloud. Thus, they think God's Kingdom will be revealed in all its glory by such happenings rather than through a gradual transformation from evil conditions into God's righteous Kingdom through corrective trouble-plagued stages.

As mentioned before, we are not to look for miraculous changes occurring overnight, we then fail to note that the unprecedented social, material, medical, communication, religious, financial, and etc. now taking place in the world from year to year, and decade to decade, have been and are advancing humanity into Kingdom conditions as Bible prophecy speaks of, an increase in knowledge of truth and righteousness in every area (physical, medical, mental, social, political, and religious) that steadily transforms the world into the Kingdom Jesus promised.

Why have so many Christians interpreted the prophetic end of the world as frightful, marked by sudden, fiery, worldwide destruction? Doesn't prophecy point to God's Kingdom appearing gradually like the rising of the sun, and with healing effects? Clouds of trouble do accompany the transition into the Kingdom, but the thick darkness of ignorance is gradually being replaced with the light of peace and knowledge. The answer lies in interpreting prophetic scriptures, whether they are meant literally or symbolically. For example, the following scriptures attain harmony with seemingly contradicting scriptures when we understand that pictorial is often symbolic of the natural or materialistic.

Then to, the intended meaning of the Prophet Joel telling of the emerging of the kingdom becomes clearer when helpful interpretation is added:

"A day (period) of darkness and of gloominess (ignorance amidst controversy), a day of clouds (trouble) and of thick darkness (much ignorance), as the morning (righteousness, justice, and truth) spread upon the mountains (governments): a great people and a strong

(social demands for change); there hath not been ever the like, neither shall be any more after it, [even] to the years of many generations." —Joel 2:2

And Zephaniah:

"That day [is] a day (period) of wrath (controversy and destruction), a day of trouble and distress (wars and dislocation), a day of waste (environmental destruction and of human life) and desolation (bleakness), a day of darkness (ignorance) and gloominess (despair), a day of clouds (troubles) and thick darkness (much ignorance)."— Zephaniah 1:15

And Malachi:

"But unto you that fear (have reverence for) *my name shall the Sun of righteousness* (Jesus the Christ) *arise* (spiritual presence) *with healing* (knowledge) *in his wings* (rule); *and ye shall go forth, and grow up as calves of the stall* (learn righteousness)."—*Malachi 4:2*

It is a process of growing in righteousness, truth, mercy, and love, as learned in the Gospel Age by faithful Christians, who in the spirit, assist others up the highway of holiness as the world moves into the Kingdom promised.

And apostle John:

"Behold, he comes with clouds (trouble); *and every eye* (mind) *shall see* (discern, be aware of) *him* (his righteous spiritual presence), *and they [also] which pierced him* (Israel): *and all kindred's of the earth shall wail* (be troubled) *because of him* (his spiritual presence

of knowledge and truth brings change). *Even so, Amen."*—Revelation 1:7

And Matthew:

"Then shall the righteous shine forth (righteousness, justice, mercy, and truth, virtues necessary for life) *as the sun in the kingdom of their Father. Who hath ears to hear, let him hear."*—Matthew 13:43

"He (truth) *shall come down* (be understood) *like rain upon the mown grass: as showers (truth) [that] water the earth* (society)."—Psalms 72:6

Knowledge and truth of God's justice, righteousness, and mercy refreshingly increases in societies during Jesus the Christ's Kingdom. As Isaiah wrote:

"They shall (learn to) *not hurt nor destroy in all My holy mountain* (government)*: for the earth* (societies) *shall be full of the knowledge of the LORD, as the waters cover the sea."*—Isaiah 11:9 (When the Kingdom is fully established.)

Before the beginning of the twentieth century, nations were already beginning to experience the trying and troubling transition of the Gospel Age into the Millennial Age of Jesus the Christ's Kingdom—a time of enlightenment spanning decades, even centuries, of gradually increasing knowledge awakening recognition of righteousness and elimination of evil. The unprecedented movement towards better living conditions for the poor is due to people acknowledging the need and doing something about it, whether from government, private, or commercial interest.

The tumultuous gathering of nations is also part of the process that will eventually lead to peace and prosperity. Christians have been blessed with hope, as the Church or little flock prove them selves faithful. The Gospel Age has been a time of calling out for his name during centuries of oppressive evil, a time for those who hear to seek truth in Jesus the Christ. Thus, the Gospel has generated hope and confidence as faithful and chosen Christians from the Gospel Age have been prepared through the spirit to reign in the Kingdom during restitution blessings.

The momentum of learning and growth in justice, righteousness, mercy, love, and respect for those during the transition into the Kingdom involves differences in ideas and cultural beliefs of individuals and nations, which at times produces a time of trouble as never before. The past century has been violent, but today, nations can see light at the end of the tunnel. Public demand for change causes heads of states to negotiate with one another in the best way to make changes. There is a strong reluctance by citizens to wage war, which forces leaders to employ diplomacy. Violence is moderating as nations learn to respect one another no matter the size of the country.

The "have" nations are more willing to aid the "have-not" nations with diplomatic efforts at the forefront to prevent any misunderstanding. As the years pass, the increase of knowledge in most cases leaves behind discarded methods and socially destructive ideas as the world moves into unprecedented, unimaginable living conditions that are more advanced than ever thought possible a hundred years ago. *Forbes'* ninetieth anniversary issue of May 7, 2007, has an article titled "The Inside-Out Web" that tells of a coming electronic information beam. The World beam, which is expected to replace today's Web, will update and store information on every past and present subject ever recorded. Everyone will have a personal beam for information.

There will be sub-beams that everyone will have access to. New technology will encourage markets without boundaries, where buyers find perfect sellers, or vice-versa, no matter where they are or what they trade. The World beam involves moral and social as well as commercial implications, while strengthening the world's responsible governments against terrorists and criminals and protecting the individual against busybodies, including the government, for each person will have controlling access to his or her own sub-beam.

Also in *Forbes'* ninetieth anniversary issue, an article titled "Guts and Glory" tells of another revolutionary advancement, referred to as "global collaboration," which has already begun and will continue to grow, fundamentally changing business models, relationships, political networks, innovation, and learning. History shows that wars do not take place unless there is adequate financing. The day is upon this world in which international businesses will not support or allow destructive wars to take place, for war ruins business and trade. Corporations do not want any disruption that would endanger employees living in various nations.

Such advances do not mean that conflict and war will cease overnight; no, the beginning of the Millennium (the Judgment Day or the Kingdom of God) "brings an end to the Day of Jehovah," a period of time in which humanity has suffered long and hard from their hardness of heart under the evils of selfishness, lust, greed, and ignorance of God's will. Today, mankind is experiencing the beginning of God's Kingdom under Jesus the Christ as it gradually becomes established upon earth, even as the evil powers and concepts supporting the old world pass away.

Jesus the Christ said:

"I am the way, the truth, and the life: no man comes unto the Father, but by me."—John 14:6

No matter what religious or secular background a person is from, everyone, to have life, is to have opportunity and encouragement to accept and follow the path of righteousness, justice, love, mercy, patience, and kindness as the World's Redeemer: Jesus the Christ gave example As the apostle Paul wrote:

"For as in Adam all die, even so in Christ shall all be made alive."—1 Corinthians 15:22

(To be made alive involves the opportunity to go up the highway of holiness as prophesied by Isaiah.)

"And an highway (opportunity) shall be there, and a way, and it shall be called the Way of Holiness; the unclean (evil-minded people) shall not pass over it; but it [shall be] for those: the wayfaring men (but willing people), though fools, shall not err [therein]."—Isaiah 35:8

Therefore, the world, under a progressive increase of knowledge, is experiencing change from age-old, destructive concepts to growing in brotherhood and care, leaving behind the power and influence of evil (Satan, Devil, Serpent, or Dragon). This is the binding process of evil (Satan, Devil, Serpent, or Dragon). The past era is described as a dark day of intense trouble and distress and perplexity upon mankind:

"...a time of trouble such as never was a nation—no, nor ever shall be again." —Daniel 12:1–3/Mathew 24:21–22

As knowledge and understanding progressively cover the earth, the quality of life improves for increasing numbers of people through the spirit of peace, assistance, and sharing, which benefits the many nations. Not a week goes by that most people in the USA do not receive at least one appeal for a donation for the needy in this country or in other countries, whether by mail, the Internet, at church, at work, or personally. Today, nations that do not cooperate in improving civil rights and limiting armaments face trade restrictions by other nations.

Most Christians are aware that some prophecies are being fulfilled today. One of which is in Paul's second letter to Timothy, in which he writes:

> *"This know also, that in the last days perilous times shall come. For men shall be lovers of their own selves, covetous, boasters, proud, blasphemers, disobedient to parents, unthankful, unholy, without natural affection, trucebreakers, false accusers, incontinent, fierce, despisers of those that are good, traitors, heady, high-minded, lovers of pleasures more than lovers of God, having a form of godliness, but denying the power thereof: from such turn away. For of this sort are they which creep into houses, and lead captive silly women laden with sins, led away with divers lusts, ever learning, and never able to come to the knowledge of the truth."* —2 Timothy 3:1–7

The listing of evil that the apostle speaks of seems to portray the day we live in. But, humanity has always been afflicted with these evils. It can be heavier and more prevalent today, for problems are worldwide. The evil characteristics appear more common in societies that place emphasis on religion, politics, business, education, and finance; thus the prophecy of Malachi is also taking place in societies:

> *"For, behold, the day* (Millennium, Kingdom, Judgment Day or Restitution) *comes, that shall burn*

(be destructive) *as an oven; and all the proud, yea, and all that do wickedly, shall be stubble: and the day that comes shall burn them up* (destroy them), *said the LORD of hosts, that it shall leave them neither root nor branch. But unto you that fear* (reverence) *my name shall the Sun of righteousness* (spirit of the Lord) *arise with healing in his wings* (power); *and ye shall go forth, and grow up as calves of the stall. And ye* (through righteousness and justice) *shall tread down the wicked; for they shall be ashes under the soles of your feet in the day that I shall do [this], said the LORD of hosts."*   —Malachi 4:1–3

Though evil is common in societies, restitution blessings continue to improve conditions to when the tide will turn and the virtues that our Lord and the apostles taught and lived by will overwhelm the evils that Paul listed as well as any other evil. Then, in God's due time, the resurrection of the dead will begin. By then, evil will be undesirable and unwelcome and have little attraction to people going up the highway of holiness, in which righteousness, justice, mercy, and love for God and fellow man will motivate people to appeal in prayer to God for the restoration of loved ones. In that day, as the resurrection begins, generations of the dead will come forth from the grave in a reverse of the sequence in which they went into death. As the decades and centuries pass by, it may be possible that though the resurrection of the dead will be joyous and emotional, it may also be seen as natural or common, even as death, though sad and heart wrenching, seems natural or common today because of its daily occurrence.

Scriptures Related to the Lord's Presence

Prophecies that describe present world conditions, but also as the day of the Lord's spiritual presence, are:

> *"To the end he may establish your hearts with out blame in holiness before God, even our Father, at the coming* (presence) *of our Lord Jesus Christ with all his saints* (Church)."—1 Thessalonians 3:13   (Paul is addressing Christians)

> *"But who may abide the day of his coming? And who shall stand when he appears (spiritual presence)? For he (his spirit) [is] like a refiner's fire (searches the heart), and like fuller's soap (character of willing people)."* —Malachi 3:2

> *"For as the lightning (light) comes out of the east, and shines even unto the west, so shall also the coming (presence) of the Son of man be."*—Matthew 24:27

(The sun shines from east to west; lightning does not.)

(note: Repeated quotation of prophecy alludes to a particular time period or change)

"And then shall appear the sign (troubling changes) of the Son of man in heaven (religion): and then shall all the tribes (nations) of the earth (society) mourn, and they shall see (discern) the Son of man coming (spiritual presence) in the clouds (trouble) of heaven (religion) <u>with power and great glory</u>.—Matthew 24:30

"Jesus said unto him, Thou hast said: nevertheless I say unto you, Here after shall ye see the Son of man sitting (rule) on the right hand of power, and coming (spiritual presence) in the clouds (troubles) of heaven (religion)."— Matthew 26:64

"Verily, verily, I say unto you, the hour is coming, and now is, when the dead (all are dead in sin or in the grave) shall hear the voice of the Son of God: and they that hear (do his will) shall live."—John 5:25

"Marvel not at this: for the hour is coming, in the which all that are in the graves shall hear his voice And shall come forth; they that have done good, unto the resurrection of life; and they that have done evil, unto the resurrection of judgment." —John 5:28

"But every man in his own order: Christ the first fruits (plural, i.e. the Church, little flock, chosen or faithful); afterward they (that learn of Jesus the Christ) that are Christ's (learn righteousness and justice) at his coming (spiritual presence)." —1 Corinthians 15:23

"For what [is] our hope, or joy, or crown of rejoicing? [Are] not even ye in the presence of our Lord Jesus Christ

at his coming (spiritual presence)*?"*—1 Thessalonians
2:19

*"And then shall that wicked be revealed, whom the Lord
shall consume with the spirit of his mouth (truth), and shall
destroy with the brightness (righteousness and justice) of
his coming (spiritual presence)." *—2 Thessalonians 2:8

*"Looking for and hasting unto the coming of the day
of God, wherein the heavens (religion) being on fire
(religious controversy and destruction of erring doctrine)
shall be dissolved (religious differences fade away), and the
elements (rules, rituals, and false doctrine) shall melt with
fervent heat (intense trouble)."*—2 Peter 3:12

We are to remember that most of these prophecies are fulfilled
during the first part of the Kingdom, also as the restitution
progresses, length of life increases as Adamic death ceases and
the dead are resurrected, thus, all are to have full opportunity
to learn righteousness, justice, love and mercy and live. Those
who attain life, will cope with memories of loved ones who
died a second death due to not seeking righteousness, justice,
love and mercy, characteristics required to live. The following
prophecies depict the changing conditions of what the World
is to experience in the next few centuries.

"And the nations were angry, and thy wrath (nations
judged) *is come, and the time of the dead* (dead in
the grave), *that they should be judged, and that thou
should give reward* (crown of life) *unto thy servants the
prophets, and to the saints* (faithful chosen from Gospel
Age), *and them that fear thy name, small and great; and
should destroy them* (reprobates) *which destroy the earth*
(society)."—Revelation 11:18

"*And I John saw the holy city, New Jerusalem* (the faithful and chosen), *coming down from God out of heaven* (religion), *prepared as a bride* (truth, righteousness, and love) *adorned for her husband* (Jesus the Christ)."
—Revelation 21:2

"*And the seventh angel* (message of restitution and the Lord's spiritual presence) *sounded, and there were great voices in heaven* (religion), *saying: The kingdoms of this world are* (to) *become [the kingdom] of our Lord, and of his Christ; and he shall reign for ever and ever.*"
—Revelation 11:15

"*And there was war* (conflict) *in heaven* (religion)*: Michael* (truth in Jesus the Christ) *and his angels* (messengers of truth) *fought against* (opposed) *the dragon* (evil)*; and the dragon* (evil) *fought and his angels* (messengers of error and hate)*, and prevailed not; neither was their place found any more in heaven* (religion)*. And the great dragon* (evil) *was cast out, that old serpent* (evil)*, called the devil* (evil)*, and Satan* (evil)*, which deceives the whole world* (religious and secular society)*: he* (evil) *was cast out into the earth* (secular society)*, and his angels* (messengers, followers) *were cast out with him* (evil)*. And I heard a loud voice* (clear revelation) *saying in heaven* (religion)*, <u>Now is come salvation, and strength, and the Kingdom of our God, and the power of his Christ</u>: the accuser of our brethren is cast down, which accused them before our God day and night.*"—Revelation 12:7–10

"*And I saw another angel* (message) *fly* (proclaimed) *in the midst of heaven* (religion)*, having the everlasting gospel* (good news) *to preach unto them that dwell on the earth* (society)*, and to every nation, and kindred, and* *tongue, and people, saying with a loud voice* (powerful message of God's love), *Fear* (reverence) *God, and give glory to Him; for the hour of His judgment is come* (during the time of restitution and resurrection): *and worship* (reverence) *Him that made heaven, and earth, and the sea, and the fountains of waters."* —Revelation 14:6–7

"And I (John in vision) *saw a new heaven* (no evil in religion) *and a new earth* (righteous society): *for the first heaven* (evil in religion—check history) *and the first earth* (evil-led society) *were passed away; and there was no more sea* (restless masses in society). *And I John saw the holy city* (faithful and chosen under Jesus the Christ), *New Jerusalem* (faithful and chosen), *coming down* (faithfulness recognized) *from God out of heaven* (religion), *prepared as a bride adorned* (having virtuous and truthful characteristics) *for her husband* (Jesus the Christ). *And I heard a great voice* (strong message) *out of heaven* (religion) *saying, behold, the tabernacle* (favor) *of God [is] with men, and He* (Spirit of righteousness, justice, love and mercy) *will dwell with them, and they shall be His people, and God himself shall be with them, [and be] their God. And God shall wipe away all tears from their eyes; and there shall be no more death, neither sorrow, nor crying, neither shall there be any more pain for the former things are passed away."* —Revelation 21:1–4

Using many of prophetic scriptures shows how understanding of pictorial words increase when interpretation is also harmonious; thus, the increase of knowledge reveals major signs of our Lord's spiritual presence or return, consisting of truth, justice, righteousness, mercy, and so on, all fundamental characteristics that grow, permeate, enlighten, and rule in due time over every aspect of the new world. The Bible tells us that the spirit of God is manifested by love, patience, joy, peace, long-suffering, gentleness, goodness, faith, meekness, temperance, and the like.

These virtuous qualities reflecting the Lord's spirit from the heart bring to fruition God's plan for mankind. We see the process of restitution all around us today as many nations make efforts to solve tremendous social problems in a cooperative spirit of justice and righteousness such as has never been seen before in the history of mankind. It is in this expanding and developing spirit that Israel and the USA lead the world, providing assistance and provisions to needy nations while encouraging liberty, justice, and peace.

Often, the principles of the USA constitution are used as the example to follow when bringing a new nation through a struggling transition from bondage and tyranny to liberty and justice for its people. The fundamental culture of the USA, having its roots in the Christian religion, is a significant factor in the progress. Though a long-fought change is occurring in the area of civil rights of race, religion, workers, and women, the process has created numerous secular and religious organizations to aid the needy locally and around the world with food, medical aid, clothing, and shelter while promoting justice and righteousness. Such helpful and enlightening efforts are part of strong influences that are overcoming the worldwide evils of greed, lust, hate, etc.

Thus, from prophecy, we see that learning and practicing of just and righteous principles are leading nations into God's Kingdom; it is these values that inspire the hearts of people to seek peace and appreciate life. An example of this is seen in an article in *The Grand Rapids Press* of February 17, 2007. The article tells of a local college (Calvin) receiving a substantial grant to help the Chinese improve their nation's moral breach. Chinese scholars credit western science, religion, and philosophy with keeping free enterprise's darker side (greed) in check. Science and religion are considered new to them.

The college philosophy professor in charge of the program, said it is not Christian values they (the Chinese) want, but a means to control corruption at all levels that will eventually put a drain on the Chinese economy. The following scriptures point to more of such appeals in the future. The basic reason is that societies cannot improve under the forces of evil. Truth, righteousness, justice, and knowledge raise cultural conditions, while ignorance, greed, and other evils stunt growth. The following scriptures speak of this:

> *"Keep thy heart with all diligence; for out of it [are] the issues of life."* —Proverbs 4:23

> *"For as he thinks in his heart, so [is] he."*—Proverbs 23:7

The growth of the Kingdom is offering people the opportunity to learn godliness under increasing conditions of righteousness and justice. People of every nation are to have opportunity to learn and live, which includes both the living and those resurrected. It involves a change of heart in the individual, not a Satan, Devil, Serpent, or Dragon changing its activity. As the prophet Jeremiah said:

> *"The heart [is] deceitful above all [things], and desperately wicked: who can know it?"* —Jeremiah 17:9

Jesus said:

> *"For out of the heart proceed evil thoughts, murders, adulteries, fornications, thefts, false witness, blasphemies."*—Matthew 15:19

> Paul wrote: *"Flee also youthful lusts: but follow righteousness, faith, charity, peace,* with them that call on the LORD out of a pure heart." —2 Timothy 2:22

> *"But as it is written, Eye hath not seen, nor ear heard, neither have entered into the heart of man, the things which God hath prepared for them that love Him."* —1 Corinthians 2:9

> *"That in the dispensation of the fullness of times he might gather together in one all things in Christ, both which are in heaven* (religion)*, and which are on earth* (society)*; [even] in him."*—Ephesians 1:10

The above scriptures help in understanding the complexities of human character. Some people in a culture may desire peace, love, and prosperity, while others in the same culture may lust for power, wealth, and esteem. As the blessings of restitution increase, the news media, cell phones, and Internet are major blessings that draw attention to the needy and to positive events, even as they also bring news and ads relating to lust, crime, and selfishness. People thus reveal their character by what they consider important in their lives. The prophet Isaiah wrote:

> *"Thus said the LORD, Keep ye judgment, and do justice:* <u>*for my salvation [is] near to come, and my righteousness to be revealed*</u>."—Isaiah 56:1

The Scriptures provide clues as to what to watch for that signals our Lord's return (presence). Increasingly, revelations of unjust and unrighteous conditions upon earth show the need for social progress, an article written in the 1920's, described the increasing wonders of that day, it said:

> "Are we not at the time when the whole world is on the move as never before in the past? Steamboats, steam and electric railways, etc., are only a century old and are only reaching their climax of efficiency. It would seem as though God had prospered human intelligence along these lines just at the opportune moment to bring in the running to and fro at the appropriate time—in the end of this Age. How about the increase of knowledge? Is it not true that greater increase has been made in knowledge within the last fifty years than ever before? Not only is this knowledge exemplified in tunnels, bridges, buildings, machinery, electric lighting and power, and in every conceivable device for human comfort, but; it is especially marked in human education. Within the past thirty years free schools, yea, compulsory education, have seemingly been forced upon the people of every land, as though to fulfill the prophecy 'Knowledge shall be increased."

The above comments were made almost a century ago… what do we think will happen during this next century: will there be more people making this planet into a better world, or do we expect more people involved in selfish, alcohol-related depravity? The Bible speaks of God's judgment as fair. For example, in Jeremiah we read:

> *"I the LORD search the heart, [I] try the reins, even to give every man according to his ways, [and] according to the fruit of his doings."*—Jeremiah 17:10

Paul wrote in Romans about the judgment of God:
"Who will render to every man according to his deeds"
—Romans 2:6

God will allow every person the freedom to express his or her mind without any hindrance. For only when the individual has complete liberty to do with out hindrance of his or her desire without any obstruction, can the person be judged on his or her own merit. The apostle Peter wrote of this transition from the Gospel Age into the Judgment Day or the Kingdom of God, saying:

> *"But the day* (kingdom) *of the Lord will come as a thief in the night* (the world unaware of what the changes mean)*; in the which the heavens* (evil in religion) *shall pass away with a great noise* (conflict), *and the elements* (evil doctrines and rituals) *shall melt with fervent heat* (controversy), *the earth* (evil society) *also and the works (evil activity) that are therein shall be burned up* (destroyed)."—Peter 3:10

Peter is describing conditions that bring about change from the old world *(evil society)* to the new world *(just and righteous society)*. In verse 13, he writes:

> *"Nevertheless we, according to his promise, look for new heavens* (truthful and just religion) *and a new earth* (truthful and just society), *wherein dwells righteousness."*

Then there are the prophetic words of Daniel 12:4, which also apply to present changing conditions:

"But thou, O Daniel, shut up the words, and seal the book, [even] to the time of the end (of evil)*: many shall run to and fro, and knowledge shall be increased."*

And as Peter wrote: *"...new heavens (truth in religion) and a new earth* (truth in society)*, wherein dwells righteousness."* —2 Peter 3:13

The transformation from an evil world into a new world, which Peter said to expect (as mentioned before), is advancing throughout the earth through instant communication, fast travel, modern housing, electronics, etc. Today, these modern marvels are commonly accepted, and they are instrumental in the increasing awareness and desire for justice, civil liberties, better living conditions, environmental needs, and so forth. The changes involve public participation and approval in both the secular and religious sectors of societies, resulting in a gradual transition from control by a few to leadership employed by democratic process as educational institutions teach values that include assisting and encouraging those in need.

The Kingdom of God is materializing in a manner that appears normal. Unlike centuries ago, religious or civil differences are appropriately settled in a court of law or negotiated in a manner that is publicly acceptable. In other words, societies prosper when justice, mercy, cooperation, and peaceful means are employed. Increasing numbers of TV, Internet, and radio shows are sources of information and learning. Universal education is increasing and becomes a very important factor in the development of the Kingdom of God. Problems of pollution, overcrowding, and global warming are given increasing attention as nations' leaders, working together, try to decide what is best for everyone's welfare. The goal of a better and healthier planet is attracting increasing numbers of supporters even as healthcare institutions under government observation work towards healthier and longer lives. Worldwide efforts are made to help or improve many situations and conditions that a few centuries ago went unnoticed because of the lack of communication and knowledge that Daniel prophesied would come. Also, the promise our Lord made to his followers of the Gospel Age. He said:

> *"Fear not, little flock; for it is your Father's good pleasure to give you the Kingdom."*—Luke 12:32

The first advent of Jesus, through his death and resurrection, not only brought redemption from Adamic death, but also initiated the spark of God's righteousness and hope in the hearts of believers. The words of Jesus and the apostles have been as a spiritual compass in guiding and building the foundation of righteousness, justice, love, mercy, and the like during the Gospel Age through faithful followers and will reach its fulfillment during the Millennial Age, which is the Judgment Day or God's Kingdom.

Thus, the objective of our Lord's second advent (spiritual presence) leads the heart of those willing into knowledge of God's spirit of righteousness, mercy, justice, and love. These changes (during the Kingdom) transform a sinful world into one of righteousness and justice, as Jesus promised. However, some people will continue their evil ways even while the knowledge of God's purpose increases; for their character, hardened by greed and self-deception, will continue in wickedness to eventually bring second death.

As Jesus the Christ said:

> *All that are in the graves shall hear his voice, and shall come forth; they that have done good* (the chosen, faithful), *unto the resurrection of life; and they that have*

done evil (the rest of mankind), *unto the resurrection of judgment."* —John 5:28–29

"And before him shall be gathered all nations (during restitution)*: and he shall separate them* (those who learn righteousness from those who do not) *one from another, as a shepherd divides [his] sheep from the goats."* —Matthew 25:32

"Then shall he say also unto them on the left hand (the reprobates), *Depart from me, ye cursed, into everlasting fire* (destruction), *prepared for the devil* (evil, Satan, Serpent, or Dragon) *and his* (its) *angels* (messengers or followers)*."*—Matthew 25:41

"Then shall the righteous shine forth as the sun in the Kingdom of their Father."—Matthew 13:43

The development of God's Kingdom, under the rule of Jesus the Christ and his Church, involves the world first going through dark and trying circumstances, which, over time, results in the spirit of justice and righteousness sweeping away evil and wickedness. In God's appropriate time, the resurrection will begin, and those who have slept or died, the rest of *"all flesh"* (Jeremiah 25:31), will have the opportunity to understand and learn righteousness that brings life. However, as mentioned before, some people will persist in following evil and thus die the second death—that is, will be destroyed. The prophet Jeremiah wrote of this:

"I the LORD search the heart, [I] try the reins, even to give every man according to his ways, [and] according to the fruit of his doings."—Jeremiah 17:10

Other prophecies also describing Kingdom or Judgment Day conditions are found in the books of Jeremiah and Isaiah, in the Gospels, and in the letters of the apostles:

> "*A noise shall come [even] to the ends of the earth; for the LORD hath a controversy with the nations, He* (through Jesus the Christ) *will plead with all flesh* (at end of the Gospel Age); *He will give them [that are] wicked to the sword* (destruction), *said the LORD.*" —Jeremiah 25:31

> "*And the glory of the LORD shall be revealed, and all flesh shall see [it] together* (during time of restitution and resurrection): *for the mouth of the LORD hath spoken [it].*"—Isaiah 40:5

> "*As Thou (God) hast given him* (Jesus the Christ) *power over all flesh, that he should give eternal life to as many as Thou hast given him.*"—John 17:2 (Gospel Age and the Kingdom.)

> "*And all flesh shall see the salvation of God.*" —Luke 3:6 (During the Kingdom.)

> "*Then [comes] the end, when he (Jesus the Christ) shall have delivered up the Kingdom to God, even the Father; when he (Jesus the Christ) shall have put down all rule and all authority and power (evil).*"—1 Corinthians 15:24

As knowledge of God's love increases, desire for justice and righteousness also increases, which is fundamental to the transition from the Gospel Age to Kingdom conditions. The positive changes alter societies and religious organizations, especially among Christians. Traditional doctrines that have been absolute for centuries are being questioned and challenged. Increasing numbers of Christians are recognizing their right and responsibility to prove all things, to openly discuss morals, character, and doctrine as they determine Scripture harmony and objectivity for direction in righteousness, justice, and mercy.

Each passing year brings greater recognition in Christian circles that the Bible's central theme of righteousness, justice, and mercy echoes, first within the Church and then throughout the world; thus, God's plan involves all people. The day will come when people who continue in immorality and injustice will cease to exist, for, as the Kingdom of God under the righteous, just, and merciful rule of the spirit of Jesus the Christ and his Church envelops the earth. Evil will gradually cease and be bound, and all desiring life will have learned to love God with all their hearts and their neighbor as themselves. The following scriptures describe the effect that the Lord's return or spiritual presence is to have on societies during the thousand years of restitution:

"And, behold, I come quickly (second advent); and my reward [is] with me, to give every man according as his work shall be (during the Kingdom)." —Revelation 22:12

"The LORD preserves all them that love him: but all the wicked will he destroy (during the Kingdom)." —Psalms 145:20

"And then shall that wicked be revealed, whom the Lord shall consume (destroy) with the spirit of his mouth (truth) and shall destroy with the brightness (righteousness and justice) of his coming (spiritual presence during the Kingdom)." —2 Thessalonians 2:8

Many Christians, in the search for truth, have been able to discern that fear, superstition, ignorance, and lust for power among Christians over the centuries have confused and distorted the vision God has in store for mankind when the Gospel Age (evil world) fades away. Today, significant fulfillment of Bible prophecy is alerting vigilant Christians to recognize that unparalleled, worldwide changing conditions increasingly reveal that personal responsibility to the Lord is required, which frees the liberated heart from repressive, dominating religious control and doctrines of the Dark Ages. The opportunity presents alert Christians a choice in how to handle the freedom: whether to enthusiastically take to the streets with the news of this revelation or to calmly and faithfully encourage others in knowledge of God's Word, which brings freedom from fear of eternal torment and of an evil spirit being instigating evil into our minds. The apostle Peter wrote of this day and how to deal with it, saying:

> *"But the heavens (religion) and the earth (society), which are now, by the same word are kept in store, reserved unto fire (destruction) against the Day of Judgment and perdition of ungodly men."* —2 Peter 3:7

> *"[Seeing] then [that] all these things* (evil and wickedness) *shall be dissolved, what manner [of persons] ought ye to be in [all] holy conversation and godliness."* —2 Peter 3:11

The following scriptures speak of our Lord's enlightening presence seen in increase of justice and righteousness in the hearts of men:

> *"Thus said the LORD, Keep ye judgment, and do justice: for my salvation [is] near to come, and my righteousness to be revealed."*—Isaiah 56:1

"Clouds (trouble) *and darkness* (ignorance) *[are] round about him* (the Lord's spiritual presence*): righteousness and judgment [are] the habitation of his (Jesus the Christ) throne."*—Psalms 97:2

The times appear to be in a flux of contradiction in that the darkness of ignorance and wickedness covers the earth, yet the light of truth and knowledge abounds as never before, and that light is to shine brighter as the promises of God are fulfilled, as Isaiah and John prophesied:

"Of the increase of [his] government and peace [there shall be] no end, upon the throne of David (name for Jesus the Christ)*, and upon his kingdom, to order it, and to establish it with judgment and with justice from henceforth even for ever. The zeal of the LORD of hosts will perform this* (through the enlightened hearts of men)." —Isaiah 9:7

"And God shall wipe away all tears from their eyes; and there shall be no more death, neither sorrow, nor crying, neither shall there be any more pain: for the former things are passed away (during the Kingdom)." —Revelation 21:4

Spiritual enlightenment is a gradual process in which the Lord's spiritual presence (return) is seen in the inquisitive and eager attitude of concerned people all over the earth for righteousness and justice. A fleshly presence (return) of Jesus in a physical, forceful, and commanding manner would be contrary to how the spirit of God has operated in the past, namely, working in the hearts of people having desire for peace, righteousness, and justice, while abhorring evil or wickedness. Thus, the Kingdom under Jesus the Christ develops through knowledge, truth, and love in the hearts of people, at times, in troubled stages as the prophet Joel predicted. As the reign of Jesus the Christ's Kingdom grows in power and glory, people will recognize a literal fulfillment of John's metaphoric prophecy:

> *"And I heard a loud voice (worldwide declaration) saying in heaven (religion), Now is come salvation, and strength, and the Kingdom of our God, and the power of His Christ: for the accuser (evil, Satan, Devil, Serpent, or Dragon) of our brethren is cast down (restrained), which accuse (has been blamed by) them before our God day and night."*
> —Revelation 12:10

Lastly, the prophecy of the apostle Paul points to the finality of the work of Jesus the Christ and his Church in his Kingdom, saying:

> *"Then [comes] the end, when he (Jesus the Christ) shall have delivered up the kingdom to God, even the Father; when he (Jesus the Christ and the chosen faithful) shall have put down all rule and all authority and power."*
> —1 Corinthians 15:24

Truth Transforms Christians

In the nineteenth and twentieth centuries, numerous errors were uncovered in traditional beliefs and doctrines of Christendom that hid the loving and just plan of God. Independent Bible study groups brought about enlightened perception amidst religious controversy—their findings were a major problem that threatened traditions of structured Christianity. The increase in knowledge revealed to many studious Christians that a number of traditional doctrines and methods of worship were not Scriptural and were counter to the recently discovered loving objective of our Creator, that restitution opportunity was for all humanity including the thousand-year Judgment period that was imminent through the spiritual presence of Jesus the Christ. This caused staunch supporters of Dark Age concepts to uniformly oppose such revelations as being of the Devil. Thus, traditional-minded Christians supported their leaders in limiting the spread of the wonderful news of God's Kingdom upon earth.

The good news of our Lord's Kingdom commencing was strongly opposed by traditional Christendom; opposition was similar during the enlightenment period, which brought about change in the lives of many Christians during the Reformation. Years later, advancement in understanding Bible prophecy brought forth the Miller movement and the Seventh Day Adventists, followed by the non-denominational Bible Student movement that encouraged further in-depth study among interested Christians in both Bible prophecy and doctrine. Studious Christians of various religious backgrounds recognized and rejoiced in Bible prophecy telling of God's loving plan of restitution and resurrection for all people. The good news was not acceptable by traditional religion, but the newly formed Bible study groups continued to search the Scriptures under the main leadership of a studious spiritual Christian, Charles T. Russell. Upon his death, the resulting leadership altered main doctrines within a decade, which caused division. The organization then took on the name of "Jehovah's Witnesses." Many Christians then left the organization to form independent Bible study groups, which today exist under local Ecclesia control of leadership, while associating with groups nationally and internationally. For centuries, Christians, under the eyes of tradition-led religion, have endeavored to study and pray to understand more fully the picture language of the Bible. In many cases, prophetic interpretation led to the absurd when allegorical, metaphorical, or symbolic intent was interpreted as literal.

Studious Christians realized that prophecy, when viewed in the light of traditional, fear-inducing doctrine, presented a horrible future of torment for ignorant and unrepentant people, a future that was to be dominated by a frightful, evil spirit being called Satan. This concept, formed against a background of fear, caused many to have great anxiety over "the Evil One" and his many evil assistants. This imagined, evil spirit being also caused fearful reluctance in Christians to question how the concept of an evil spirit being developed in the first place. The apostle Paul cautioned about subscribing to this:

*"For God hath not given us the spirit of fear; but of power,
and of love, and of a sound mind."*—2 Timothy 1:7

Nevertheless, over the centuries fear of a Satan set in among Christians because the Scriptures said so, resulting in the majority being afraid to investigate this threat that countered God's love; it was unscriptural to question how circumstances brought this evil, mystical character, whose main objective was to tempt people into doing evil, into existence. It seems that this evil spirit being named Satan, Devil, Serpent, or Dragon firmly occupies a throne of power and Christians are to think that God does not want Christians to question the subject further. Isn't it odd, though, that nowhere in the Bible is there even a hint that belief in an evil spirit being named Satan is necessary for salvation? Rather, the apostle Peter clearly said:

*"And it shall come to pass, [that] whosoever shall call on
the name of the Lord shall be saved."*—Acts 2:21

When our Lord came on the scene, he saw the culture of the Jews had a history of using the name of Satan or Devil in reference to evil. It appears that he did not want to cause controversy over the matter, as it would disrupt his message of the Gospel and his mission to die as a ransom for Adam. But, he is quoted in Matthew in regards to the source of evil saying:

*"A good man out of the good treasure of the heart brings
forth good things: and an evil man out of the evil treasure
brings forth evil things."*— Matthew 12:35

When Matthew, Mark, and Luke recorded what they understood about the temptation of Jesus the Christ in the wilderness, they used the aphorisms or idioms of their cultural language in recording it. According to Matthew,

"Then was Jesus led up of the Spirit into the wilderness to be tempted of the devil (Satan, Serpent, or Dragon)." —Matthew 4:1

Mark, likewise, wrote:

"And he was there in the wilderness forty days, tempted of Satan (Devil, Serpent, and Dragon)." —Mark 1:13

Also, Luke wrote: *"Being forty days tempted of the devil (Satan, Serpent, and Dragon)."* — Luke 4:2

Either the translator slipped up on the statement of Mark, or Mark preferred using the idiom Satan rather than Devil or Serpent or Dragon. History offers strong evidence that religious leaders and most teachers, in their fear and arrogance, intentionally promoted error and violence by reinforcing people's fearful belief in the existence of an evil spirit being or persona called Satan or Devil, but not with the other two names. Such endeavors to scare others are evil, and those teaching such beliefs ignore God's love for humanity.

Throughout the Gospel Age, the darkness of fear that an evil spirit being haunted mankind caused not only physical and emotional harm, but also led to useless and deceptive religious concepts and rituals. Even today, fearful and superstitious proclamations from pulpits and religious publications continue to scare many as they describe an unrealistic, catastrophic end in hell under the supervision of Satan while the world is destroyed by a literal firestorm. In contrast, a thorough and fair interpretation of Bible prophecy does not portray the world turning into a fireball under the jurisdiction of an evil spirit being, for the Bible tells us in a very clear manner:

"[One] generation passes away, and [another] generation comes: but the earth abides for ever." —Ecclesiastes 1:4

The changes taking place upon earth will eventually lead to life upon earth without sickness and Adamic death, the very opposite of the deceptive and destructive evil expectations produced by fear-filled ignorance, greed, and misconceptions taught over thousands of years. For centuries, the majority of Christians have recognized the moral aspect of the Bible's message, but not its comforting, long-term restoration of humanity.

The Bible is read daily for encouragement in the faith, but many Christians have failed to understand God's objective of man's future existence upon earth. They have not understood that the new world is to develop through a newness of attitude and belief in the hearts of people even as fiery, destructive troubles consume, or gradually bring to an end, the evil conceived in the hearts of men upon earth. This is the fundamental intent of the apostle Paul's message to Christian Jews in Rome:

> *"But now the Law no longer applies to us; we have died to what once controlled us (Gspd); that we should serve in newness of spirit (righteousness, justice, love, mercy, kindness, patience, and so on), and not [in] the oldness of the letter (under the law)."*—Romans 7:6, KJV

To the Ephesian brethren he wrote:

> *"Put on the whole armor of God* (righteousness, justice, love, mercy, kindness, patience, and the like) *that ye may be able to stand against the wiles of the devil* (evil, Satan, Serpent, or Dragon)." —Ephesians 6:11

Thus, during this process of change into the Kingdom of God, people are encouraged to seek righteousness, justice, love, mercy, kindness, patience, and so on. Christians, searching the Scriptures for direction in present life, can fail to perceive the overall prophetic harmony of God's Word relating to future life. This happens because they have not perceived that traditional concepts of future life are handicapped by imaginings of specific destinations for the immortal souls of saints and sinners. This concept creates confusion, for the reality is that we are living souls (breathing creatures, Strong, #5313); we don't have a soul, as we read:

> *"And the LORD God formed man [of] the dust of the ground, and breathed into his nostrils the breath of life; and man <u>became</u> a living soul."*—Genesis 2:7

> *<u>"And if a soul</u>* (person*) <u>sins, and commits any of these things</u> <u>which are forbidden</u> to be done by the commandments of the LORD; though he wished it not, yet <u>he</u>* (person or living soul) *<u>is guilty</u>, and shall bear his iniquity."* —Leviticus 5:17

> *"Behold, all souls are mine; as the soul of the father, so also the soul of the son is mine: <u>the soul that sins, it shall die.</u>"* —Ezekiel 18:4

> *And so it is written, the first man <u>Adam was made a</u> <u>living soul</u>; the last Adam [was made] a quickening spirit."*—1 Corinthians 15:45

As living souls or humans with an ability to reason, we want to hear convincing words of future existence, and it does not help when a preacher, educated in an "approved" seminary, delivers a traditional, hazy viewpoint on the destiny of an immortal soul. When a "living soul" is said to be a spiritual essence in a body, it gives a different perspective to the loving and delightful message Jesus and his apostles preached about the message of resurrection from the dead, which is: first the Church (chosen faithful) and then, according to each generation, the millions of people (souls) who have lived and died. Many Christians fail to understand that Judgment Day consists of progressive restitution blessings, which, over approximately a thousand years, brings utopia to humanity upon earth. Just think of the billions in money used for warfare, often supported by fear-led Christian's that will instead be used to benefit societies when nations learn—and it is beginning to happen—to eliminate war:

> *"And he shall judge among the nations, and shall rebuke many people: and they shall beat their swords into plowshares, and their spears into pruning hooks: nation shall not lift up sword against nation, neither shall they learn war any more."*—Isaiah 2:4/Micah 4:3

The judgment upon nations appears to have started in the last century, for it has been calculated that the evil of man's destructiveness has killed more people in the twentieth century than in all previous centuries put together. The World is experiencing judgment of nations, which precedes the judgment of individuals. Nations are seeking avenues of peace, trust, diplomacy, to change from the race in armaments to the quietness of peace by negotiated settlements made often under troubling transition. Leadership has the choice between ways of war or of living peacefully and fairly with one another. A prophesy of the Psalmist has echoed the world's future:

> *"O let the nations be glad and sing for joy: for you* (Jesus the Christ under the authority of the Heavenly Father) *shall judge the people righteously, and govern the nations upon earth."*—Psalms 67:4

In contrast, for centuries, this good news (Gospel) has been ignored in preference to the demeaning idea that our Creator is going to send everyone (except the Church or chosen ones) to eternal torment, while the earth is destroyed by literal fire. The concept is also prevalent that He has allowed an evil spirit being called Satan, with many demon assistants, to tempt people to sin so they can end up in eternal torment. How a Satan tempts people to sin is subject to opinion, never reasonably explained, but is firmly believed. When we read the Bible in the context of God's love and interpret it in the context of God's wisdom, justice, and power, the Gospel (good news) is that people are to learn that they are responsible for sin through their lust, anger, hate, jealousy, and greed and that only through the ransom sacrifice of our Lord Jesus the Christ does mankind have opportunity to learn righteousness and justice that bring life from condemnation under Adam's sin. As the apostle Paul wrote:

> *"Wherefore, as by one man sin entered into the world, and death by sin; and so death passed upon all men, for that all have sinned."*—Romans 5:12

> *"For as in Adam all die, even so in Christ shall all be made alive."*—1 Corinthians 15:22

And James supports the above with:

> *"Then when lust is conceived, it brings forth sin: and sin, when it is finished, brings forth death."* —James 1:15

Because of God's love and mercy, the Gospel of Jesus the Christ declares the answer to the awful dilemma of sin and death. It is a wonderful message of resurrection and restitution opportunity through the World's Redeemer,: Jesus the Christ, which brings life for the repentant in God's Kingdom upon earth. This is explained in Revelation:

"And the Spirit and the bride (chosen faithful) say: Come. And let him that hears say, Come. And let him that is athirst (for righteousness, justice, and truth) *come. And whosoever will, let him take the water of life* (truth in Jesus the Christ) *freely."*—Revelation 22:17

This verse refers to the Judgment Day, the Kingdom, the Millennium or thousand years of restitution, which is being established throughout the world; it is an educational process that grows worldwide under the spirit led oversight of Jesus the Christ and his bride, the Church, the little flock, the chosen, the faithful Christians from the Gospel Age who live and reign with Jesus the Christ in the spirit encouraging nations and mankind. The bride, through the spirit of truth, justice, righteousness, mercy, and love assist and lead willing hearts in every nation as they progress up the highway of righteousness, justice, and love as prophesied. In Proverbs:

"The highway of the upright [is] to depart from evil: he that keeps his way preserves his soul (life)." —Proverbs 16:17

From Isaiah:

"In that day shall there be a highway out of Egypt to Assyria, and the Assyrian shall come into Egypt, and the Egyptian into Assyria, and the Egyptians shall serve with the Assyrians."—Isaiah 19:23

Again from Isaiah:

> *"And an highway* (consisting of righteousness, justice, love, and mercy) *shall be there, and a way, and it shall be called: The way of holiness; the unclean* (reprobates) *shall not pass over it; but it [shall be] for those* (the repentant): *the wayfaring men, though fools, shall not err [therein]."*—Isaiah 35:8

Again from Isaiah:

> *"The voice of him (prophecy of John the Baptist) that cries in the wilderness, Prepare ye the way of the LORD, make straight in the desert* (of sin and death) *a highway* (of righteousness and justice) *for our God."*—Isaiah 40:3

Thus, the knowledge of the Lord in spirit and truth requires years to spread across every continent. Today, people of every Christian denomination are sending missionaries and Bibles wherever possible, as television, the Internet, and fast travel increase the prospects of people hearing and learning of God's love through Jesus the Christ. Interest and results are growing to the extent where knowledge of the Lord can literally be visualized to cover the earth as water covers the seas. It is reasonable to suggest that knowledge of God's saving grace through Jesus the Christ will spread and be understood throughout the earth before the start of the general resurrection. It would not be beneficial for those having been resurrected to have evil still rule in the hearts of men.

As mentioned before: the Bible states there are two resurrections: the first is the resurrection of the Church, the faithful of the Gospel Age; the second or general resurrection is of humanity, likely in reverse generational sequence, raised from the grave with full opportunity to learn to overcome their sinful nature and attain life in the Kingdom of Jesus the Christ.

"Blessed and holy [is] he that hath part in <u>the first</u> <u>resurrection</u>: on such the second death hath no power, but they shall be priests of God and of Christ, and shall reign with him a thousand years."—Revelation 20:6

"Marvel not at this: for the hour is coming, in the which all that are in the graves shall hear his voice and shall come forth; they that have done good, unto the resurrection of life (the Church or chosen); and they that have done evil *(the rest of humanity),* unto the resurrection of judgment (trial period of learning righteousness)."*—John 5:28–29

The Bible, when read in the spirit of wisdom, justice, truth, and love, presents a bright picture of God's equitable and compassionate purpose. It is ignorance and fear, especially from the Dark Ages, that have clouded this inspirational prospect with the dark dogma of fabricated phobic and erring ideas that project a human destiny of bliss in heaven for those approved by the religious systems and of eternal torment in hell for the rejected or unbelievers under the direction of an evil spirit being called Satan, Devil, Serpent, or Dragon. In correcting these erring teachings and to understand present and future human existence according to Scripture, the historical and Biblical verification of prophecy must harmoniously substantiate and assure that the Judgment Day; being approximately a thousand years, is an opportunity for all humanity, the living as well as the dead.

Then, both the millions who have heard of salvation in Jesus the Christ and did not understand and the millions who have not actually heard of salvation in Jesus the Christ will have their opportunity to hear, learn, and be judged to have life in God's promised paradise upon earth. A search through the Bible gives confirmation that Jewish writers wrote the Scriptures in the spirit of justice and righteousness, in the context of God's love. Much of it was composed in the picture language of their day, but, over the centuries, imaginations, religious politics, and fearful ideas of Judgment Day was believed to bring harsh retribution from God that cast a dark shadow of fear over God's loving promise to Abraham. In contrast to the traditional idea of eternal torment, we read:

> *"And I will bless them that bless thee* (Israel)*, and curse him that curses thee* (Israel)*: and in thee (Abrahamic faithfulness) shall all families of the earth be blessed."*
> —Genesis 12:3

Thus, the increase of knowledge, led by the spirit of truth, love, justice, and righteousness is bringing attention to the Bible's comforting message of God's promise of the resurrection and restitution blessings in His Kingdom. Unfortunately, most Bible translations and commentaries still contribute to the fear that an evil spirit being called Satan initiates evil in humans, which sadly, gravely distorts the loving objective of our Creator. To fully comprehend the context of God's plan for humanity, our faith is to rest in Jesus the Christ without fear of an evil spirit being named Satan, Devil, Serpent, or Dragon or the thoughts of people being hampered by the interference of an imagined, evil spirit being.

We can see God's objective for humanity in a much brighter light (truth) when questions such as below are answered relative to God's nature of justice, righteousness, mercy, and love:

Does Satan actually exist, or is he a product of human imagination?

Must a Christian accept the existence of an evil spirit being called Satan in order to have salvation?

Is evil conceived in the minds of men, or does an evil spirit being instigate evil in a person's mind?

If the character of God consists of wisdom, justice, love, and power, why would He have people ignorant of the salvation message end up in eternal torment?

Why would God create a devil to plague people if the Prophet Jeremiah said:

> *"The heart [is] deceitful above all [things], and desperately wicked."*—Jeremiah 17:9

Why do Christians have bad things happen to them in this life?

If God hates evil, why does evil exist?

Why would God send an evil spirit upon Saul if a Satan has jurisdiction over evil?

> *"And it came to pass, when the evil spirit from God was upon Saul"*—1 Samuel 16:23

There are harmonious and reasonable answers to the above questions in the Bible, but the average reader needs help in interpreting and finding the answers, keeping in mind that it is God's plan to have all the earth filled with His glory:

> *"But [as] truly [as] I live, <u>all the earth shall be filled with the glory of the LORD</u>."*—Numbers 14:21

Search for Truth

Using the King James Bible, the NIV translation, and *Strong's Complete Concordance*, the reader can find many helpful answers. Answers do not always come from traditional, seminary-trained leadership, who are prone to proclaim the message of dual responsibility for evil—a troubling error taught for thousands of years. Sometimes a Devil or Satan is cited as the source of evil, while at other times, people, whether religious or non-religious, are blamed. Numerous authors of religious articles and books have offered persuasive evidence the Bible teaches that evil originated with a spirit being called Satan who infiltrates the minds of humans, making them think and act wickedly.

Having been taught this doctrine in youth, I was overjoyed to discover that there are harmonious answers in Scripture contrary to that traditional doctrine. Harmonious answers are found in the summation of non-denominational Christian writers of the nineteenth and twentieth centuries. During that time, as mentioned before, numerous newly-formed Bible study groups, consisting of people from every possible denomination, studied and accumulated considerable knowledge of the Lord's return and realized God had a wonderful plan for people upon earth. They examined traditional doctrines and found them inconsistent and out of harmony with the objective of God to have paradise upon earth for mankind.

Their main leader, Charles T. Russell, published articles raising critical questions among members of traditional churches. Although certain traditional doctrines (Immortal soul, Eternal Torment, Triune God and Lord's Return in the Flesh) were evaluated and rejected by the new Christian Bible Student movement, the fear-inspired doctrine of the Devil (Satan, Serpent, or Dragon) remained intact. Today, in searching for the justice in God's love, we find reliable information on how evil originated and how sin is a people product and not instigated by an imagined, evil spirit being—that history and the Bible reveal evil is of the hearts of men.

The ideas of men have altered original doctrine and added useless ritual in the Christian faith that is opposite to the generous and truthful spirit of Jesus the Christ. He was our example of how to resist the evils of lust, fear, pride, ignorance, and the like, all destructive characteristics of eroded values, submissiveness to temptation, and sin. The World's Redeemer: Jesus the Christ paid the ransom required by his Heavenly Father through death on the cross, Our Lord's life was an example for all Christians in rejecting evil thoughts that tempted him. His thoughts were guided by God's attributes of wisdom, justice, love, and power, and was faithful in preaching God's love, and the resurrection of the dead, the time when evil and the sting of Adamic death will be past.

Jesus the Christ used the names Satan and Devil in reference to the powerful, evil temptations of hate, lust, and pride. His statements were in parables and symbols that did not blame an imagined, evil spirit being as the source of man's evil. He did not claim that a Satan instigates evil behavior in people. People are responsible for their sin (evil) and must repent of their sin in his name in order to attain life. Unfortunately, over the centuries, Christian writers have emphasized ideas of torment and retribution of God, rather than His justice, righteousness, and love.

An excellent book on history, titled *Great Issues in Western Civilization, Vol. 1*, published by Random House, New York, tells of Martin Luther, founder of the Lutheran faith, as having a confused view of the source of evil. Its author noted that Luther's concept of evil coming from people, with the devil as instigator, is contrary to other statements he made.:

> "It is therefore true that man, being a bad tree, can only will and do evil."

And:

> "It is false to state that man's inclination is free to choose between either of two opposites. Indeed, the inclination is not free, but captive. This is said in opposition to common opinion."

And:

> "It is false to state that the will can by nature conform to correct precept"

And:

> "As a matter of fact, without the grace of God, the will produces an act that is perverse and evil."

And:

"It does not, however, follow that the will is by nature evil, that is, essentially evil, as the Manicheans maintain. It is nevertheless innately and inevitably evil and corrupt."

Though Martin Luther recognized evil as being of a person, he could not shake his strong conviction that a devil was heavily involved. This has also been a troublesome puzzle for many Christians, past and present. The belief that an evil spirit being tempts humans is a contradiction to Scripture that proclaims the heart of man is the source of evil. It is not only confusing but also unreasonable.

In his book titled *World History at a Glance*, published by The Garden City Publishing Co., 1942, Joseph Reither offers a commendable background to the Martin Luther of the Renaissance and the Reformation:

"Martin Luther was a loyal Catholic and had no thought of separating himself from the Catholic Church. In accordance with the custom of the time, Luther posted upon the door of Castle Church at Wittenberg a list of 95 theses in which he stated his position on indulgences and allied questions.

Sure of the rightness of his original stand, Martin Luther was led to insist he would not submit against the dictates of his conscience. It occurred shortly after the printing press was invented, and Luther flooded Germany with articles attacking every sort of abuse. Luther called upon the Germans to unite and destroy the power of the Pope over the German states. Because Martin Luther insisted he had to follow his conscience according to Scripture, he soon found himself opposing ecclesiastical authority."

But, like the rest of us, the attitude and actions of Martin Luther were not always above reproach; at times, his prejudice (evil) restrained him from being just and righteous. For instance, *Free Inquiry* magazine of October/November 2004 has an article by Gregory S. Paul, titled "The Great Scandal, Christianity's Role in the Rise of the Nazis." The author writes:

> But his (Luther's) differences with the Pope and Church council did not alter his condemnation of the Jews. In his publication 'On the Jews and Their Lies,' Luther wrote, 'But since I learned that these miserable and accursed people, to lure themselves even to us... I have published this little book... Our Lord calls them a 'brood of vipers' ... Therefore the blind Jews are truly stupid fools ... Wherever they have their synagogues, nothing is found but a den of devils in which sheer self-glory, conceit, lies, blasphemy, and defaming of God and men are practiced most maliciously... They are nothing but thieves and robbers who daily eat no morsel and wear no thread of clothing which they have not stolen and pilfered from us by means of their accursed usury.'

Martin Luther's denunciation of the Jews continued on, but the above quote illustrates how a professing Christian, who holds common prejudices of his day, brings forth evil but is still looked upon as a means of enlightenment of God's Word. A sad and destructive consequence of evil (prejudice) coming from a Christian is that it can become a curse or evil to others. The problem is not of an evil spirit 'being' placing evil thoughts in a person's mind; the problem is that the individual allows his or her prejudice to devise evil of greed, lust, hate, jealousy, and the like. In allowing evil to dominate one's mind concerning a particular topic or of culture, a person's speech or writings can contaminate the thoughts of other people: Thus, Hitler used the prejudice of Martin Luther against the Jews in his crusade to destroy the Jews. Gregory S. Paul writes:

> Hitler professed being a Christian and was well acquainted with the writings of Martin Luther and once told General Gerhart Engel in 1941: 'I am now as before a Catholic and will always remain so.' In a 1944 speech, Hitler said: 'I may not be a light of the church, a pulpiteer, but deep down I am a pious man and believe that whoever fights bravely in defense of the natural laws framed by God and never capitulates will never be deserted by the lawgiver, but will, in the end, receive the blessings of Providence.' ... The standard biographies of the principal Nazi leaders state that all were born, baptized and raised Christian. Most grew up in strict, pious households, where tolerance and democratic values were disparaged. Nazi leaders of Catholic background included Adolf Hitler, Heinrich Himmler, Reinhard Heydrich, and Joseph Goebbels.

The point here is that Martin Luther and Adolf Hitler, along with others who have professed the Christian faith and who are used here as examples, allowed their minds to generate evil thoughts and acted upon that evil in word and deed. The evil of Martin Luther in directing condemnation upon the Jews was used by Hitler to help justify extermination of the Jews.

If I judge my neighbor unjustly and others follow my judgment to harm their neighbor, all have done evil. This is the basic problem with humanity—we all have evil thoughts, but we also are able to choose whether or not to act upon our evil thoughts. It is when we learn of and commit ourselves to Jesus the Christ as our Redeemer and Savior that we raise our values and goals to a higher plane by applying his teachings in our lives. This includes change from thinking only of our needs, but also to think of needs of others. Primarily, it involves steady progress of not acting upon evil thoughts and is often called "becoming Christ-like." The apostle Paul described the change as mainly a self-control situation in the spirit of God of righteousness, justice, love, and mercy as Paul wrote:

"But now ye also put off all these; anger, wrath, malice, blasphemy, filthy communication out of your mouth."— Colossians 3:8

"And above all these things [put on] charity (love), *which is the bond of perfection."*—Colossians 3:14

"Now the works of the flesh are manifest, which are [these]: adultery, fornication, uncleanness, lasciviousness, idolatry, witchcraft, hatred, variance, emulations, wrath, strife, seditions, heresies, envyings, murders, drunkenness, revellings, and such like; of the which I tell you before, as I have also told [you] in time past, that they which (continue to) *do such things shall not inherit the kingdom of God."*—Galatians 5:22–25

The Christian goal therefore is to change oneself, to avoid in every way the temptation to act upon evil thoughts. We are to think upon what is righteous and just and not allow evil to linger in our minds or to be our choice, no matter what the circumstances or occasion. As James wrote:

"A double minded man [is] unstable in all his ways."— James 1:8 And:

"Out of the same mouth proceeds blessing and cursing. My brethren, these things ought not so to be."—James 3:10

We then see there is no gray area, that an evil spirit being does not cause us to choose evil; we are solely responsible for our evildoing. Fortunately, since Martin Luther's time, there is a much greater understanding as to how the human mind functions. Today, increased knowledge offers a solution to the long troublesome problem of whether it is of God, our lust, or Satan that initiates evil. Why would evil acts conceived and committed by humans be blamed upon imagined demons, a Satan, or even God? Surely, our Creator would not handicap humanity by making their minds subject to the schemes of an external and invisible, evil spirit being. In all fairness and justness, people do not need an evil spirit being to tempt them; we are fully capable of tempting ourselves.

In religious organizations, it is common to hear or read of a Devil or Satan as the source of evil, while at the same time people are accused of being its source. As said before, the authors of numerous religious articles and books have offered persuasive evidence that the Bible teaches that evil originates with a spirit being called Satan who infiltrates the minds of humans. But what happens when a Satan (Devil, Serpent, Dragon, or evil) is bound with chains? It thus makes sense that Satan, Devil, Serpent, and Dragon are pictorial names for evil, and we are to look for the manner or process of binding as symbolic meaning.

Since evil is conceived in the minds of people, it is when we desire to attain knowledge of truth, righteousness, and justice and live accordingly that evil is bound, a process of commitment to change one's character from acting upon evil thoughts to following the ways of righteousness, justice, love, mercy, and so forth. This requires time, as all Christians learn, to eliminate the evil of lust from their mind and to not think evil of others or do evil to others. Remember the old saying; "garbage in, garbage out"? We cannot expect to have clean, helpful thoughts if we feed our mind with lusts of the flesh.

When a person learns to respect and do what is righteous towards others and others learn to respect and do righteously in turn, the activity of evil thinking and doing eventually becomes dormant; it is the many little links of righteousness, justice, and love that binds evil, Satan, Devil, Serpent, and Dragon. This is basic to people experiencing restitution blessings; it becomes fundamental knowledge as the Kingdom of God, the spiritual direction of our Lord Jesus the Christ and his Church, leading willing, loving hearts up the highway of holiness to life.

We are to remember, life expectancy is to increase during the approximately one thousand years, as opposed to life expectancy decreasing before and after the flood, when people's life span was over nine hundred years. Soon after the flood, a few generations lived over a couple of hundred years; Abraham's father is recorded to have been 205 at his death. The book entitled *The Divine Plan of the Ages* (previously mentioned), published in 1896, may have a few statements a person may differ on, but as a whole it is very helpful to understanding the changes going on around us. Ironically, long-established Christian organizations (mostly leadership) strongly oppose any change in long-held traditions and doctrine, which, as the book points out, many are not logical and err as to God's objective for humanity upon earth.

However, even with their impressive insight and ability in summing up the abundance of discovered knowledge of the Bible in their day, Bible students did not investigate doctrine relating to Satan and demons. As Christians, we should be able to see that evil behavior is of people and out of harmony with the attributes of wisdom, justice, love, and power of our Creator. It is because Adam chose to disobey that God provided a way for man's redemption from evil of sin and wickedness.

Paul explains God's loving, all-encompassing objective for all who learn to love and listen to His Word with the following statement:

> *"For this [is] good and acceptable in the sight of God our Savior; Who; will have all men to be saved, and to come unto the knowledge of the truth."*—1 Timothy 2:3–4

God's love reveals a compassionate and just objective. Contrarily, the vindictive, traditional teaching of a devil or Satan as instigator of evil is far from being reasonable or in harmony with God's loving objective. Jesus told of a future change when he said:

> *"When the Spirit of truth, is come, he (it) will guide you into all truth."*—John 16:13

The spirit of truth is not a spirit being, but is the spirit of God of righteousness, justice, mercy, love, compassion, and so forth, which guides the thoughts of submissive Christians over the years. In contrast, it is the spirit of evil hate, jealousy, greed, lust, etc. that restrains some professing Christians from growing in the spirit of the Lord. The spirit of God is also the spirit of truth, which is an opening of the mind to examine all things to see if what is said or written harmonizes with all Scripture, which then destroys the mystifying doctrine of a Satan, Devil, Serpent, or Dragon. Today, in most cultures, it is common in religious circles to refer to an evil spirit being as instigating or manipulating the thoughts of people and compelling them to commit evil, but the secular court of law is clear that people are themselves responsible for conceiving and committing evil. Thus the courts do not recognize evil spirit beings as the cause of a person's evil acts.

But even then, evil, Satan, Devil, Serpent, or Dragon) remains a deeply embedded personal belief of many religious people, including some judges and lawyers who interpret the law. In defense of Martin Luther, records show that though he believed in a Satan, his writings reveal his struggle against the evils of men, as his Treaty, published in 1520, disclosed some of the evil corrupting the Roman religious system. Eventually, his opposition to the evils of Church leadership made his break with Rome irreconcilable. And In an excerpt from his Treaty we read:

> "The Romanists, with great adroitness, have built three walls about them, behind which they have hitherto defended themselves in such wise that no one has been able to reform them and this has been the cause of terrible corruption throughout all Christendom.
>
> First, when pressed by the temporal power, they have made decrees and said that the temporal power has no jurisdiction over them, but on the other hand, that the spiritual is above the temporal power. Second, when the attempt is made to reprove them out of the Scriptures, they raise the objection that the interpretation of the Scriptures belongs to no one except the pope. Third, if threatened with a council, they answer with the fable that no one can call a council but the pope. In this wise they have slyly stolen from us our three rods, that they may go unpunished, and have ensconced themselves within the safe stronghold of these three walls, that they may practice all the knavery and wickedness which we now see."

Thus, Martin Luther recognized the evil of professing Christians practicing politics in the Roman Church and confronted the leadership of the Church about it. But the hypocrisy and deceitfulness built up in the Roman Church over the centuries made it incapable of change. Even today, the hierarchy of the Roman Church struggles to maintain control in the wake of sex scandals committed by its priests. Under the relentless scrutiny of lay members and news media, some Cardinals appear incapable of applying corrective action. *Time* magazine, in its May 6, 2002, issue, contained intense criticism on this subject by a reporter named Andrew Sullivan, who wrote:

"We have learned one simple thing from last week: the highest officials of the largest Christian denomination on earth have lower standards with regard to the protection of children and minors than secular law does. The endorsement of 'zero tolerance' by Philadelphia's Anthony Cardinal Bevilacq last Saturday (good post-Rome spin) is still not official policy. I can't believe I'm writing this—but they still don't get it. And if they cannot get the enormity of the crimes their clergy have committed, they are even further from acknowledging their own role in enabling them. No one has resigned. No one has taken responsibility. And on the two central issues behind this scandal, there is no movement.

The first is the authoritarian governing structure of the church, whereby a self-selected elite makes every decision for hundreds of millions of people. When you have a structure like this—immune from outside input—it is bound to create crises like this one. It has no real means of self-correction. The system creates incentives for secrecy and cover-ups that are often just as bad as the crime. But none of that is on the table. In fact, a critical element for recovery—boards of inquiry composed of lay people, not just clergy—was not even mentioned in the text."

Mr. Sullivan points out the inability of the authoritarian governing structure of the system to change. It lacks self-correction in that no one takes responsibility for secrecy and cover-ups. Jesus and his apostles had no intention of forming such a controlling system—it has developed ways to slyly operate around the principles he taught. This religious system has a history of abuse and deceit, in which many of its members look the other way as they keep supporting the system (Church) which, for centuries, has persecuted dissenters and repressed the spirit, truth, and love of our Savior Jesus the Christ.

Recognizing some of the evil aspects of this system in his day, Martin Luther had the courage and fortitude to oppose the evils that he was aware of. However, since he had been raised under the schooling of Roman Catholicism, some of its doctrinal and structural baggage affected his efforts to preach the grace of God in its fullness. Nevertheless, he was very instrumental in drawing the attention of Christians to some truths in Scripture.

In contrast, at a later date and in a less controversial manner, a Bible scholar named Benjamin Wilson, in his approach to attaining a more truthful perspective of Scripture for the consecrated spirit, offered his expertise to increase understanding of Scripture. In his dedicated style, he compiled a book titled *The Emphatic Diaglott*, a word-for-word translation of the New Testament from Greek into English. His rendition has been of great assistance to many Christian Bible students in comprehending Scripture in its authenticity (comments in parentheses are of this author):. An example from the "Diaglott" is John 14:16–17, where Jesus explains how the spirit of truth will guide his followers.

> *"And I will ask the Father, and He will give you another helper, that He* (the Father) *may be with you to the age, the spirit of truth, which the world cannot receive. Because*

> *it* (the world) *beholds it not* (spirit of truth), *nor knows it* (spirit of truth)*: but you know it* (spirit of truth)*; because it* (spirit of truth) *abides with you, and <u>will be in you</u>.*"

This translation of Jesus' statement corresponds with many other scriptures relating to the "spirit of truth" as not a spirit being, but as the desire, will, attitude, and aspiration of Christian's to trust in the Lord as they spread the good news of the Kingdom as Jesus commanded. The question then confronts us: How can the spirit of truth be evaluated in contrast to the spirit of evil? Remember the advice of Jesus and his apostles that Christians are to express justice, righteousness, honesty, kindness, mercy, love, patience, and so on every day. A Christian applying these virtues will not commit evil or will not fear that an evil spirit called Satan, Devil, Dragon, or Serpent is hovering about to intervene in his or her life.

In Ezekiel, we are told that evil thoughts appear in the mind because of lust:

> *"Thus said the LORD God, It shall also come to pass, [that] at the same time shall things come into your mind, and <u>you shall think an evil thought</u>."*—Ezekiel 38:10

To counter this possibility, the apostle Paul said to be aware of what we think and do virtuously, that we are to conquer the temptation of doing evil:

> *"Finally, brethren, whatsoever things are true, whatsoever things [are] honest, whatsoever things [are] just, whatsoever things [are] pure, whatsoever things[are] lovely, whatsoever things [are] of good report; if [there be] any virtue, and if [there be] any praise, think on these things."*—Philippians 4:8

As followers of Jesus the Christ, we are to develop the characteristics he displayed to build and maintain a trusting and loving relationship with others and our Creator. We are comforted and assured that an evil spirit being is not the source of any evil that separates us from God's love; rather, it is the evil conceived in our own minds that will do this. Therefore, when we allow lust or anger or jealousy to take root in our minds, sin is ready to be activated—not because evil thoughts come from enticement or directive by an evil spirit being, but because evil resides in us, and it is our responsibility to be aware of it so as to not act upon it. We read in Genesis:

> *"And the LORD God said, Behold, the man is become as one of us, to know good and evil."*—Genesis 3:22

Having knowledge of evil but not acting with evil is important; thus, we want to habitually think positive thoughts so as to counter evil. Our efforts to follow the advice of the apostle Paul (Philippians 4:8) can be similar to the struggles of the moth larva as it metamorphoses into a beautiful moth as described in 2 Corinthians, where the Amplified New Testament reads:

> *"And all of us* (believers), *as with unveiled face because we continue to behold as in a mirror the glory of the LORD, are constantly being transfigured into his very own image in ever increasing splendor and from one degree of glory to another; for this comes from the LORD who is the Spirit."*—2 Corinthians 3:18

To help clarify what the apostle wrote: we are to see our minds transformed from the influence of a worldly spirit into awareness not to think of or do evil. Paul was not saying that an evil spirit being instigates evil within us, but that a negative thought process can lead to failure to act with righteousness and love.

It is a spiritual warfare that goes on inside every Christian. As he wrote:

> *"For though we walk in the flesh, we do not war after the flesh: For the weapons of our warfare [are] not carnal, but mighty through God to the pulling down of strong holds. <u>Casting down imaginations</u> and every high thing that exalts itself against the knowledge of God, and <u>bringing into captivity every thought</u> to the obedience of Christ."*—2 Corinthians 10:3–5

We then understand that Paul's statement does not refer to literal weapons of warfare, though some Christians may mistakenly advocate the use of literal weapons to oppose apparent evil. The apostle is projecting the warfare as being of a spiritual nature—that we not allow our thoughts to justify evil, that we be aware of our desires, our attitudes, or our lusts in order to combat the evils of lust, impatience, hate, arrogance, prejudice, or evil imaginations that corrupt our relationship of love and peace with our neighbor and with our Heavenly Father. Since evil (Satan, Devil, Serpent, or Dragon) is conceived in the mind, Christians are to be alert to thoughts (not the interjection of thought by an evil spirit being) that leads to evil action. The apostle Paul quoted Isaiah as to how evil developed amongst Jews:

> *"For the heart of this people is waxed gross, and their ears are dull of hearing, and their eyes have they closed; lest they should see with [their] eyes, and hear with [their] ears, and understand with [their] heart, and should be converted, and I should heal them."*—Acts 28:27

Paul later pointed out, in his letter to the Galatian brethren, that Christians are to be aware of such self-defeating characteristics that will restrict them from attaining life eternal through Jesus the Christ our Lord:

> *"[This] I say then, walk in the spirit, and ye shall not fulfill the lust of the flesh. For the flesh lusts against the spirit, and the spirit against the flesh: and these are contrary the one to the other: so that ye cannot do the things that ye would. But if ye be led of the spirit, ye are not under the law. Now the works of the flesh are manifest, which are [these]: adultery, fornication, uncleanness, emulations, lasciviousness, idolatry, witchcraft, hatred, variance, wrath, strife, seditions, heresies, envyings, murderers, drunkenness, revellings, and such like: of the which I tell you before, as I have also told [you] in time past, that they which do such things shall not inherit the kingdom of God. But the fruit of the spirit is love, joy, peace, longsuffering, gentleness, goodness, faith, meekness, temperance: against such there is no law. And they that are Christ's have crucified the flesh with the affections and lusts."*—Galatians 5:16–24

The words of Jesus and the apostles are clear as to where evil originates. Therefore, though evil thoughts may occur momentarily, our goal is to not allow evil to remain in our minds or be expressed in our words and actions. Jesus could have retaliated with evil, but he did not do so. He knew that not to act upon evil thoughts was extremely important in carrying out the objective set before him. This is why he said to Peter:

> *"Get thee behind me, Satan* (evil, Devil, Serpent, or Dragon)*: you are an offence unto me, for you savor not the things that be of God, but those that be of men."*— Matthew 16:23

Jesus was saying that Peter's counsel were of evil thoughts, as it was contrary to God's will, not the action or direction for Jesus to follow. Likewise with us, it is essential that we be aware of our desires and our attitudes in order to combat the evils of impatience, hate, arrogance, prejudice, and lustful imaginations that would corrupt our character. Again, since evil (Satan, Devil, Serpent, or Dragon) originates in the mind, Christians are to learn to be aware of their evil thoughts.

Differences in Interpretation

A preacher may be zealous and devoted to the Lord and accepted by many Christians as a reliable source of Bible interpretation, but some of his visions or expectations may not be Scriptural. The objective here is not to question a Christian's integrity, but to question statements that echo a tradition or superstitious interpretation of Scripture. For example, the age-old claim "Satan made me do it" is not acceptable, because such a statement conveys tradition and superstition.

A number of concepts common or traditional in religious circles are quoted and commented on in this chapter. Again, the idea here is not to condemn a person for views and beliefs, nor to cast unpleasant insinuations on character—the person may be a sincere and dedicated Christian—but, in all fairness, we can understand the Gospel more clearly if popular ideas often held by Christians that inspire or cause fear according to traditional interpretations of Scripture are examined. Also, some statements may fail to harmonize with the teaching of the ransom as put forth by the apostle Paul in 1 Corinthians:

> *"For as in Adam all die, even so in Christ shall all be made alive."*—1 Corinthians 15:22

The point is to seek a positive "Thus says the Lord" with the objective to shine light on unexamined traditions or an imaginary spirit being called Satan. The non-biased reader can benefit from the following statement of Pastor Charles T. Russell, who, over a century ago, made the following statement (words in parentheses are of this author):

> "As we (Christians) proceed to set forth our understanding of the symbols of Revelation *(Scripture)*, we wish to state most emphatically that we are saying nothing whatever against godly Christians anywhere, at any time, whether in any church or out of any church. We have nothing to say respecting people. We discuss principles, doctrines, always; individuals, never! God has not commissioned us to discuss people; it is ours to discuss His Word."

With his comment in mind concerning fellow Christians, we will examine and compare, without judging others, Scriptural evidence that reveals Satan, Devil, Dragon, and Serpent are symbolic names for evil. For millennia, the traditional concept of evil has darkened the vision of God's objective through the Messiah of Israel and mankind: 'Jesus the Christ.' Today, we are blessed with greater clarity in understanding the goal of our Creator, in which the idea of an evil spirit being hovering about and waiting to intrude into a person's life is not of God but comes from fears of men. Thus, the following statements of traditional teachings or beliefs are commented upon, at times using quotes from other authors and from Scripture.

Traditional belief holds: The activity of Satan is evident on every side; we can see it in the wars and other crises that affect people daily. We can also see it in the attacks of Satan against individual members of the body of Christ.

Comment! = The doctrine of an evil spirit being assailing or causing people to do evil contradicts the words of Jesus and of the prophet Jeremiah:

> *"Out of the heart of men proceed evil thoughts."*—Mark 7:21

> *"The heart [is] deceitful above all [things] and desperately wicked: who can know it?"* —Jeremiah 17:9

Why then is an imagined, evil spirit being blamed for instigating evil?

Traditional belief holds: Satan acts only by the permissive will of God; he is on a leash. God has provided Christians with both offensive and defensive weapons. One of Satan's sly devices is to divert our minds from the help God offers us in our struggles against the forces of evil.

Comment! = This is an example of blaming an evil spirit being for manipulating the human mind. What happened to free moral nature? Some time ago, a writer in the paper called the "Jewish Chronicle" stated:

> "God works His will through the will of men; and if the prophecies are to be fulfilled, it will be by human wills and energies."

This statement tells us that the Lord's spirit functions in people who apply the precepts of righteousness and justice in daily living, which the Bible says brings into existence the Kingdom of Jesus the Christ. The statement also echoes the words of Peter:

> *"And in the last days it shall be, God declares, that I will pour out My spirit upon all flesh."*—Acts 2:17

And Jesus said:

> *"Neither shall they say, Lo here! Or, lo there! For, behold, the kingdom God is within you."*—Luke 17:21

Also, Paul cautions the followers of Jesus:

> *"[This] I say then, walk in the Spirit, and ye shall not fulfill the lust of the flesh."*—Galatians 5:16

> *"We all once lived in the passions of our flesh, following the desires of body and mind."*—Ephesians 2:3

The words of Jesus, Peter, and Paul confirm that the mind can allow itself to be led by passions, desires, selfishness, and lustful characteristics and that it is not an evil spirit being that initiates malicious and evil thoughts. We are to be aware of our emotions and thoughts in order to control our passions and desires.

The author Wilfred Peterson, in his book entitled *The Art of Creative Thinking*, suggests:

"We must discipline ourselves to create mental pathways for the direction in which we want our lives to move. We must keep repeating over and over again thoughts, which will deepen the pathway of constructive living. To make a deep mental path we must think and think, again and again, the kind of thoughts we want to dominate our lives. A person cannot think good thoughts for a week or a month without influencing his life."

Wilfred Peterson's advice is reflected in the following words of Proverbs:

"The thoughts of the righteous are right, but the counsels of the wicked are deceitful."—Proverbs 12:5

Therefore, honorable thoughts expressed in word and action builds the path to righteous living. The apostle Paul encourages this practice, saying:

"See that <u>no one renders evil for evil</u> to anyone: but <u>always pursue the good,</u> both towards each other and towards all. Rejoice always. Pray without ceasing. In every thing give thanks; for this is God's will by Jesus Christ, concerning you."—1 Thessalonians 5:15–18

In following this advice, the mind creates positive thoughts of appreciation, justice, love, mercy, goodness, patience, and so forth and thus responsibly chooses good rather than evil. Each person thinks and chooses for himself or herself—it is not an evil spirit being that manipulates the mind into doing evil; evil comes from lust or derogatory thoughts. This also is a convincing reason why prayer is necessary in motivating and maintaining a loving and healthy attitude towards God and others. It is written:

"Love works no ill to his neighbor."—Romans 13:10

"Speak evil of no man."—Titus 3:2

On the topic of angels, we find the spiritual concept of angels often misunderstood. So <u>there is the need</u> to have a reasonable idea of who or what the Bible speaks of as angels. The conventional interpretation of the Living Bible (paraphrased), in Deuteronomy, refers to saints as angels, but the King James translation reads:

> *"And he said, The Lord came from Sinai, and rose up from Seir unto them; he shined forth from mount Paran, and he came with ten thousands of saints: from his right hand [went] a fiery law for them."*—Deuteronomy 33:2

"His right hand" refers to Moses. In the first and third verses of the chapter, 'saints' applies to the people of Israel, not to spirit beings. This is the only verse in the Old Testament where the Hebrew word translated as 'saints' is of a different connotation. Professor Strong interprets it (#6944) as meaning a "sacred place / thing." Also, "ten thousands" literally means "abundance in number" (#7233)

The next verse states:

> *"Yea, he loved the people; all his saints [are] in thy hand: and they sat down at thy feet; [every one] shall receive of thy words."*—Deuteronomy 33:3

Here "saints" (#6918, Strong) applies to the people and basically means 'holy ones.' The above verses are better understood if the Lord's spirit (justice, righteousness, mercy, and love) is looked upon as the spiritual guide of Israel; thus Israel, through the spirit, was guided through the desert and also from Seir (where the children of Esau dwelt). In finding their way through the wilderness near the mountain of Paran, the Israelites became abundant in number.

In seeking the dos and don'ts of God's will, they were given the Law, which the people found impossible to keep. (In due time, Jesus, begotten of and filled with God's holy spirit, fulfilled the Law.) Instead of understanding the scripture as referring to Israel's leadership and messengers as people, the reader is led to believe that 'spirit beings' are meant. But, the account refers to

Moses as God's right-hand man giving them (the people) fiery (troublesome) laws to keep.

Traditional belief holds: The following scripture from Psalms is verification that spirit beings guard the Christian's welfare:

> *"He will give His angels charge of you, to guard you in all your ways. They shall bear thee up in [their] hands, lest thou dash thy foot against a stone."* —Psalms 91:11–12

Comment! = The commonly held idea that angels are to literally provide protection from all harm to believers is an assumption made from the context of Psalms, which was written in the picture language of that day:

> *"Only with thine eyes shall you behold and see the reward of the wicked. Because you have made the Lord, [which is] my refuge, [even] the most High, thy habitation; there shall no evil befall thee, neither shall any plague come nigh thy dwelling, For He shall give His angels* (message of righteousness and truth) *charge over thee, to keep thee in all thy ways. They* (it) *shall bear thee up in [their]* (its) *hands* (spiritual guidance), *lest thou dash thy foot against a stone. Thou shall tread upon* (overcome) *the lion and adder* (power and evil): *the young lion* (power) *and the dragon* (evil) *shall thou trample under."*—Psalms 91:8–13

In picture language, "lion" stands for power and "adder" depicts evil or the venomous, malicious sting of death.

The above scripture is highly figurative and is better appreciated when the text is understood as relating to spiritual understanding and direction, which imparts confidence in weathering opposition and trials in life. If these scriptures are viewed as

literal, they would not apply to Jesus—let alone his followers—
for evil did befall him: he suffered a violent death at the hands
of his enemies. But, being a perfect example, Jesus became our
role model in maintaining faithfulness and confidence by doing
according to God's Word. As followers of Jesus, we also are
subject to evil (Satan, Devil, Serpent, and Dragon): temptations
to think evil thoughts or act in evil ways as a consequence of
our lusts and desires, even acceptance of another person's evil
thoughts.

Traditional belief holds: Frankly, we may always know the
agent or means God is using—the Holy Spirit or the angels.

Comment! = Traditional belief understands the Holy Spirit to
be a spirit being and "angels" to always refer to spirit beings. This
differs from the intent of Scripture. Harmony of Scripture is seen
when we interpret "Holy Spirit" to mean "spirit of God"—that
is, the spirit of righteousness, justice, mercy, power, and truth.
The word translated as "angel" generally means "message" or
"messenger." "Angel" may also mean "responsiveness to God's
will" or refer to a person. Examples of this are seen in the
following verses:

> *"If ye then, being evil, know how to give good gifts unto
> your children: how much more shall [your] heavenly Father
> give the Holy Spirit* (spirit of righteousness, justice,
> truth, etc.) *to them that ask Him?"*—Luke 11:13

> *"But this spoke he of the Spirit (righteousness, truth,
> justice, etc.), which they that believe on him should receive:
> for the Holy Spirit (righteousness, truth, justice, etc.) was
> not yet [given]; because Jesus was not yet glorified."*—
> John 7:39

"But when Herod was dead, behold, an angel (message, inspirational understanding) *of the LORD appeared in a dream to Joseph in Egypt."*—Matthew 2:19

"For there stood by me this night the angel (message) of God, whose I am, and whom I serve. Saying, Fear not, Paul; you must be brought before Caesar: and, lo, God has given you all them that sail with you."—Acts 27:23

The Diaglott, word for word from Greek, in both accounts, renders "angel" as "messenger." This basically means a message or communication of the Lord. It was a dream (message of understanding) that Joseph had about the birth of Jesus. The vision (message of understanding) Paul had in a dream helped him realize it was God's will for him to appear before Caesar and therefore not to fear, that everyone on the boat would survive the shipwreck.

Traditional belief holds: The holy angels will never die; angels are sexless. This may indicate that angels enjoy relationships that are far more thrilling and exciting than sex.

Comment! = Since spirit beings do not have physical bodies and there are no scriptures relating to the longevity of angels or their relationship to one another except the verse quoted below, it is questionable that angels would experience something more exhilarating than a husband and wife mutually enjoying a loving relationship. In the Gospel of Matthew, Jesus said:

"For in the resurrection they (people) *neither marry, nor are given in marriage, but are as the angels* (messengers) *of God. ('In heaven')"*—Matthew 22:30

The words "in heaven" in this statement are considered spurious, as they are not found in the oldest manuscripts. Also, Jesus was discussing the general resurrection, when the world of mankind, including the woman with seven husbands, would be raised to life. The reference to angels appears to refer to preachers or pastors as religious messengers, for they bring encouragement and understanding of the Bible. Jesus said in Luke:

> *"And Jesus answering said unto them, The children of this world marry, and are given in marriage: But they which shall be accounted worthy to obtain that world* (Kingdom of Jesus the Christ), *and the resurrection from the dead, neither marry, nor are given in marriage."* —Luke 20:34–35

The first resurrection involves the body of Christ, the Church, whom God chooses to live and reign with Jesus in His kingdom at the second resurrection over mankind. This is affirmed in the following verses:

> *"For if we have been planted together in the likeness of his death* (faithful unto death), *we shall be also [in the likeness] of [his] resurrection."*—Romans 6:5

It is not clear whether Jesus the Christ meant those of the first resurrection—the Church—or the general resurrection—rest of mankind—that do not marry.

In Revelation, Jesus the Christ told the apostle John:

> *"Blessed and holy [is] he that hath part in the first resurrection: on such the second death hath no power, but they shall be priests of God and of Christ, and shall reign with him a thousand years."*—Revelation 20:6

The general resurrection *(of the world)* is mentioned in other scriptures:

"Because he hath appointed a day, in the which He will judge the world in righteousness by [that] man (Jesus the Christ) *whom he hath ordained; [whereof] he hath given assurance unto all [men], in that He hath raised him* (Jesus the Christ) *from the dead."*—Acts 17:3

"Do ye not know that the saints shall judge the world and if the world shall be judged by you, are ye unworthy to judge the smallest matters?"—1 Corinthians 6:2

"Marvel not at this: for the hour is coming, in the which all that are in the graves shall hear his voice, and shall come forth; they that have done good, unto the resurrection of life; and they that have done evil, unto the resurrection of judgment."—John 5:28–29

Those resurrected to life are the body or Church of Christ; those resurrected to judgment are the rest of mankind.

Traditional belief holds: God made no provision for evil angels. Their sinfulness cannot be changed, their evil cannot be forgiven, and salvation is not possible.

Comment! = Some Christians base a statement as this upon two quotations, the first from 2 Peter, which is a quote from Enoch, a book not acceptable to Protestants as part of the Bible:

"For if God spared not the angels that sinned, but cast [them] down to hell, and delivered [them] into chains of darkness, to be reserved unto judgment."—2 Peter 2:4

The second scripture is from Jude:

"And the angels which kept not their first estate, but left their own habitation, he hath reserved in everlasting

chains under darkness unto the judgment of the great day."—Jude 1:6

These two scriptures are considered by some Bible scholars as interjections into the text of the two letters, 2 Peter and Jude, They do not belong in either letter. Both times, the statements about the angels appear to be additions by someone who felt obligated to add the thought based upon conjecture that perfect spirit beings became evil rather than human messengers did evil. If translators had used the word "messenger" rather than "angel" in the following scriptures (just a few of many), the original thought could have been preserved:

"He cast upon them (Israel) *the fierceness of his anger, wrath, and indignation, and trouble, by sending evil angels [among them]."*—Psalms 78:49

Young's literal translation helps a little more:

"He sent on them (Israel) *the fury of His anger, wrath, and indignation, and distress—a discharge of evil* (messages)."

This occurred through rumors and lack of faith. Dissent arose among the people, and rebellion and distress spread throughout the nation:

"Then the devil, (Satan, serpent, dragon) (evil temptations) *left him, and, behold, angels* (human messengers between Jesus and John the Baptist) *came and ministered unto him."*—Matthew 4:11

Jesus, spiritually strengthened through prayer and meditation of prophecy, saw that his choice of action must be accomplished in truth, righteousness, and love, in accordance with God's will, not with spectacular displays of God's power to convince people.

> *"For the Son of man shall come in the glory of his Father with his angels* (messengers, or chosen Church)*; and then he shall reward every man* (in the general resurrection) *according to his works."*—Matthew 16:27

> *"Know ye not that we shall judge angels (messengers, pastors, or prophets), how much more things that pertain to this life?"*—1 Corinthians 6:3

Judgment would not refer to "fallen" angels, because if there were "fallen" angels, they would not have redemption under the blood of Jesus. This would better apply to prophets, pastors, or evangelists as messengers who are judged by their character, faithfulness, and the message they preach.

Traditional belief holds: Angels who never sinned need no salvation ... Angels, unspoiled by sin, do not need the holy spirit ... Obedient angels do not die.

Comment! = This statement is speculation. The explanation in the footnote of the *Harper Study Bible*, while speculation, p. 14, on Genesis 6, provides a more reasonable and scriptural interpretation of these verses, as explained after quoting Genesis 6:1–4:

> *"When men began to multiply on the face of the ground, and daughters were born to them, the sons of God* (priests) *saw that the daughters of men were fair; and they took to wife such as they chose. Then the Lord said, 'My spirit shall not abide in man forever, for he is flesh, but his days shall be a hundred and twenty years.' The Neph-ilim was*

on the earth in those days, and also afterward, when the sons of God (priests) *came in to the daughters of men, and they bore children to them. These were the mighty men that were of old, the men of renown."*

The footnote says (comment in parentheses is of this author):

"The KJV reads, 'There were giants in the earth.' Many have construed this to mean that angels (as the sons of God) were joined in marriage to human beings and spawned a mixed race. The Nephilim were strong, violent, tyrannous men of great wickedness, but it is far more likely that 'sons of God' refers to those descendants of Seth who trusted in the Lord but whose children intermarried with children descended from Cain. The marriage union was not with angels then, but one consummated between the godly and ungodly families of men. Angels neither marry nor are given in marriage so the verse hardly applies to them. On the other hand, Peter speaks of angels—2 Peter 2:4 and apparently referred to the Book of Enoch 20:2 where 'sons of God' is interpreted 'angels.' It may be then that the explanation of the original meaning of Genesis 6:1–4 has been lost to us."

Traditional belief holds: The rebellion of Lucifer resulted in insurrection and war in heaven.

Comment! = This viewpoint echoes the common concept of a Lucifer as Satan in a spiritual realm, conceiving evil and acting in opposition to God. If there is "war" in heaven between an evil spirit being and the Creator, why did Jesus, in recommending how to pray, say:

"Thy kingdom come, Thy will be done, on earth as it is in heaven."—Matthew 6:10

Why didn't he say: as it will be in heaven? "As it is in heaven" suggests a spiritual condition of peace, cooperation, love, and righteousness, with no hate, anger, disloyalty, and rebellion. The word "heaven" in Mathew 6:10 has the same metaphorical designation that is used in Revelation: " ...there was war in heaven." The apostle John, "in the spirit" (Revelation 12:7), was able to visualize and record the future religious scenario relating to God's objective on earth. While in a trance-like state and thinking of the Lord, he visualized future conditions or developments that appeared strange and abstract. This is recorded in Revelation as follows:

"The Revelation of Jesus Christ, which God gave unto him (Jesus), *to show unto his servants things which must shortly come to pass; and he sent and signified [it] by his angel* (message) *unto his servant John, who bare record of the Word of God* (Jesus the Christ), *and of the testimony* (truth and prophecy) *of Jesus Christ, and of all things* (righteousness and evil) *that he saw."* —Revelation 1:1–2

John records in Revelation:

"I was in the Spirit on the LORD'S Day and heard behind me (unknown source) a great voice (message), as of a trumpet (loud, clear message)." —Revelation 1:10

John then prophesies:

"And there was war in heaven (in religion)*: Michael and his angels* (truth and its messengers) *fought against the dragon* (evil, Satan, Devil, or Serpent)*; and the dragon*

(evil, Satan, Devil, or Serpent) *fought* (used deceit, fear, hell fire, threats, condemnation, etc.), *and his angels* (evil messengers)."—Revelation 12:7

"And the great dragon (evil) was cast out, that old serpent (evil), called the devil (evil), and Satan (evil), which deceives the whole world: he (evil) was cast out into the earth (society), and his angels (evil messengers) were cast out with him." —Revelation 12:9

It is suggested that the statement italicized in the above verse, *"which deceives the whole world,"* applies to the names Satan, Devil, Serpent, and Dragon given by men, thus deceiving the whole world into believing an evil spirit being exists with those names. In support of the above suggestion, the following verse referring to the serpent has to be symbolic of evil, for its mouth, water, flood, and woman are symbolic of something; thus 'serpent' is symbolic of evil.

"And the serpent (evil, Satan, Devil, or Dragon), *cast out of his mouth water* (truth) *as a flood after the woman* (religious system), *that he* (Serpent, evil, Satan, Devil, or Dragon) *might cause her* (religious system) *to be carried away of the flood* (truths)."—Revelation 12:15

The apostle Paul had said:

"And no marvel, for Satan (evil, Devil, Serpent, or Dragon) *is transformed into an angel of light* (message of truth)."—Revelation 12:15

A point to remember is that we are dealing with pictorial terms and abstract allusions describing the Kingdom of God materializing upon earth. We are to decipher these symbolic meanings to make sense to us as Christians. For example, the words war, heaven, great voice, Michael, angels, Dragon, Serpent, Devil, Satan, flood, mouth, and woman depict organization, activity, condition, or character. From a symbolic point of view, the statement that "The rebellion of Lucifer (light bringer) resulted in insurrection and war in heaven (religion)" has led to misinterpreting the meaning of Revelation 12:15.

Traditional belief holds: We would describe unrighteousness and transgression against God as "self-will" or being against the will of God. This definition applies to human beings and to angels.

Comment! = This statement raises the question: How can the sinner blame a Satan or an evil spirit being for the sinner's transgression if the sinner conceives and wills his or her own transgression? Did not Jesus say:

> *"Out of the heart of men proceed evil thoughts"*—Mark 7:21?

Or Proverbs:

> *"The thoughts of the righteous are right, but the counsels of the wicked are deceitful."*—Proverbs 12:5

Why blame criminals for crimes if demons initiate the thought that precedes the act? It is not fair or just to hold a person responsible for evil if an evil spirit being suggests or inveigles evil thoughts into the mind. This would eliminate the fact that we are free moral agents.

Traditional belief holds: Satan and his demons are known by the discord they promote as with wars, hatred, and murder in opposition to God and His commandments.

Comment! = This statement implies the ancient myth that evil spirit beings are responsible for initiating thought that leads to acts of evil by people. The question again is: Why hold people responsible if evil spirit beings do that?

Traditional belief holds: Satan's objectives are to bring the downfall of nations, to corrupt moral standards, and to waste human resources. He uses his destructive power to create havoc, fire, flood, earthquake, storm, pestilence, disease, and devastation of peoples and nations.

Comment! = God (not Satan) told Noah:

> *"For behold: I will bring a flood of waters upon the earth."*—Genesis 6:17

And didn't Abraham ask the Lord:

> *"Wilt Thou indeed destroy the righteous with the wicked?"*—Genesis 18:23?

Isaiah said of God:

> *"I form the light, and create darkness; I make peace, and create evil. I am Jehovah, that doeth all these things."*
> —Isaiah 45:7

Thus, God occasionally uses His power over nature to change conditions, as with the flood or Daniel in the furnace. Otherwise, the laws of nature continue to operate according to "the laws of nature "God established.

Traditional belief holds: Our senses of hearing, seeing, smelling, and tasting are there that Satan may work, prod, and inject his deadly "direction."

Comment! = This suggestion does not harmonize with scriptures such as:

> *"His* **(man's)** *heart shall work iniquity."*—Isaiah 32:6

> *"Everyone walked in the stubbornness of his evil heart."*—Jeremiah 11:8

> *"The heart [is] deceitful above all [things], and desperately wicked: who can know it?"*—Jeremiah 17:9

Traditional belief holds: If Adam and Eve had not sinned, our world would be a paradise today.

Comment! = This is a common assumption. But isn't it God's purpose to allow the experience of both good and evil so that, during Judgment Day (time of restitution), most individuals, having had experience with evil and desiring life, will, having fair opportunity, choose righteousness over evil under Kingdom rule? If the statement were true, each individual committing evil or sin would die without promise of a resurrection because the ransom of Jesus the Christ would not be available, as the next two scriptures indicate:

> *"Even as the Son of man came not to be ministered unto, but to minister, and to give his life a ransom for many."*—Matthew 20:28

> *"For as in Adam all die, even so in Christ shall all be made alive."*—1 Corinthians 15:22

All of humanity is included under the ransom because all were not yet born when Adam sinned. This also covers Eve, for she came from Adam.

Traditional belief holds: The designation "God's host" means spirit beings met Jacob, for the verse says, *"The angels of God met Jacob … And when Jacob saw them, he said, This [is] God's host."* —Genesis 32:2

Comment! = Strong's concordance interprets "angel" (Hebrew), #4397, as "messenger," meaning "to dispatch as a deputy" or (#4399) as "ministry, employment, work or property as result of labor: business, cattle, etc."

Why assume angels materialized to converse with Jacob? Would not the phrase "The angels of God met Jacob" make more sense if Jacob met travelers or messengers who gave him the idea or vision (message) of what God would have him do when he met Esau? We should be aware that myths or cultural beliefs might have affected the choice of words of translators or copiers over the ages. For instance, we read in Genesis:

> *"And Jacob went on his way, and the angels* (messengers) *of God met him. And when Jacob saw them, he said, This [is] God's host: and he called the name of that place Mahan aim."*—Genesis 32:1–2

The statement is understood better if Jacob figured the solution after meeting the travelers and before meeting Esau. He then acknowledges the solution as coming from God. Verse 3 says:

> *"Jacob sent messengers before him."*

The word "messenger" comes from the same Hebrew word for "angel"; thus "angel" can also refer to a servant, messenger, pastor, or prophet.

The Greek for "angel" (Strong, #32) means "messenger" or "pastor," which comes from the Greek #71 meaning "to lead" or "to bring. "This fundamentally implies that the meaning of the word "angel" (message) is to lead to or bring encouragement to endure, persuade, support, or even visualize a solution. In 1 Corinthians, we read:

> *"Do you not know that we are to judge angels (messengers)?"*
> —1 Corinthians 6:3

This pictures the Church, those chosen, as judging angels (messengers) who are pastors or leaders that preach the Word of God. The context implies the judging as pertaining to this life (Gospel Age), for pastors have greater responsibility as God's messengers and are thus judged and selected by the congregation.

Traditional belief holds: At the end of the age, angels will execute judgment on those who have rejected God's love.

Comment! = The angels (messengers) are the saints or the faithful who have followed Jesus the Christ during the Gospel Age and who are chosen to live and reign with him, as the following scriptures affirm:

> *"Do ye not know the saints shall judge the world?"*—1 Corinthians 6:2

> *"Know ye not that we shall judge angels* (messengers, pastors)*? How much more things that pertain to this life?"*—1 Corinthians 6:3

> *"Do not ye judge them that are within* (other professing Christians in the Church)*?"*—1 Corinthians 5:12

> *"And with them we are sending our brother whom we have often tested* **(judged)** *and found earnest* **(sincere**

and faithful) *in many matters."*—2 Corinthians 8:22

The testing or judging the apostle Paul refers to is not only of doctrinal matters, but also of just and righteous character. The person being sent by the Church is not to be temperamental, argumentative, insulting, deceitful, lustful, or whatever else is contrary to the Gospel in Jesus the Christ. The person would be familiar with the love and harmony of the Bible and the Hebrew and Greek expressions and idioms as follows:

<u>Subtle</u> *"The serpent* **(evil, Satan, Devil, and dragon)** *was more subtle."*—Genesis 3:1 = Hebrew; Strong's #6175—crafty, cunning (lust of the mind) Sin develops from lust.

<u>Beguiled</u> *"But the serpent* **(evil, Satan, Devil, and Dragon)** *beguiled me."*—Genesis 3:13 = Hebrew; Strong's #5377—Beguile: to lead astray (self-deception)

> *"And God saw that the wickedness of man [was] great in the earth, and [that] every imagination of the thoughts of his heart [was] only <u>evil (Satan, Devil, Serpent, and Dragon)</u> continually."* —Genesis 6:5

No need for an evil spirit being.

"As the serpent (evil thoughts, Satan, Devil, Serpent, or Dragon) *beguiled Eve."*—2 Corinthians 11:3 = Greek; Strong's #1818—to seduce (allowing evil of lust to affect judgment)

Lust

"The lusts of your father ye will do."—John 8:44 = Greek; Strong's #1939—longing for what is forbidden

"Ye are of [your] father the devil (evil, Satan, Serpent, or Dragon) *and the lusts of your father (evil) ye will do. He* (evil, Devil, Satan, Serpent, or Dragon) *was a murderer (evil, anger of Cain) from the beginning, and abode not in the truth, because there is no truth in him (evil). When he* (evil) *speaks a lie, he* (evil) *speaks of his own: for* he (evil, Satan, Devil, Serpent, or Dragon) *is a liar, and the father (conceiver) of it."*—John 8:44

The above scripture projects an allegorical picture describing how evil affects mankind from the beginning. The following words are explained so as to help interpret meaning correctly.

Deceitful: *"Corrupt according to deceitful lusts."*—Ephesians 4:22 = Greek; Strong's #539—delusion (false belief)

Fiery darts: *"Quench fiery darts of the wicked."*—Ephesians 6:16 = Greek; Strong's #4448—to be led astray by anger, jealousy, hate, lust,

Spoil: *"Beware lest any man spoil you."*—Colossians 1:8 = Greek; Strong's #4812—to lead away, seduce.

Fables: *"Not to occupy themselves with myths and fables."* —1 Timothy 1:4 = Greek; Strong's #3454—fiction (not reality)

Error: *"Error of the wicked."*—2 Peter 3:17 = Greek; Strong's #4106—fraud, deceit

Traditional belief holds: Fallen angels cannot even be saved from their own sins.

Comment! = The term "fallen angels" comes from the preconceived idea that evil spirit beings exist or is a result of error in translation. The Bible declares mankind is to experience

287

evil because of Adam's sin, but, in due time, willing men (and women) will be reconciled to God through the ransom by the Lord Jesus the Christ. Below are some scriptures that speak of the resurrection, restitution, and Judgment Day:

> *"And all flesh shall see the salvation of God (at the resurrection)."*—Luke 3:6

> *"For God's mercy has appeared with salvation* (the Gospel) *for all men* (even pagans).*"*—*Titus 2:11, Gspd*

> *"Who will have all men* (even pagans) *to be saved* (from Adamic death)." —1 Timothy 2:4

> *"I will ransom them* (humanity) *from the grave."* —Hosea 13:14 (The ransom has been paid.)

> *"Who will render to every man according to his deeds."* —Romans 2:6

(The above verses apply during the Judgment Day to mankind during restitution or Judgment Day under Jesus the Christ and his Church, a period of approximately a thousand years.)

> *"Whom the heaven must receive until the times of restitution of all things."*—Acts 3:21

Signs of restitution are appearing all about us, for the Lord's return is a presence of the spirit with countless blessings and a gradual restoration to righteousness within of justice, love, mercy, and the like. These virtues are increasing, which were lost in Adam.

"And it shall come to pass, [that] every soul, which will not hear that prophet (truth in Jesus the Christ), *shall be destroyed from among the people."*—Acts 3:23

During the Judgment period of approximately one thousand years, the dead are resurrected and those unwilling to seek and practice righteousness are destroyed. We read that all, except those who have sinned deliberately against the Holy Spirit, receive a resurrection.

"For [it is] impossible for those who were once enlightened, and have tasted of the heavenly gift, and were made partakers of the Holy Spirit, and have tasted the good word of God, and the powers of the world to come, if they shall fall away, to renew them again unto repentance; seeing they crucify to themselves the Son of God afresh, and put [him] to an open shame."—Hebrews 6:4–6

According to this next verse, not everyone during the Day of Judgment will attain eternal life:

"And the nations were angry, and thy wrath is come, and the time of the dead, that they shall be judged, and that You (God, through Jesus the Christ) *shall give reward unto thy servants the prophets, and to the saints, and them that fear* (revere) *Your name, small and great; and shall destroy them* (second death) *which destroy the earth* (society)."—Revelation 11:18

Traditional belief holds: At the moment of death, the spirit departs from the body and moves through the atmosphere, where the Devil lurks. He is the "prince and power of the air" (Ephesians 2:2). We visualize the air filled with demons, the enemies of Christ.

Comment! = This statement is based upon the erring theory of the immortal soul and a Satan as a literal, evil spirit being. The following scriptures describe a quite different state of affairs upon death:

> *"Nevertheless, man being in honor abides not: he is <u>like the beasts that perish</u>."*—Psalms 49:12

> *"For that which befalls the sons of men befalls beasts; even one thing befalls them<u>: as the one dies, so dies the other;</u> yea, they have all one breath (need breath); so that a man has no preeminence above a beast: for all is vanity. All go into one place; all are of the dust and all turn to dust again."*—Ecclesiastes 3:19–20

Also, a <u>literal</u> Satan, Devil, Serpent, or Dragon is not the prince and power of the air; it is evil that is the prince and power of the air.

Traditional belief holds: When Christ came to earth, he had to pass through the Devil's territory and open up a beachhead here. That is one reason he was accompanied by a host of angels when he came.

Comment! = This statement comes from applying literal meaning to the following scriptures rather than pictorial or symbolic meanings. A Devil and his territory are imagined, and applying literal meaning to imagination is misleading.

> *"Wherein in time past ye walked according to the course of this world, according to the prince of the power of the air, the spirit (evil attitude) that now <u>works in the children of disobedience</u>."* —Ephesians 2:2

"Fear none of those things which you shall suffer: behold, the devil (evil people) shall cast [some] of you into prison, that ye may be tried."—Revelation 2:10

"By which also he (Jesus the Christ) went and preached unto the spirits in prison."—1 Peter 3:19 (meaning, he was an example of faithfulness to everyone in the prison house of Adamic death.)

"The prince and power of the air" alludes to evil ideas and attitudes people of the world live by, often ignoring—or not knowing of—righteousness in Jesus the Christ. Also, an evil spirit being cannot literally cast people into prison. Rather, it was evil-minded people that ordered Christians to be cast into prison, where their faith was sorely tried. Jesus died and was laid in the tomb a dead soul (person) waiting to be restored to life. He was in the grave for three days. Resurrected in the spirit, he ascended into the clouds after appearing to his followers, but, while in the grave, he was dead, unaware of anything. Thus it is asked, Are the dead really dead? And the Bible tells us:

"The dead know not anything."—Ecclesiastes 9:5

Peter was aware of the following scripture in Isaiah, in which Isaiah prophesies of the Messiah in the prison of death:

"He (Jesus the Christ) *was taken from prison (death) and from judgment: and who shall declare his generation? For he was cut off out of the land of the living: for the transgression of my people was he stricken."*—Isaiah 53:8

"To open the blind eyes, to bring out the prisoners from the prison (of ignorance and sin), *[and] them that sit*

in darkness out of the prison house (Adamic death condition)."—Isaiah 42:7

In regard to the moment of death, *Parade* magazine of March 7, 1993, published an article by Carl Sagan entitled "What's Really Going On." Mr. Sagan wrote:

> Repeated surveys have shown that 10 to 25 percent of ordinary, functioning people have experienced at least once a vivid hallucination—hearing a voice, usually, or seeing a form when there is no one there. In some cases, these are profound religious experiences. Such hallucinations may occur to perfectly normal people under ordinary circumstances. But there are various circumstances in which they can be elicited: by a campfire at night, or under great stress, or by prolonged fasting or sleeplessness or sensory deprivation, or through hallucinogens such as LSD, psilocybin, mescaline, hashish or alcohol. These hallucinations have a vivid and palpable reality.

But a traditional-minded Christian may argue that, in 2 Corinthians, the Bible says:

> *"While we are at home in the body, we are absent from the Lord."*

The quotation is of 2 Corinthians in which the apostle also wrote:

> *"Now he that hath wrought us for the selfsame thing [is] God, who also hath given unto us the earnest (beginning or part) of the spirit. Therefore [we are] always confident, knowing that, while we are at home in the body, we are absent from the Lord."* —2 Corinthians 5:5–6

And further on in 2 Corinthians, we read:

> *"Wherefore henceforth know we no man after the flesh:*
> *yea, though we have known Christ after the flesh, yet*
> *now henceforth know we [him] no more. Therefore if*
> *any man [be] in Christ, [he is] a new creature: old things*
> *are passed away; behold, all things are become new."*—2
> Corinthians 5:16–17

Paul's words "absent from the body but present with the Lord" refer to the Christian's objective and thoughts as being in harmony with God's will as his or her mind seeks righteousness and justice as the Lord requests. But if the Christian allows lust, desire, habit, anger, jealousy, and so forth to activate his evil upon others or self, that Christian's thoughts are not present with the Lord's will.

Traditional belief holds: Dying patients are given so many drugs today that many of these stories are not experienced, but of those who die in Christ, some do claim the experience. The Bible tells of every believer being escorted into the presence of Christ by holy angels.

Comment! = The New Testament is consistent in its treatment of the death condition. It often uses the words "sleep" or "asleep" in referring to having died or of the dead. "Sleep" and "asleep" express the opposite of being awake or alive. There are no references to a "soul" going up to heaven. The objective of the death and resurrection of Jesus the Christ is confirmation to us that all in the grave (the dead) are to be raised to life to experience a judgment period along with the rest of mankind as the Kingdom grows on earth. Thus, under the reign of righteousness, justice, and mercy, the continuing unrepentant wicked (reprobates) will be cut off or die a second death. The following scriptures support the principle that the person (soul, sentient being, or individual) dies or ceases to exist until the resurrection.

> *"Marvel not at this: for the hour is coming, in the which all that are in the graves shall hear his voice, and shall come forth* (be resurrected); *they that have done good, unto the resurrection of life* (reign with Jesus); *and they that have done evil, unto the resurrection of judgment* (trial period to attain life in the Kingdom)."—John 5:28–29

> *"Jesus said unto her, I am the resurrection, and the life: he that believeth in me, though he were dead (having died), yet shall he live (be resurrected)."* —John 11:25

> *"Men [and] brethren, let me freely speak unto you of the patriarch David, that he is both dead and buried, and his sepulcher (grave) is with us unto this day."* —Acts 2:29

> *"For David (soul) did not ascend into the heavens."* —Acts 2:34

> *"And when he* (Stephen) *had said this, he fell asleep* (died)."—Acts 7:60

> *"Some have fallen asleep* (died)."—1 Corinthians 15:6

> *"Then those who have fallen asleep in Christ have perished* (died, have no resurrection if Jesus the Christ is not resurrected)."—1 Corinthians 15:18

> *"Concerning those who are asleep* (dead)."—1 Thessalonians 4:13

"For if we believe that Jesus died and rose again, even so them also which sleep in Jesus (have died) will God bring with him."—1 Thessalonians 4:14

"We which are alive—shall not precede (ASV) those who have fallen asleep (died)."—1 Thessalonians 4:15

"The dead in Christ shall rise first."—1 Thessalonians 4:16

"Since the fathers fell asleep (died)."—2 Peter 3:4

<u>**Traditional belief holds**</u>: God will cast Satan in the lake of fire and brimstone, there to be tormented forever (Revelation 20:10)

Comment! = The literal interpretation of this scripture does not harmonize with all Scripture, but a symbolic interpretation will harmonize. The following are symbolic names used relative to evil, Satan, Devil, Serpent, or Dragon:

"Lake of fire" = symbol of destruction

"Brimstone" = symbol of everlasting destruction of evil

"Torment" = symbol of memory of past evildoers

"Beast" = symbol of "controlling evil religious system"

"False prophet" (in Revelation) = symbol of other religious systems

"Death" = non-existence (lifelessness, destroyed)

"Hell" = the grave (death, lifelessness)

In the following scriptures, the beast, the false prophet, the Devil, and wicked people end up in the same place, the lake of fire, which means non-existence or everlasting destruction:

> *"And the devil (Satan, Serpent, Dragon, or evil) that deceived them was cast into the lake of fire and brimstone, where the beast and the false prophet [are] and shall be tormented day and night forever and ever (sad memories of those in death to the living)."*—Revelation 20:10

The evil religious systems ("beast" and "false prophet") are utterly destroyed but remembered forever for their evil characteristics, which are restrictive, controlling, and condemning, even as they gloried in power.

> *"And whosoever was not found written in the book of life was cast into the lake of fire* (destroyed, eliminated, non-existent, or dead)."—Revelation 20:15

> *"But the fearful, and unbelieving, and the abominable, and murderers, and whoremongers, and sorcerers, and idolaters, and all liars, shall have their part in the lake which burns with fire and brimstone: which is the second death (nonexistence, destroyed)."* —Revelation 21:8

A fair trial under conditions of righteousness and justice (which are to be learned) is promised to all—the faithful from the Gospel Age and the rest of mankind—during the Resurrection, Millennium, Kingdom, Restitution, or Judgment Day.

Traditional belief holds: Thousands of wicked people have been evil and perpetrated their evil acts upon others without being judged for their misdeeds.

Comment! = This reflects the traditional, inconsistent position many Christians hold that people are free moral agents, able to choose between good and evil, who conceive and act upon their ideas, while claiming that an evil spirit being initiates the evil that they choose to act upon. This dualism of doctrine comes from misinterpreting symbolism of Scripture and its picture language. This error happens by misunderstanding the following scriptures:

> *"In that day the LORD with His hard and great and strong sword* (truth in Jesus the Christ) *will punish Leviathan* (evil) *the fleeing serpent* (evil), *Leviathan* (evil) *the twisting serpent* (evil of half truths) *and He will slay* (eliminate) *the dragon* (evil) *that is in the sea* (society)."—Isaiah 27:1

> *"And the great dragon* (evil) *was thrown down, that ancient* serpent (evil), *who is called the devil* (evil) *and Satan* (evil), *the deceiver* (evil) *of the whole world* (society)."—*Revelation 12:9*

> *"The waters* (society) *that you saw, where the harlot* (evil religious system) *is seated* (in power), *are peoples and multitudes and nations and tongues."* —*Revelation 17:15*

Leviathan, the Serpent

Leviathan, the fleeing and twisting Serpent, is a symbolic term for evil (wickedness) that deeply permeates and infects society (the sea). The word "leviathan" basically means "to twist" or "a snare." Its principal effect or consequence is of the mind dwelling on immoral, twisted, distorted, and ensnared thoughts, that they become strongly rooted in the thinking process. Mankind has been plagued with thoughts of evil, the Leviathan—a fleeting and twisting Serpent, which is also called Satan, Devil, Dragon, and evil—through lust, ignorance, superstition, and fear. The binding of Satan, Devil, Serpent, Dragon, or evil pictures the gradual self-restriction from lust, ignorance, superstition, fear, and sin in God's Kingdom through the influence and growth of knowledge, truth, righteousness, justice, mercy, love, and so on, which is the spirit of God in Jesus the Christ and his bride (the Church or the chosen).

A very dark period in the history of humanity gives example of how evil, a Leviathan, fleeting and twisting Serpent (evil, Satan, Dragon, or Devil), has affected society during the reign of evil. A part of the era is reviewed by Richard Erdoes in his book titled *AD 1000: A World on the Brink of Apocalypse*, published by Berkeley, Ca. The semimonthly booklet the *Herald, News Views* of January/February 2000 quoted a few paragraphs of Erdoes' book:

"The tenth century has been called the Century of Lead and Iron. The Saracens, the Spanish Moors, the Vikings, the Bulgars and the Magyar horsemen all invaded Europe. Land barons slaughtered each other over pieces of property, killing rival baron's serfs, burning villages and crops in order to weaken enemies. In Rome, rival popes imprisoned, starved, mutilated and assassinated each other. Recurrent famines produced starvation in region after region, resulting in widespread cannibalism. Famines were followed by epidemics caused by eating infected grain. Medicine was still a matter of magic and illness was looked upon as divine punishment. Life was so difficult and so challenging that men believed the orderly laws of nature had been suspended, that the natural flow of seasons had fallen into utter disorder, foretelling the end of all mankind.

Thus it was in the year 999 that an epidemic terror of the end of the world spread throughout the earth. The author Raoul Glaber wrote, 'Though the people quarreled about the exact day and hour, they all agreed that Satan will soon be unleashed because the thousand years have been completed.' Buildings, edifices, churches, all were allowed to deteriorate as people from all walks of life made their way towards Jerusalem with their 'eyes on the sky,' expecting the Son of God to descend in glory at any moment.

On the last day of 999 in Rome, a mass of weeping and trembling worshipers waited for the dreaded

Day of Wrath. Many poor entered the church of St. Peter's in sackcloth and ashes, having spent months doing penance and mortifying the flesh. Their fears were only heightened as they looked at the new pope celebrating the mass. He was Sylvester II, also known as Gerbert, who many worshipers believed to be Antichrist (!) appearing in the shape of a pontiff. Gerbert had risen from humble beginnings to the papacy through the influence of his pupil Emperor Otto III. The Frenchman had learned much in Spain as a young man that was as yet unknown in the superstitious west. He had invented a steam-powered organ, a new system of writing music and even Arabic numerals. Accusations abounded that he had sold his soul to the devil at an early age in order to get this magical ability. Now he was head of the church.

This chilling historical account of the days leading up to and just after the year 1000 holds up a dark mirror to our own society and gives an interesting and early perspective on how the Roman Catholic Church rose to such power during a mysterious time in history. Told through the perspective of Gerbert of Aurillac, who became Pope Sylvester II in February, 999, the book recounts a time of almost unbelievable ignorance and superstition. Gerbert was a prolific letter writer and left a great legacy that author Erdoes analyzes and describes in a fascinating account of the early medieval world. The account of Gerbert's attempts to reform the abusive powers of the church may not be as interesting to Bible Students as the understanding that comes from Erdoes' description of the environment of inequity, injustice and ignorance that allowed such power to develop. As a sideline, Bible students will find it interesting that the only pope to attempt some reform to the papal system was eventually disowned and buried without note. Later that century the church would show its total corruption with the most horrendous of all its activities—the Crusades."

This bit of history reveals how Leviathan or evil, composed of ignorance, superstition, and fear, afflicted society. Author Flora Lewis gives another forceful example of how evil is a Leviathan of ignorance, superstition, and fear leading to extremism in "true" believers:

"From the Red Guards of Mao to the Islamic disciples of Khomeini, the Orthodox Militants of Israel and even the Fundamentalists of the Moral Majority, all have profound similarities. They all feel they know better than others what is good and what is bad for society. They have simple rules defining good and evil to save their world from devilish confusion, calling for a higher order while bringing disorder, and may be called intolerant, unreasonable and unenlightened. Such fundamentalism can be a search for lost ignorance."

Flora Lewis' statement effectively describes the part "religious extremists" have played. They quickly blame others for being wicked while proclaiming Satan the instigator of the evil. This raises some questions: Why do "believers" who see Satan or the Devil as instigating evil fail to take into account personal beliefs and feelings activated by an attitude of anger, fear, hostility, hate, jealousy, or deceit? Why do they hold people responsible for evildoing while blaming an imagined Satan as the instigator of the immorality or evil?

In contrast, *The Washington Post* published an interesting article about a possible physical aspect of moral responsibility, which can result in evil choices. It is titled "Neuroscientists See Center for Morality in the Brain." It said:

"In 1848, a dynamiting accident drove an iron bar through the skull of a railroad worker named Phineas Gage. Miraculously, Gage survived with no apparent damage to his intellect. His personality, however, changed dramatically. Once a diligent worker, Gage became an irresponsible drifter. Gage's misfortune provided neuroscientists with what have become landmark insights into how the brain works. The spike damaged Gage's prefrontal cortex, indicating that this part of the brain is critical for social and moral decision-making.

Now, researchers have found new evidence supporting that idea. Antonio Damasio of the University of Iowa and colleagues found two subjects who suffered damage to their prefrontal cortices before the age of 16 months. Both children seemed to recover. But as they aged, the two began to behave aberrantly, stealing, lying, abusing other people, poorly parenting their out-of-wedlock children, showing a distinct lack of remorse, and failing to plan for their futures. There were no obvious environmental explanations—both came from stable, middle-class families and had well-adjusted siblings.

'Early dysfunction in certain sectors of the prefrontal cortex seems to cause abnormal development of social and moral behavior, independently of social and psychological factors, which do not seem to have played a role in the condition of our subject,' the researchers conclude in the November 1999 issue of Nature Neuroscience. 'This suggests that antisocial behavior may depend, at least in part, on the abnormal operation of a multi-component neural system which includes ... sectors of the prefrontal cortex.'"

The *U.S. News & World Report* of November 20, 2000, included an article titled "Seeds of a Sociopath, Violence in the Brain?" The author, Josh Fischman, wrote:

"You wouldn't want your child to date either of the two British teens identified only as Case I and Case II. Perhaps you would blame derelict parents—or a lax society—for the teenagers' school failures, fighting, drug abuse, and arrests.

But if you were a neuroscientist like Faraneh Vargha-Khadem, you'd instead blame serious head injuries that in both cases damaged a tiny spot in the brain, just above the eyes. 'It turned the boys into walking time bombs, because the trouble didn't show until years after the injuries,' says Vargha-Khadem of University College London Medical School. 'It's the first time we've seen this.'

The part of the brain in question is a tiny area in the orbital frontal cortex. Researchers surmise this region plays a big role in judgment and impulse control. It allows people to balance their needs and desires against morality and values. Normally, the brain's two hemispheres cover for one another if one is hurt. But with the British boys, brain scans showed lesions involving both hemispheres. Vargha-Khadem suspects, that as various brain areas became more active in the teen years, there wasn't enough frontal lobe left on either side to exert control.

The study raises the possibility—disturbing to many at last Week's meeting of the Society for Neuroscience in New Orleans—of screening brain-damaged children to identify 'bad seeds.' Or the possibility that juvenile delinquents will someday be able to stand up in court and say, 'My brain made me do it.'"

Neither article suggests the persons having the damaged brain were subject to the influence of demons. It is not reasonable to have it both ways; either the will or desire is produced in the brain, or it is initiated by an outside source. The apostle Paul writes in Ephesians:

"That ye put off concerning the former conversation of the old man, which is corrupt according to the deceitful lusts."—Ephesians 4:22

The apostle is quite definite about the human mind as subject to lustful delusion. One might also quote 2 Thessalonians, where Paul writes that God sends strong delusions:

"And for this cause God shall send them strong delusion, that they should believe a lie." —2 Thessalonians 2:11

Paul's statement suggests that strong delusion is a result of willful blindness to truth and righteousness. It is from God in the sense that He created Adam with the ability to sin; to rebel; and to delude himself with self-aggrandizement, lust, or callousness of heart. God does not interfere with the thoughts and desires of humans. If He did, we would not be free moral agents. Reason cautions us that people out of harmony with

God's spirit of truth, justice, and righteousness bring judgment and consequences upon themselves.

Good morals are learned and reflect character. Some people are deficient in decent morals, but the opportunity opens wide for anyone desiring life to learn of righteousness, justice, love, and mercy during the restitution in Jesus the Christ's Kingdom. An article in *Bible Study Monthly* of Jan./Feb.1998 (p. 11) gives insight into that "time of judgment" as the world rises out of the stumbling, confusing days now upon it. The unidentified author wrote:

> "The words about a 'strong delusion' or 'working of error' are an example of what is taught as clearly in the New Testament as in the Old, that judicial hardening follows willful blindness and persistent sin. God will never send any delusion upon those who have not first deluded themselves. Thus Pharaoh hardened his own heart before it was ever said that the Lord hardened his heart. God has so ordered things that sin brings its own judgment in this way, and the Hebrew writers were so greatly impressed with the basic fact of the sovereignty of God that they expressed themselves in the most direct language about it. The conviction that all things were under divine ordering and control saved them from a pagan dualism such as would regard evil as existing under separate authority beyond Divine control. In this conviction, they represent everything as directly within the sphere of Divine action—not that God is the author of evil or desires evil for anyone, but that Divine ordering inevitably brings its own judgment; and it is a real judgment of God, because God has so ordered things as to involve this inevitable consequence."

This explanation can help us understand how belief in an evil spirit being hovering at the ready to lead humans into sin, is of pagan, dualistic teaching and was readily accepted into Judaism and Christianity. The imagined, powerful Satan is viewed as a persuasive spirit being, immune to God's purpose, causing evil thoughts and conditions. Such a delusion cancels human responsibility for conceiving and acting upon evil from desire or lust and causes many Christians to take literally the account of God talking to a Serpent (Genesis 3:14–15).

If it were a "literal" incident, the Serpent would crawl on its belly and eat dust, but it is a metaphor that portrays the mental struggle of Adam failing to control his lust or desire, which solidified into disobedience. Adam did not realize that this failure would also bring feelings of guilt and shame. The account thus provides in picture language how sin and death began through Adam when he chose to disobey God and submitted to his desire to know good and evil, thus conceiving and acting upon evil thoughts, which led to disobedience. Here, the metaphor refers to evil as Serpent, but John also identifies it as Satan, Devil, or Dragon:

> *"In that day the LORD with his sore and great and strong sword (truth) shall punish Leviathan the piercing serpent, even Leviathan that crooked serpent; and he shall slay the dragon that [is] in the sea (society)."* —Isaiah 27:1

> *"And He* (truth) *laid hold on the dragon, that old serpent, which is the devil, and Satan, and bound him a thousand years."* —Revelation 20:2

In Genesis, this depiction of lust as evil (Satan, Devil, Serpent, or Dragon) action continues with an abstract implication, not a literal one:

> *"And the LORD God said unto the serpent, Because thou hast done this, thou [art] cursed above all cattle, and above every beast of the field; upon thy belly shalt thou go, and dust shalt thou eat all the days of thy life. And I will put enmity between thee and the woman, and between thy seed and her seed; it shall bruise thy head, and thou shalt bruise his heel."*—Genesis 3:14–15

Adam gained knowledge about good and evil, but it altered his relationship with God. By submitting to lust, he gained the knowledge, but his innocence left him; he then understood the difference between good and evil from his own experience. As we read in Genesis:

> *"And the LORD God said, Behold, the man is become as one of us, to know good and evil: and now, lest he put forth his hand, and take also* (learn) *of the tree of life, and eat, and live for ever:"*—Genesis 3:22

In Proverbs, it says:

> *"The fruit of the righteous [is] a tree of life; and he that wins souls [is] wise."*—Proverbs 11:30

This scripture, when applied to Adam's situation, raises the question: If Adam had decided not to sin again, but repented and followed righteousness, would he have continued to live? If that situation had been possible, it would have voided God's plan for mankind because Adam, having been contaminated by sin, required a ransom, a life for a life. Adam, a perfect man who sinned, was sentenced to death, and God's justice required that another perfect man die to redeem Adam. Repenting for his sin was not a possibility, for the ransom for Adam required payment for the death penalty; thus the ransom for Adam was a life for a life. The law to Israel demanded that if someone causes the death of or kills another person, that responsible person must pay with his own life. We read of this in Deuteronomy:

> *"And thine eye shall not pity; [but] life [shall go] for life, eye for eye, tooth for tooth, hand for hand, foot for foot."—* Deuteronomy 19:21

Thus, in due time our Heavenly Father would send His son (Jesus the Christ) as that ransom. When reality set in, Adam's awareness of his sin revealed his failure to trust God; Adam's understanding of his and Eve's predicament was reflected in their guilt, as told in Genesis:

> *"And the eyes of them both were opened, and they knew that they [were]naked; and they sewed fig leaves together, and made themselves aprons."*—Genesis 3:7

Adam and Eve were not aware of their nakedness until after they disobeyed. Standing before God, Adam realized their negative feelings about their nakedness came about as a result of their choice to disobey, by an act of evil and sin.

"The eyes of them both were opened" is a way of stating they became fully aware that disobedience was evil. For the first time, awareness of their nakedness brought feelings of remorse, shame, guilt, and blame, which, becoming part of their thought processes, changed their relationship with God. The evil act caused their hearts to be troubled and to lack the joy, peace, and innocence they once held, and they tried to make excuses when confronted with the truth. Adam blamed Eve, and Eve blamed her tempting thoughts, thus claiming that lust or evil (Serpent, Satan, Devil, or Dragon) enticed her.

The implication is that Eve was fascinated by and enticed with the temptation to know (take of the tree of) good and evil and convinced Adam to take part, and Adam, despite his understanding of what God had said, chose to act upon his lust to follow Eve's suggestion:

> *"But of the tree of the knowledge of good and evil, thou shalt not eat (partake) of it: for in the day that thou eatest (partake) thereof thou shalt surely die."*—Genesis 2:17

The word "tree" in Hebrew, means "from its firmness," does not signify a literal tree, but points to the firm, unchangeable reality that knowledge demands responsibility. Eating of the tree was to test God's firm command to Adam not to test God, thus, his disobedient choice brought "firm" certainty that their lives had changed—not maybe or possibly, but absolutely—as fear entered their relationship with God. The lust or desire to acquire knowledge of what evil was like and to be like God fostered the decision to disobey. Eating of the tree was not a literal digesting of an eatable object, but a succumbing to temptation and choosing to disobey.

The entire setting of the incident is described in a figurative way. The characters, Adam and Eve, existed. They were living in a secure, delightful environment and experienced a dependent, trusting relationship with their Creator, but they allowed lust to replace trust and responsibility. The whole account informs the reader in picture language, which was a style of communication familiar to the culture of the time, both of what occurred and the result of the occurrence.

We are to be mindful that the ancient writing of Egypt were probably in hieroglyphic inscriptions in the documents. Moses, who wrote the first five books of the Bible, was trained in all the ways of the Egyptians and could well have used the Egyptian hieroglyphic method of recording the five books, which later would be translated into the Hebrew language and, thousands of years later, into English. But no matter how it was recorded, the account of Adam's sin resulted in the penalty of death, which is the reason the ransom of Adam by Jesus the Christ was necessary. This is clearly expressed by the apostle Paul:

> *"For as in Adam all die, so also in Christ shall all be made alive."*—1 Corinthians 15:22

If Adam and the Garden of Eden is a myth and his choosing to disobey did not actually happen, the ransom sacrifice of Jesus the Christ would not be required, the whole objective of the Old and New Testament would fall apart, the Bible would not be true, and all mankind would be in the position as the apostle Paul wrote in 1 Corinthians 15:19,

> *"If in this life only we have hope in Christ, we are of all men most miserable."*

But we see these things through faith, for the Bible gives solid reason and evidence for why and how the ransom is necessary and believable. Continuing his account in Genesis, Moses, using figurative speech, writes of the lust that led Adam to sin:

> *"And the LORD God said unto the serpent* (Satan, Devil, Dragon, or evil), *because you have done this, you* (evil) *[art] cursed above all cattle, and above every beast of the field; upon your* (its) *belly* (scorn) *shall you go, and dust* (destruction) *shall you eat* (exist on) *all the days of your life. And I will put enmity between you* (evil, Serpent, Satan, Devil, or Dragon) *and the woman, and between your seed* (greed, lust, hate, jealousy, etc., in people) *and her seed* (truth, righteousness, justice, mercy, love, etc.)*; it shall bruise* (destroy) *your head, and you shall bruise* (harm) *his heel."* ---Genesis 3:14–15

This explanation describes a changed condition. The Serpent, a symbol of opposition to God, depicts the deviousness of evil that can turn intentions into adversity. Thus evil, in all its devious connotations, is to be feared above all cattle or domestic creatures and beasts of the field or wilderness. The account is not of God literally speaking to a Serpent or an evil spirit being, but describes, in a symbolic manner, that Adam's choice to disobey his Creator resulted in an unfamiliar feeling, a feeling of knowing evil *(Serpent, Satan, Dragon, or Devil)*, and that he faced the dire consequences of his choice. The picture of a Serpent crawling upon its belly, eating dust with its head bruised conveys the idea that acting upon evil thoughts is destructive to life while also hinting at the limited existence of evil (Serpent, Satan, Devil, or Dragon), for it says *"all the days of your* (its) *life."*

As mentioned before, when the Serpent (Satan, Devil, Dragon, or evil) is spoken of as an evil spirit being, it is not thought of as crawling and eating dust. But in pictorial language the account portrayed how deceitful, contemptible and harmful evil is to be perceived by mankind. Therefore, the word "enmity" is used in Genesis:

> *"And I will put enmity between thee (evil) and the woman, and between thy seed (evil minds) and her seed (Messiah, truth, and righteousness)"* —Genesis 3:14–15

"Enmity" denotes a condition of hostility. The greatest fear a mother can experience is for evil to come upon her child. This hostility (enmity) of evil occurring to her child has remained with mothers ever since, and spiritually it depicts the enmity between righteousness and evil.

The enmity between "thy seed and her seed" is fully evident in Jesus the Christ, the Messiah, as the truth and the way; the "seed of the woman" triumphs over the insidious evil (Satan,

Devil, Serpent, or Dragon). Our Lord's character remained holy, not begotten or tainted by the evil of men. Because our Lord exhibited the spiritual and moral characteristics of God in every situation, he fulfilled prophecy and his mission. It was of the highest importance that his life be sinless in order to offer it as a perfect ransom price for Adam and all humanity who are of Adam, including those not yet born.

Jesus the Christ understood from prophecy, what the menacing failure of his mission meant if he were to react to evil with evil. He was to do no evil, for that would be destructive in accomplishing God's will. He therefore resisted sin and evil in every aspect of his life and displayed enmity (hostility) toward evil (Serpent, Satan, Devil, and Dragon). He did not, as Adam chose to do, allow his mind to dwell or act upon evil or allow the ways of men to be his choice. As the apostle Paul said:

> *"The carnal mind is enmity against God."*—Romans 8:7

Another interesting account of comparable symbolic nature of the Serpent of Genesis 3:14–15 is Job 1:6–7:

> *There we read: "Now it came to pass on the day when the sons of God came to present themselves before Jehovah, that Satan* (evil, Devil, Serpent, or Dragon) *also came among them. And Jehovah said unto Satan* (evil, Devil, Serpent, or Dragon), *Why are you here? Then Satan* (evil, Devil, Serpent, or Dragon) *answered Jehovah and said: From going to and fro in the earth, and from walking up and down in it."*

Again, there are two ways to interpret this verse: the account is either literal or figurative. If it is literal, in that God asks an evil spirit being what it has been doing or why it was there, it is only consistent to conclude that Satan (Serpent, Devil, or Dragon) was actually walking upon the earth at the time of Job. The question then arises, how can a spirit being walk upon the earth? We realize that a spirit being does not literally walk on the earth. So, what then does this mean, and who or what is Satan? Since the word "Satan" means "to attack," "to accuse," "to resist," or "to be an adversary," the statement is to be considered figurative and depicts humanity faced with the temptation either to conceive and act with evil or to choose to act with righteousness and justice.

Holy Spirit Versus Evil Spirit

The following excerpt from the book: The *Divine Plan of the Ages* provides a reasonable explanation how the Holy Spirit is to emanate from the Christian and also, in opposite manner, the spirit of evil (Satan, Devil, Serpent, or Dragon) that emanates from those who care not to follow the Lord in righteousness and justice. It says:

> "Someone long ago asserted that spirit beings were omnipresent; that is to say, spirit beings could be present everywhere at the same time. This unscriptural declaration has been fruitful to much confusion and error. Nevertheless, Jesus did promise to be with his disciples wherever they might meet in his name throughout this Gospel age, and we inquire, in what sense is he present with us? The answer comes from the Master's own words. He informs us that he and the Father take up their abode in the minds of those who are truly consecrated to the divine will, but how? The answer is—by his spirit, which dwells in us.

The Holy Spirit is the spirit or influence or power of the Father and of the Son, and this power or influence, we readily see can be exerted by the Lord everywhere. When we think of the meaning of the word spirit—in the Greek, 'pneuma'—and that it signifies that which is powerful but invisible, we can see why angels are called spirits and why God Himself is declared to be a spirit, and how the Lord Jesus is called a spirit—because all of these have power but are invisible to men.

But the word spirit has still further reaching signification; it applies to any influence or power proceeding from any human being or a spirit being, because that power or influence is invisible. Thus, for instance, the Truth has power over the minds of men and thus over their conduct; hence it is spoken of as the spirit of Truth, the power of the Truth. So we read of the spirit of man, the power or influence of a man; so we read of the spirit of life, the power or energy of life; and again we read of the spirit of a sound mind, or a well-balanced disposition or judgment. These are illustrations of the Scriptural use of the word spirit; and we find on the other hand that the same word spirit, with the same meaning, is used in an evil sense, as, for instance, the spirit of wickedness, the spirit of sloth, the spirit of evil, the spirit of deceit, the spirit of dishonesty, the spirit of untruth, the spirit of the devil.

Is it unreasonable to believe that the Great Creator, Himself a spirit being of the highest order, is able to exercise an influence upon the hearts of men through the Truth, or through a thousand agencies or channels, which He may use? And would not this influence or power proceeding from God be; like Himself, holy? And is it not therefore properly called the Holy Spirit, the spirit of the Father? And since the Son is in full accord with the Father, is it not appropriate that we read that the spirit proceeds from the Father and from the Son? And can we not distinguish between this power and influence exerted by the Father and the Son upon us and by a spirit being? We can see how this influence can be exerted throughout the whole world upon all of the Lord's people everywhere and at one time. But it would be monstrously unreasonable to ask anyone to believe that a spirit being could be present in all hearts, in all minds, the world over.

We remember that our Lord, in consoling His disciples, promised that after He had ascended to the Father He would send them the Holy Spirit, which would comfort them and be with them as His representative. His words are: "I will not leave you comfortless; I will come unto you." Thus it is the Holy Spirit in the Lord's people that signifies the Lord's presence throughout the Gospel age. And what comfort they have received! What a blessing! What rest of heart! Not through believing that a spirit being should be in each one and everywhere at once, but with the right understanding and attitude, this spirit, or power or energy as the Lord Jesus displayed will lead us for our comfort, guidance and edification. What beauty and simplicity we find in this message from the Word."

This explanation is an excellent description of God's spirit as the power or influence of our Creator working in the hearts of believers. In a similar manner, Christians may manifest an evil spirit, but if they do so unexpectedly, they are to request forgiveness of the Lord as they also forgive. The following scriptures illustrate that Christians are to display the spirit (attitude) of the Lord, but doing so means keeping under control the spirit of evil that had risen in the past. It is the new will that follows the Lord, a spirit that replaces the old spirit that had centered on self, had ignored the love of God.

"And he that keeps his commandments dwells in him, and he in him. And hereby we know that he abides in us, by the Spirit (attitude) *which he has given us."*—1 John 3:24

"But the fruit of the Spirit (attitude) *is love, joy, peace, longsuffering, gentleness, goodness, faith, meekness, temperance: against such there is no law. And they that are Christ's have crucified the flesh with the affections and lusts. If we live in the Spirit, let us also walk in the Spirit."*—Galatians 5:22–25

"Hereby we know that we dwell in him, and he in us, because he has given us of his Spirit. And he that keeps his commandments dwells in him, and he in him. And hereby we know that he abides in us, by the Spirit which he has given us."—John 4:13

"We are of God: he that knows God hears us; he that is not of God hears not us. Hereby know we the spirit of truth, and the spirit of error."—1 John 4:6

"Now the works of the flesh (evil) *are manifest, which are [these]; Adultery, fornication, uncleanness, lasciviousness, idolatry, witchcraft, hatred, variance, emulations, wrath, strife, seditions, heresies, envying, murders, drunkenness, reveling, and such like: of the which I tell you before, as*

I have also told [you] in time past, that they which do such things (manifest an evil spirit) *shall not inherit the kingdom of God."* Galatians 5:19–21

"Ye ask, and receive not, because ye ask amiss, that ye may consume [it] upon your lusts. Ye adulterers and adulteresses; know ye not that the friendship of the world (evil) *is enmity with God? Who so ever therefore will be a friend of the world* (evil) *is the enemy of God. Do ye think that the scripture said in vain: The spirit that dwells in us lusts to envy?"*—James 4: 2–4

As the Holy Spirit is not a spirit being, but is the attitude of righteousness, justice, mercy, and so on—that is, the spirit of God working in us—so, in contrast, an evil spirit or attitude of hatred, prejudice, selfishness, unthankful ness, and lust is not of an evil spirit being but is the spirit of evil conceived in our minds by allowing lust or evil ideas to control our thoughts. Our Lord is quoted in the Gospel of Matthew as saying:

"A good man out of the good treasure of the heart brings forth good things: and an evil man out of the evil treasure brings forth evil things."—Matthew 12:35

But in Isaiah we read:

"I form the light, and create darkness; I make peace, and create evil. I am Jehovah, that doeth all these things."— Isaiah 45:7

In this case, evil of God relates both to destruction through nature and to humans' ability to conceive evil. While God can alter the laws He has established, He has created the earth and heavenly bodies to function under those laws. There have been times when He used nature to carry out His purpose, as in the parting of the Red Sea or the flood in Noah's day. God also does not direct or rule over humans, as the doctrine of predestination would have it. Since people are free moral agents, people are responsible for choosing either good or evil, as recorded in Genesis:

> *"And the LORD God said, Behold, the man has become as one of us, to know good and evil."—Genesis 3:22*

And to the Hebrews, God said:

> *"See, <u>I have set</u> before thee this day life and good, and <u>death and evil.</u>"* —Deuteronomy 30:15

The people of Israel were unable to keep the law; thus a Messiah was promised to release Israel and all mankind from the death penalty of Adam. For a long time, evil dominated the heart of man, while good was ignored. But this bleak condition began to change when Jesus the Christ, the Messiah, came upon the scene. He fulfilled the law (Israel was unable to keep the law) and gave his life as a ransom for Adam, which includes everyone born of Adam or, as Paul wrote in 1 Corinthians:

> *"For as in Adam all die, even so in Christ shall all be made alive."*—1 Corinthians 15:22

> Thus, Jesus the Christ could lead the way, saying: *"Seek ye first the Kingdom of God and its righteousness."*— Matthew 6:33

Jesus the Christ revealed the way to life eternal in all he said and did, first to Israel only, but when they rejected and crucified him, his message of salvation went to the Gentiles, as the apostle Paul declared:

"For I am not ashamed of the gospel of Christ: for it is the power of God unto salvation to every one that believeth; to the Jew first, and also to the Greek (Gentiles).*"—* Romans 1:16

The prophet Habakkuk said of God:

"[Thou art] of purer eyes than to behold (condone) *evil, and canst not look* (approve of) *on iniquity: wherefore do you look upon them that deal treacherously?"* —Habakkuk 1:13

The prophet reminded Israel that God does not act with evil intent, nor is He tempted by evil, and He does not approve of the evil of men. But, compassionately, God has prepared a judgment day, which is also the Kingdom and time of restitution for mankind, wherein some people, born in sin and shaped by iniquity in life, will not care to seek justice and righteousness under the rule of Jesus the Christ's Kingdom and thus will be destroyed—the second death. The character and attitude each person develops in this life under the rule of evil will be either an asset or a liability toward attaining life in the Kingdom. This is indicated in the following verses:

"When the wicked spring as the grass, and when all the workers of iniquity do flourish; [it is] that they shall be destroyed for ever."—Psalms 92:7

"Whoso despises the Word shall be destroyed: but he that fears (reveres) *the commandment shall be rewarded."*— Proverbs 13:13

"Even as I have seen, <u>they that plow iniquity, and sow wickedness, reap the same</u>."— Job 4:8

The following commandment is of Jesus the Christ: *"Love God with all your heart and your neighbor as yourself."*

> *"And it shall come to pass, [that] every soul* (person), *which will not hear that prophet* (Jesus the Christ), *shall be destroyed from among the people."*—Acts 3:23 (During the Judgment Day, Kingdom, Thousand Years, or Restitution)

> *"But **these** (people), as natural brute beasts, made to be taken and destroyed, speak evil of the things that they understand not; and shall utterly perish in their own corruption."*—2 Peter 2:12 (During the Judgment Day)

People continuing in wickedness in the Kingdom of Jesus the Christ, not desiring or caring to live righteously in truth and love, will die a second death. This is to occur as people are resurrected upon earth and judged under conditions of righteousness, justice, and equity. The faithful Christians, chosen from the Gospel Age, have their part in the first resurrection and do not face further trial or the second death, as mentioned in the following scripture:

> *"He that hath an ear, let him hear what the Spirit* (of truth) *said unto the churches; He that overcomes* (the chosen) *shall not be hurt of the second death."* —Revelation 2:11

The above scripture applies to faithful Christians of the Gospel Age. It also indicates that unfaithful Christians of the Gospel Age, having confessed Jesus as their Savior and experienced love and truth in Jesus the Christ but then having disowned him, have shamed the Lord and have committed sin against the Holy Spirit of God. The apostle Paul writes of this in the Book of Hebrews:

"For [it is] impossible for those who were once enlightened, and have tasted of the heavenly gift, and were made partakers of the Holy Spirit and have tasted the good word of God, and the powers of the world (restitution and judgment) *to come, if they shall fall away, to renew them again unto repentance; seeing they crucify to themselves the Son of God afresh, and put [him] to an open shame."*—Hebrews 6:4–6

The apostle John saw the glory of the faithful in a vision: "Blessed and holy [is] he that hath part in the first resurrection: on such the second death hath no power, but they shall be priests of God and of Christ, and shall reign with him a thousand years."—Revelation 20:6

As mentioned, this verse applies to Christians of the Gospel Age who are chosen to live and reign with Jesus the Christ in his Kingdom. Having been faithful, they are not subject to the second death, which is eternal destruction:

"And death and hell were cast into the lake of fire. This is the second death." —Revelation 20:14

The lake of fire depicts destruction or elimination, hell (the grave) or death (destruction) and also comes to those who were once enlightened by the Holy Spirit in the Gospel Age but who turned away from the truth in Jesus the Christ; they will not be resurrected. The second death will claim as well those who have been resurrected but ignore seeking righteousness and continue in wickedness in the Kingdom of Jesus the Christ.

> *"But the fearful, and unbelieving, and the abominable, and murderers, and whoremongers, and sorcerers, and idolaters, and all liars, shall have their part in the lake which burns with fire and brimstone (eternal destruction): which is the second death."* —Revelation 21:8

Man's first death is inherited from Adam; the second death is self-inflicted by continuing in sin or not having any desire to go up the highway of righteousness, justice, and love that leads to life.

> *"until the times of restitution of all things."*—Acts 3:21

The times of restitution Peter spoke of is also the time of resurrection and judgment Jesus prophesied of:

> *"Marvel not at this: for the hour is coming, in which all that are in the graves shall hear his voice, And shall come forth; they that have done good* (in the Gospel Age) *to the resurrection of life; and they that have done evil, to the resurrection of judgment."*—John 5:28–29

The above scriptures confirm that a literal Devil, Serpent, Dragon, or Satan is not the basis or source of sin. The statements are clear as to where the responsibility lies in devising wickedness. As Jesus said:

> *"Out of the heart proceeds evil."*—Matthew 15:19

However, even with much evidence and reasoning, some Christians will not want to change from traditional doctrine that an evil spirit being inveigles a person's mind to do wickedness. Such Christians can find it difficult to grasp the pictorial language of the Bible. When the Bible's pictorial language is viewed as literal, it is evident to the traditionalist that a Satan,

Devil, Serpent, or Dragon is the source of evil, rather that evil is conceived in the minds of men. An evil spirit being does not suggest or initiate wickedness in the believer or unbeliever's mind, for the apostle Paul says:

> *"And for this cause God shall send them* (the wicked) *strong delusion, that they should believe a lie: That they all might be damned* (condemned) *who believed not the truth, but had pleasure in unrighteousness."*—2 Thessalonians 2:11–12

The implication in this verse is that people may willingly pursue their desires or lust into following error and giving assent to evil. But they are to be revealed and will bear the consequences as truth and righteousness confront them as the Day of Judgment develops throughout the earth.

Paul wrote:

> *"And then shall that wicked be revealed, whom the LORD shall consume with the spirit of his mouth (truth), and shall destroy with the brightness (knowledge) of his coming (spiritual presence)."* —2 Thessalonians 2:8

The listeners of Paul understood his forewarning to be aware of distorting revelations and misapplication of truth. The spirit of lawlessness or iniquity (as the Webster translation has it) was beginning to permeate the teachings of the early Church. Some leaders were deviating from the Gospel (good news) and failed to understand what the apostle spoke of in his letter to the Hebrews, as the fundamentals or "milk": the wisdom to discern between righteousness and evil, which is necessary before undertaking the meatier teachings of prophecy and the plan of God:

> *"For when by reason of the time ye ought to be teachers, ye have need again that some one teach you the rudiments of the first principles of the oracles of God; and are become such as have need of milk, and not of solid food. For every one that partakes of milk is without experience of the word of righteousness, for he is a babe. But solid food is for full-grown men; [even those who by reason of use have their senses exercised to discern good and evil."*—Hebrews 5: 12–14

Failing to discern and teach that righteousness, justice, love, and mercy in Jesus the Christ overcomes evil, some leaders of not only the Jewish brethren, but also of Gentile converts, failed to recognize the depth of God's purpose in Jesus the Christ. Again, this was not a condition of an evil spirit being penetrating their minds and causing them to think badly of and to belittle one another; it was their failure to perceive the importance of the spirit of righteousness, love, and truth. Likewise, the apostle in his letter to the Ephesians cautioned them, saying:

> *"That we may be no longer children, tossed to and fro and carried about with every wind of doctrine, by the sleight of men, in craftiness (not by a Satan, Devil, Serpent, or Dragon), after the wiles of error; but speaking truth in love, we may grow up in all things into him, who is the head, [even Christ."* —Ephesians 4:14–15

The apostle's words have cautioned every generation of believers ever since, but the popular idea that a Satan, Devil, Serpent, or Dragon instigates evil thoughts in the mind neutralizes his warning about the craftiness of men who disregard truth and love as they concoct erring doctrine. Gerard Thomas Straub writes of this delusion in his book *"Salvation for Sale*:

p. 28—"Today, the oldest of the manuscripts are studied in the light of history to try to determine the meaning the Biblical writers originally intended in their own times. Of course to Fundamentalists such critical and historical study of the Bible is the work of the Devil."

p. 118—"While the idea of good and bad angels fighting for my salvation made little sense, I have come to realize that there is an unseen battle being fought, although it is very different in nature from the holy war of the Fundamentalist. A war rages within each one of us, and the two armies in conflict are all that is selfish in us pitted against all that is selfless in us. For Christianity rooted in Western culture this is a lifetime symbolic battle between the demonic and the divine. Instead of demonic and divine, the terms higher and lower are used in the East, especially among non-Christian faiths. It is interesting to note that the lower is not demonic, just material."

p. 294—"Evil exists primarily in the minds of those who wish to eliminate it. Psychologists call this 'projection.' Fundamentalists are engaged in a never-ending effort to maintain the appearance of goodness and moral purity by denying their own badness and shortcomings and projecting their own 'evil' onto others. Evil is seen everywhere but within themselves."

Mr. Straub's statements relate how some Christians are prone to blame a Satan, Devil, Serpent, or Dragon, whereas the problem is that humans conceive evil. An example of this is in a commendable article titled "The Saving Power of God!" in the May/June 2000 issue of *Bible Study Monthly*. In recognition of man's responsibility toward sin, the writer brings forth sound reason for it, but is compelled on page 61 to add," We sin because we readily fall to Satan's temptation." Why was this added? It may be because it is customary to blame a Satan, but again, isn't the individual responsible for his or her actions?

The continuous quandary of blaming a source outside of man for sin has made it essential to investigate and reevaluate this ancient belief of an evil spirit being as responsible for people's bad attitudes or acts of evil. The great increase of knowledge brings answers to many old questions in regard to this overworked inconsistency of a Satan, Devil, Serpent, or Dragon that tempts people versus lust, choice, and accountability. There is the need to examine this contradiction more objectively in the light of God's love and purpose. The traditional belief of an evil spirit being always at the ready to inject evil thoughts into a person's mind is a misconception as much as asserting that an evil spirit being hurls fiery darts of discouragement. The apostle Paul, in Ephesians tells us:

> *"Above all, taking the shield of faith, wherewith ye shall be able to quench all <u>the 'fiery darts' of the wicked.</u>"*
> —Ephesians 6:16

The apostle is not saying that the darts come from an evil spirit being, but that people say or do wicked things that may weaken another person's faith, hope, or character. Another error, widely held, is that "Satan's method of attack is to lure us into carnal strife and controversy." This assertion is not reasonable, for, as the prophet Jeremiah tells us:

> *"The heart [is] deceitful above all [things], and desperately wicked: who can know it?"*—Jeremiah 17:9

And the apostle Paul wrote:

"Let not sin therefore reign in your mortal body, that ye should obey it in the lusts thereof."—Romans 6:12

Paul also wrote:

"But they that will be rich (lust for riches) *fall into temptation and a snare, and [into] many foolish and hurtful lusts, which drown men in destruction and perdition."*—1 Timothy 6:9

Like Jesus the Christ, the prophets and apostles used metaphors when relating to evil. It is not reasonable to claim a Christian's character or mind should manifest the spirit of peace, joy, love, patience, mercy, and the like and then assert that the spirit of hate, jealousy, anger, deceit, etc. has been inveigled into the mind of a Christian by an evil spirit being. The following verse is a metaphor of how Christians, before they knew Jesus the Christ, followed their lusts and held attitudes similar to those of other non-believers in the world but, after learning of God's love in Jesus the Christ, turned over a new leaf and make every effort to develop a righteous, peaceful, loving, and patient attitude both towards others and God by trusting in their Redeemer, Jesus the Christ:

"Wherein in time past ye walked according to the course of this world, according to the prince of the power of the air (the attraction of evil that flourishes in the world), *the spirit* (selfish attitude) *that now works in the children of disobedience:"*—Ephesians 2:2

We may at times hear the statement; "The Adversary endeavors to discourage us into believing there is little use in our trying to please the Lord because we always come short of God's standard of righteousness."

This implies we are subject to an evil spirit being manipulating our thoughts, but this is not reality. When we commit evil, our minds, hearts, or characters have desired it; we are responsible because evil is conceived in our minds. In Proverbs we read:

> *"The soul (mind, mentality, or character) of the wicked desires evil."*—Proverbs 21:10

In Hebrews, the apostle writes:

> *"Strong meat* (teaching, prophecy, or interpreting) *belongs to them that are of full age* (spiritually developed), *even those <u>who by reason of use have their senses exercised to discern both good and evil.</u>"*—Hebrews 5:14

The apostle's statement in Ephesians tells us where evil comes from:

> *"Among whom also we all had our conversation in times past <u>in the lusts of our flesh, fulfilling the desires of the flesh and of the mind</u>; and were by nature the children of wrath, even as others."*—Ephesians 2:3

Therefore, our lusts or desires lead us to either acts of evil or acts of love, righteousness, and justice.

Our Emotions

In the search for answers to emotional problems facing people today, learned specialists called psychiatrists, listen to, study, and evaluate the troubling plights of their patients. Because the psychiatrist has acquired knowledge about the complexities of how human emotion affects a person's decisions, the psychiatrist does not infer in any way that emotional problems are instigated by a Devil. For example, the book entitled *Anger, Yours and Mine and What To Do About It*, written by Richard Walters, has a section with the subtitle "The Three Expressions of Anger, Rage, Resentment and Indignation." Richard Walters wrote:

> These three vigorous expressions combine emotion, physical activation, cognition and potential behavior for good or evil.
>
> Rage seeks to do wrong. Resentment seeks to hide wrong. Indignation seeks to correct wrongs.
>
> Rage and resentment seeks to destroy people. Indignation seeks to destroy evil.

Rage and resentment seeks vengeance. Indignation seeks Justice.

Rage is guided by selfishness. Indignation is guided by mercy.

Rage uses open warfare. Resentment is a guerrilla fighter. Indignation is honest, fearless and forceful defender of truth.

Rage defends itself, resentment defends the status quo and indignation defends the other person.

Rage and resentment are forbidden by the Bible, indignation is required.

Among Christians there is a fear of rage, a surplus of resentment and a shortage of indignation.

Thus, we are to be aware of our potential anger, rage, and resentment so as to do no evil and thus to be strong enough to engage others in a loving and indignant manner in God's service.

Walters continues by saying that constructive indignation is based on love and that its characteristics are:

It can identify a real injustice.

It prays, not plots.

It points at a condition, not a person.

It helps the mistreated.

It teaches, rather than destroys.

It is unselfish.

It is often reluctant.

It refuses vengeance.

Richard Walter's thoughts can be summed up in the words of Zechariah to the people of Israel:

> *"Let none of you imagine evil in your hearts against his neighbor and love no false oath, for all these are things that I hate, said the LORD."*—Zechariah 8:17

Apparently, Jesus used the words "light" and "darkness" to illustrate the difference between speaking and acting with truth, righteousness, and justice and speaking and acting with evil. In Matthew, he says:

> *"The light of the body is the eye: if therefore thine eye (your desire) be single (seeks righteousness), thy whole body shall be full of light. But if thine eye (your desire) be evil, thy whole body (thoughts) shall be full of darkness. If therefore the light that is in thee be darkness, how great is that darkness."* —Matthew 6: 22–23

By using this metaphor, Jesus is implying that, when a person's thoughts are of living a life pleasing to God, the person not only is drawn closer to God, but he or she also enhances the life of others. In contrast, to breed thoughts of fear, hate, jealousy, and so on invites evil activity, which is destructive. The apostle Paul writes in his letter to the brethren in Rome:

> *"For the wrath of God is revealed from heaven against all ungodliness and wickedness of men who hinder the truth in unrighteousness."*—Romans 1:18

In the same chapter, he writes:

> *"And even as they refused to have God in [their] knowledge, God gave them up unto a reprobate mind, to do those things which are not fitting."*—Romans 1:28

The above verses refer to lustful, destructive sexual behavior of homosexuality and immoral heterosexual acts. The point brought out here is that the wickedness of a reprobate (abandoned in sin, depraved) mind is created when one allows their mind to lust or yearn for that, which is detrimental to healthy relationships. Verse 24 says:

> *"Wherefore God gave them up in the lusts of their hearts unto uncleanness, their bodies should be dishonored among themselves."*—Romans 1:24

When lust is allowed to rule the mind, it becomes sin, and when an individual insists on continuing in sin, he or she becomes a reprobate. This means there is no hope for that person. The responsibility to change lies within the individual; one is to develop his or her mind in truth and righteousness, making it a priority in order to obtain life. It is not an invisible evil spirit being controlling a person and hindering him or her from seeking truth and righteousness, but it is the person himself or herself who allows lust to control the mind and does not want to change an evil condition.

As quoted before, Jesus said, in the Gospel of Mark:

> *"For from within, out of the hearts of men, evil thoughts proceed, fornications, thefts, murders, adulteries, coveting, wickedness, deceit, lasciviousness, an evil eye, railing, pride, foolishness: all these evil things proceed from within, and defile the man."*—Mark 7:21

As for "lasciviousness," this would apply to both heterosexuality and homosexuality. Lasciviousness means "to embrace or to desire wanton, lewd, lustful, exciting, voluptuous emotions." Whether homosexual or heterosexual, men and women are capable of eliminating the evil of lust from their minds by trusting and following Jesus the Christ. The apostle Paul tells how to do this in Philippians:

> *"Finally, brethren, whatsoever things are true, whatsoever things [are] honest, whatsoever things [are] just, whatsoever things [are] pure, whatsoever things [are] lovely, whatsoever things [are] of good report; if [there be] any virtue, and if [there be] any praise, think on these things."* —Philippians 4:8

Rick Wilson, reporter of *The Grand Rapids Press*, quoted Robin Karr-Morse, a family therapist and author of the book titled *Ghosts From the Nursery: Tracing the Roots of Violence*, in an address to nearly two hundred educators, social service workers, and business leaders:

> "During the earliest years of life, the propensity for humans to either become loving compassionate people or hardened killers is born. Violence is born in the womb. The single most amazing fact emerging from new technology is that the brain is an interactive organ requiring outside stimuli to grow. The brain requires input in order to complete itself.
>
> The latest research shows that children who are nurtured and otherwise stimulated lovingly during the first two years of life experience development in parts of their brains controlling empathy, self-regulation and problem-solving skills. Those without such nurturing experience sometimes suffer

irreparable damage to areas of the brain controlling critical functions, including the ability to resist violent impulses.

Children who are abused or otherwise experience violence firsthand are left deeply afraid. They spend more time scanning their surroundings for danger than learning. Also, substances like alcohol, nicotine and some prescription drugs taken at critical times during a pregnancy can interfere substantially with healthy brain development."

Robin Karr-Morse does not blame evil spirit beings as being responsible for violent acts of children. She provides strong evidence that the roots of violence or compassion are traced to the nursery, where "the brain requires input in order to complete itself." Research piles up more and more evidence that we are acquiring knowledge that develops our sense of personal responsibility in the choosing of righteousness over evil.

In similar fashion, it is our reasoning that compels us to believe the Bible's claim that this earth, the life upon it, and the universe has been created through God's wisdom, justice, love, and power. What clashes with the recognition of God's wisdom and justice is the claim that God has brought into existence an evil spirit being to instigate evil in humans when they already are fully capable of conceiving selfishness, lust, hate, jealousy, envy, murder, and so on. Unfortunately, theologians have us believing that evil spirit beings suggest the evil that we conceive and act upon.

Jeffrey Burton Russell, in his book titled *Satan*, published by Cornell University Press of Ithaca, New York, put together historical information regarding Satan. He wrote:

"If some new social order should be able to eliminate evil, the concept of the devil would surely die."

The Bible tells us this is precisely the objective of the Kingdom of God upon this earth, which is to consist of a new social order wherein dwells righteousness, as the following scriptures testify:

"Before the LORD: for He comes, for He comes to judge the earth (society): *He shall judge the world with righteousness, and the people with His truth."* —Psalms 96:13

"Judgment also will I lay to the line, and righteousness to the plummet: and the hail (hardness of truth) shall sweep away the refuge of lies, and the waters (truth) shall overflow the hiding place (secrets in every facet of society)."—Isaiah 28:17

"And you shall swear, The LORD lives, in truth, in judgment, and in righteousness; and the nations shall bless themselves in Him, and in Him shall they glory."— Jeremiah 4:2

"And when he (Jesus the Christ) is come (spiritual presence), he (it) will reprove the world of sin, and of righteousness, and of judgment."—John 16:8

"Because He (God) *hath appointed a day* (Kingdom, Thousand Years, Restitution), *in the which He* (God) *will judge the world in righteousness by [that] man* (Jesus the Christ) *whom He* (God) *hath ordained; [whereof] He* (God) *hath given assurance unto all [men], in that He* (God) *hath raised him* (Jesus the Christ) *from the dead."*—Acts 17:31

"Nevertheless we, according to his promise, look for new heavens (religion teaching truth in Jesus the Christ) *and a new earth* (just society), <u>*wherein dwells righteousness.*</u>"—2 Peter 3:13

"And the sea (society) gave up the dead (all are dead in sin) which were in it; and death and hell (grave) delivered up the dead which were in them (resurrection): and they were judged every man according to their works (during Restitution)."—Revelation 20:13

"And I heard a great voice (worldwide acknowledgment) *from out of heaven* (religion) *saying, Behold, the tabernacle* (family) *of God [is] with men, and He* (God's spirit) *will dwell with them, and they shall be His* (God's) *people, and God himself shall be with them* (through Jesus the Christ), *[and be] their God. And <u>God shall wipe away all tears from their eyes; and there shall be no more death, neither sorrow, nor crying, neither shall there be any more pain: for the former things are passed away</u>. And he* (Jesus the Christ) *that sat upon the throne said, Behold, I* (Jesus the Christ) <u>*make all things new*</u>. *And he* (Jesus the Christ) *said unto me* (John), *Write: for these words are true and faithful."*—Revelation 21:3–5

In describing the general belief about Satan, Jeffery Burton Russell wrote:

"Satan is the prime adversary of Christ. Satan tempts people; he causes illness and death. He obsesses and possesses individuals and tempts human beings to sin. He is a leader of a host of evil spirits. Jewish thought moved decisively in the opposite direction of giving the devil considerable importance, as the New Testament did. The Talmud consciously rejected the dualistic tendency of the apocalyptic writers and insisted upon the unity of the one benevolent Lord. Evil results from the imperfect state of the created world or from human misuse of free will, not from the machinations of a cosmic enemy of the Lord. Usually the Rabbis rejected the notion of a personified being leading the forces of evil and preferred to speak of the devil as a symbol of the tendency to do evil within humanity.

According to rabbinic teaching, two antagonistic spirits inhabit each individual: one a tendency to good (yetserhatob), the other a tendency to evil (yetser-ha-ra). … Rabbi Simon ben Lakish wrote: "Satan and the yetser and the angel of death are one." The rabbis discarded the tradition of the rebellion of the angels since angels have no evil (yetser) and cannot sin, and they did not identify Satan with the serpent of Genesis or foretell his destruction and punishment.

As Joshua Trachtenberg put it, the Jewish devil 'was little more than an allegory' of the evil inclination among humans.

Under Iranian influence, the idea that demons were of mixed nature, each fighting a spiritual struggle of his own between good and evil, was more and more replaced by the idea that some demons were inherently good and others inherently evil. In this form, Greek demon-belief became markedly congruent with Judeo-Christian ideas about good and fallen angels."

The above statements of Jeffrey Burton Russell tell when and how Satan and demons materialized in the thoughts of people, and that history reveals how strong the movements have been in placing blame for evil on an evil spirit being rather than attributing responsibility for evil to the person conceiving evil. Remember what Jesus the Christ said in Matthew:

> *"A good man out of the good treasure of the heart brings forth good things: and an evil man out of the evil treasure brings forth evil things."*—Matthew 12:35

Another aid in understanding evil is an excellent book by Paul J. Gelinas, titled *"Coping With Anger"* Rosen Publishing Group Inc. of New York, New York). He wrote;

> "If our needs are not met, we become frustrated and then angry, which tends to explain the violence in our society. In the many years as a clinical psychologist working with young adults, I cannot recall a single case of neurosis or emotional disturbance that did not have unresolved anger as the main overt or intrinsic element in the disorder.

> "The person who has rationalized his contention that he is without anger is more subject to emotional distress than he who recognizes that there is evil in all of us. In one sense, before being a good human being, one must first admit that a devil dwells within himself.

> Our ancestors created the devil as a symbol of the evil they externalized on a vast screen of their own self-deception. The 'devil' is still with us, but we have a slightly differing conception of him. He is our own evil desire, uncontrolled hate, and antisocial urges that we have refused to acknowledge fully, have repressed from our consciousness until they break

out to work havoc upon society in murders and other crimes.

People must fall back on the age-old question, what is good and what is evil? What are the criteria that should guide one's direction? Each person must will his own welfare for himself."

Paul J. Gelinas is quoted because he not only points to the benefits of people acquiring a wholesome attitude for daily living, he also does not attribute the evil in people to the machinations of a Satan. His words place emphasis upon the source of the problem, which is that people have the responsibility to not act upon evil thoughts. This knowledge can help us cultivate an attitude that controls anger, hatred, and evil.

Exorcism

Today, there are religious organizations that declare cases of demonic possession and a need for exorcism. An article in *The Grand Rapids Press* of September 30, 2000, by author Nancy Haught, titled "Interest in Exorcism Rises in Conjunction with Re-release of Movie," tells of a surge in demonic possession after the news media raised general interest in the subject. The article includes a statement by Rev. Richard Berg, a Holy Cross priest, pastor of the Downtown Chapel of Portland, Oregon, and Professor Emeritus of Psychology at the University of Portland, claiming to "differentiate between formal exorcism and deliverance ministry." He is quoted as saying:

> "The latter involves praying for protection and safety of people from evil spirits and is common, especially among charismatic groups. Before anyone would qualify for an exorcism, it would be mandatory to rule out physical and emotional or mental causes of the problems. The first thing I would do is rule out any physical reason for what was happening, any medial—including psychiatric or psychological—factors before we would even go forward with an

exorcism. In 95 percent of cases, the problems prove to be due to an illness or to environmental factors."

The article ends by saying that in January 1999 the Vatican released the first revisions in the rite of exorcism since 1614. The new rite stresses that evil is a powerful reality but warns exorcists not to mistake psychiatric illness for demonic possession. The question then before us is: If only 5 percent of the cases may be helped by exorcism and are not mentally ill or have emotional baggage from childhood, might not the 5 percent be influenced by their belief system and thus be held responsible for their actions?

The following statement was by an unidentified psychiatrist:

> "Psychological problems that involve visualizing demons or hearing voices are a different matter and evidently require counseling. The changes in treatment for mental problems are quite different from the past. Not many decades ago, the mentally ill and retarded were institutionalized in what were called Insane or Lunatic Asylums. Thousands of people restrained in such places experienced a lifetime of depression and despair when often the problem was epilepsy or retardation. Often their life was afflicted by prejudiced persons and would end in an unmarked grave."

An unknown writer said:

> "Moral responsibility cannot be attributed to an abstract principle of evil, but only to an intelligent creature capable of both moral and immoral conduct. If there is a Satan and demons, and assumed they are intelligent creatures, how could they be capable of moral conduct if they only know evil?"

From the time of Adam, man has been capable of moral or immoral conduct. When a person conceives and acts with evil, under normal conditions guilt would suggest that the evil act is sin. But, the story of Eden is an allegorical form to illustrate how the mind of Adam was seduced by evil thoughts or desire (lust), which has affected the human race ever since; thus, the evil thought or act requires positive thought and acts of repentance and prayer to God in the name of our redeemer, Jesus the Christ, to overcome it. Our efforts to do this in a mental sense are similar to the struggles of the moth larva metamorphosing into a beautiful moth; therefore the Christian's spiritual metamorphosis is portrayed in 2 Corinthians, where the Amplified New Testament reads:

> *"And all of us, as with unveiled face because we continue to behold as in a mirror the glory of the LORD, are constantly being transfigured into his very own image in ever increasing splendor and from one degree of glory to another; for this comes from the Spirit of the LORD (truth, righteousness, and justice, which Jesus the Christ manifested)."* —2 Corinthians 3:18

> *"Jesus said unto him, I am the way, the truth, and the life: no man comes unto the Father, but by me* (spirit of truth)*."*—John 14:6

The apostle Paul suggests that as Christians, we can expect to experience struggles of a spiritual nature. He does not say an evil spirit being might instigate evil within us, but rather that it is the failure to act with righteousness, justice, and love that is the problem. It is a spiritual warfare that goes on in the hearts and minds of all Christians, as the apostle writes in 2 Corinthians:

> *"For though we walk in the flesh, we do not war after the flesh: For the weapons of our warfare [are] not carnal, but mighty through God to the pulling down of strong holds. Casting down imaginations and every high thing that exalts itself against the knowledge of God, and bringing into captivity every thought to the obedience of Christ* (truth). *And having in a readiness to revenge all disobedience, when your obedience is fulfilled."* —2 Corinthians 10:3–6

We understand that Paul's statement does not relate to literal weapons of warfare. The apostle is talking about warfare of a personal nature, a spiritual battle to not allow our minds to approve or justify evil. Therefore, it is essential that we be aware of our desires, our attitude in order to combat the evils of impatience, hate, arrogance, prejudice, and evil imaginations that will corrupt our relationship of love and peace not only with others, but mainly with our Heavenly Father. Since evil (Satan, Devil, Serpent, or Dragon) is conceived in the mind, Christians must learn to be aware of their evil thoughts. In Acts, Paul quotes Isaiah as to how evil had polluted the minds of the Jews:

> *"For the heart of this people is waxed gross, and their ears are dull of hearing, and their eyes have they closed; lest they should see with [their] eyes, and hear with [their] ears, and understand with [their] heart, and should be converted, and I should heal them."*—Acts 28:27

Later, in his letter to the Galatian brethren, Paul points out that Christians need to be aware of similar self-defeating characteristics that will hinder us from gaining life eternal through Jesus the Christ:

"[This] I say then, walk in the spirit, and ye shall not fulfill the lust of the flesh. For the flesh (selfishness) lusts against the spirit (truth, righteousness, justice, or mercy), and the spirit (truth, righteousness, justice, or mercy) against the flesh (selfishness): and these are contrary the one to the other: so that ye cannot do the things that ye would. But if ye be led of the spirit (righteousness, love, justice, or mercy), ye are not under the law. Now the works of the flesh are manifest, which are [these]; Adultery, fornication, uncleanness, lasciviousness, idolatry, witchcraft, hatred, variance, emulations, wrath, strife, seditions, heresies, envyings, murderers, drunkenness, revellings, and such like: of the which I tell you before, as I have also told [you] in time past, that they which do such things shall not inherit the kingdom of God. But the fruit of the spirit is love, joy, peace, longsuffering, gentleness, goodness, faith, meekness, temperance: against such there is no law. And they that are Christ's have crucified (left behind) the flesh with the affections and lusts."—Galatians 5:16–24

The words of Jesus and the apostle are clear as to where evil originates. Therefore, though evil thoughts may occur momentarily, our goal is to not dwell on them, but to keep them from turning into words and action. For example, Jesus could have retaliated with evil, but he did not do so. He knew that it was extremely important for him to avoid acting upon thoughts of evil in order to accomplish the mission set before him, for instance, as with Peter:

"Then Peter took him, and began to rebuke him, saying, be it far from thee, LORD: this shall not be unto thee. "—Matthew 16:22

But Jesus the Christ said:

> *"Get behind me, Satan (evil, Devil, Serpent, or Dragon):*
> *you are a hindrance to me: for you are not on the side of*
> *God, <u>but of men</u>."*   —Matthew 16:23

He was saying that Peter's counsel was evil, as Peter's seemingly consoling words would have Jesus take the wrong action or direction, which would jeopardize his mission as the Christ according to prophecy. This tells us the necessity of the death of Jesus as the Messiah to pay the ransom for Adam's sin, thus providing atonement for all, for all people are of Adam. It is in due time, during the Day of Judgment or the Kingdom of Jesus the Christ, that people will come forth from the grave, and there will be ample opportunity and direction for everyone desiring to hear and make the effort of progressing up the path of truth, righteousness, justice, and mercy that leads to life. Jesus is recorded in the Gospel of John as saying:

> *"Marvel not at this: for the hour is coming, in the which*
> *all that are in the graves shall hear his voice, and shall*
> *come forth; they that have done good (during Gospel Age),*
> *unto the resurrection of life; and they that have done*
> *evil, unto the resurrection of judgment during kingdom*
> *or Judgment Day."* —John 5:28–29

The words of Jesus *"unto the resurrection of judgment"* picture the favorable conditions of restitution. The basics of restitution blessings are already changing the world even as most of the work of the Gospel Age of choosing those who reign with the Lord fades into the past. The knowledge of the Lord is in the initial stages of covering the earth as the waters cover the sea, as Isaiah tells us:

> *"They shall not hurt nor destroy in all my holy mountain*
> (government), *for the earth shall be full of the knowledge*

of the LORD, as the waters cover the sea."—Isaiah 11:9

Improving conditions of the Kingdom are recognized by the watchers, who see the spirit of the Lord growing and blessing those willing to learn righteousness and justice, with all eventually having opportunity to learn of God's love in the spirit of Jesus the Christ and his Church. Thus, the majority of people will learn and practice righteousness and, in time, be rewarded with life upon this earth as restitution and resurrection takes place over the centuries during the Kingdom and Judgment period of a thousand years. But, in both the Old and New Testaments, prophecy tells of many not wanting to change from their evil ways:

> *"But the LORD shall endure for ever: he hath prepared his throne for judgment. And <u>He shall judge the world in righteousness</u>, he shall minister judgment to the people in uprightness."*—Psalms 9:7–8

> *"<u>The LORD reigns;</u> let the earth rejoice; let the multitude of isles be glad [thereof]. Clouds (trouble) and darkness (ignorance) <u>[are] round about Him,</u>: righteousness and judgment [are] the habitation of His throne. A fire (destruction) goes before him, and burns up (destroys) his enemy's roundabout. His lightning's (truth) enlighten the world: the earth (society) saw, and trembled (fearful excitement). The hills (opposition of organizations) melted like wax at the (spiritual) presence of the LORD, at the (spiritual) presence (return) of the LORD of the whole earth. The (new) heavens (truth in religion) declare his righteousness, and all the people (desire ing righteousness and truth) see his glory."* —Psalms 97:1–6

> *"I will early destroy all the wicked of the land; that I may cut off all wicked doers from the city* (Kingdom) *of the LORD."*—Psalms 101:8

> *"For as the new heavens* (truth in religion) *and the new earth* (society without evil), *which I will make, shall remain before me, said the LORD, so shall your seed and your name remain. And it shall come to pass, [that] from one new moon to another, and from one Sabbath to another, shall all flesh come to worship before me, said the LORD. And they shall go forth, and look upon the carcasses* (remains or memories) *of the men that have transgressed against me: for their worm* (transgression) *shall not die, neither shall their fire* (destruction) *be quenched; and they shall be an abhorring unto all flesh."*—Isaiah 66:22–24

Many refusing to seek righteousness in Jesus Christ will die a second death, the penalty for insisting on following evil. They will remain a sad and disappointed memory to all who do attain life.

> *"Therefore wait ye upon me, said the LORD, until the day that I rise up to the prey: for my determination [is] to gather the nations* (United Nations), *that I may assemble the kingdoms* (nations), *to pour upon them mine indignation,[even] all my fierce anger: for all the earth* (society) *shall be devoured with the fire* (destruction) *of my jealousy. For then will I turn to the people a pure language* (truth in Jesus the Christ), *that they may all call upon the name of the LORD, to serve him with one consent."*—Zephaniah 3:8–9

> *"The men of Nineveh shall rise in judgment with this generation (Jews of Jesus' first advent), and shall condemn it: because they repented at the preaching of Jonas; and,*

behold, a greater than Jonas [is] here. The queen of the south shall rise up in the judgment with this generation and shall condemn it: for she came from the uttermost parts of the earth to hear the wisdom of Solomon; and, behold, a greater than Solomon [is] here."—Matthew 12:41–42

"And then shall that (the) wicked be revealed, whom the LORD (spiritual presence) shall consume (destroy) with the spirit of his mouth (truth and righteousness), and shall destroy with the brightness (increasing knowledge) of his coming (presence)." —2 Thessalonians 2:8

God's promises of restitution blessings are very reassuring. Not only the Bible, but also the beauty and harmony of His creation, gives this assurance. The wonders of nature are overflowing with evidence that our Creator's intent is to have people live on earth to enjoy and appreciate His love and creation. The Bible gives abundant reference of this prospect in the following verses; the first is a quotation of Jesus:

"Marvel not at this: for the hour is coming, in the which all that are in the graves shall hear his voice, and shall come forth; they that have done good, unto the resurrection of life; and they that have done evil, unto the resurrection of (judgment)."—John 5:29–28

Death is extinction of life, not a transition to a spirit life. People do not have a soul that goes to Heaven but are living souls that go into the grave (death) to await the resurrection and restitution in the kingdom of Jesus the Christ. The Psalmist David wrote:

"[Thou] (God), who has shown me great and sore troubles, shall quicken (give life to) *me again, and shall bring*

351

me up again from the depths of the earth. " —Psalms 71:20

David died, but he looked forward to his resurrection.

> *"And he shall send* (second advent) *Jesus Christ, which before was preached unto you: Whom the heaven* (religion) *must receive until the times of restitution of all things* (second advent), *which God hath spoken by the mouth of all his holy prophets since the world began. For Moses truly said unto the fathers, A prophet* (Jesus the Christ) *shall the LORD your God raise up unto you of your brethren* (Israel), *like unto me; him shall ye hear in all things whatsoever he shall say unto you. And it shall come to pass* (second advent), *[that] every soul* (person), <u>*which will not hear that prophet*</u> (Jesus the Christ), <u>*shall be destroyed from among the people."*</u> —Acts 3:20–23

Jesus died as ransom for all, and all are promised a resurrection *(faithful Christians first, the rest of mankind next)*, but, even in that day, not all will be willing to seek righteousness and justice under Jesus the Christ and his chosen Church during his Kingdom:

> *"And the city* (God's government) *had no need of the sun* (New Testament), *neither of the moon* (Old Testament), *to shine* (light) *in it: for the glory of God did lighten it* (knowledge of God), *and the Lamb* (Jesus the Christ) *[is] the light thereof. And the nations of them, which are saved, shall walk in the light* (truth) *of it: and the kings of the earth do bring their glory and honor into it."* —Revelation 21:23–24

God, through His spirit, manifested by Jesus the Christ and his chosen faithful, shall guide or watch over the willing as they learn what is called walking up the highway of holiness to life.

Any person hearing of and desiring life shall be encouraged, directed, and assisted under God's governing spiritual power upon this earth, which rises upon the ashes of the old world of evil, sin, and death. The escalating blessings through knowledge, righteousness, justice, freedom, empathy, and the like, which are beginning to envelop the world today, are indication that the old order under sin and death is being demolished to make room for constructing the new order under righteousness and justice.

> *"For the earth shall be filled with the knowledge of the glory of the LORD, as the waters cover the sea."*—Habakkuk 2:14

All nations and people will in due time have the liberty to understand and rejoice in their salvation through God's love in Jesus the Christ. A prominent sign that restitution is beginning to take place is that, over a century ago, Christian churches would not send missionaries to Africa. Today, Africa is the fastest growing area of Christianity. China and India are also seeing great expansion of interest in the Bible.

> *"And the LORD shall be king over all the earth: in that day shall there be one LORD, and his name one."*
> —Zechariah 14:9

Knowledge and trust in God's love through Jesus the Christ brings a loving, spiritual attitude with righteousness, justice, and mercy that is to fill the hearts of all who desire life.

> *"And they shall teach no more every man his neighbor, and every man his brother, saying, Know the LORD: for they shall all know me, from the least of them unto the greatest of them, said the LORD: for I will forgive*

> *their iniquity, and I will remember their sin no more."*
> —Jeremiah 31:34

> *"Every valley (social needs) shall be filled, and every mountain (government) and hill (organization) shall be brought low; and the crooked (doctrine & law) shall be made straight, and the rough ways [shall be] made smooth; and all flesh shall see the salvation of God."*
> —Luke 3:5,6

All governments, organizations, and people are to learn to reflect the caring patience, peace, love, righteousness, and truth as Jesus the Christ gave example.

> *"And to this agree the words of the prophets; as it is written. After this I will return, and will build again the tabernacle of David, which is fallen down; and I will build again the ruins thereof, and I will set it up (Jesus the Christ gave himself as ransom for all, to be testified in due time)."*—1 Timothy 2:3–6

As all die because of Adam's sin, so all are resurrected because Jesus paid the ransom price.

> *"For as in Adam all die, even so in Christ shall all be made alive."*—1 Corinthians 15:22

> *"Nevertheless we, according to his promise, look for new heavens* (truth in religion) *and a new earth* (just society), *wherein dwells righteousness."*—2 Peter 3:13

At the end of Jesus the Christ's Kingdom (a thousand years), everyone attaining life will reflect the love of God in word and deed. From the day of Adam, God has allowed people to conceive evil and use it against each other. For instance, in

Jeremiah we read of God's warning to the tribe of Judah to stop their evil ways and follow righteousness or He (not a Satan) would bring evil upon them. The prophet Jeremiah wrote:

> "It may be that the house of Judah will hear <u>all the evil</u> <u>which I purpose to do unto them; that they may return</u> <u>every man from his evil way</u>; that I may forgive their iniquity and their sin."—Jeremiah 36:3

The tribe or house of Judah failed to heed the warning and suffered the consequences. It was not until Jesus the Christ brought the Gospel with the promise of God's restitution blessings that hope of deliverance from sin, death, and evil became a reality for not only the tribe of Judah but for all of Israel and for the world. An article in *Bible Study Monthly*, a previously mentioned publication, is titled "The Saving Power of God!" It also elaborates on the hope of restitution. The author wrote:

> "If judgment was a matter of 'cause and effect in a moral universe' as Dodd wrote, then the whole human race would have been destroyed from the Earth long ago. In His great mercy, God provides opportunities for turning away from sin. In his rebellion, man frequently ignores those opportunities to repent. In the beginning, the wrath of God fell upon the whole race of mankind and the awful consequences of man's rebellion have stricken millions of innocent people. That suffering has been the direct consequence of human behavior and is more apparent in the world today than it ever was. When the curse of Eden is lifted and Earth's millions are restored to life in the resurrection they will realize that God meant it to them for good... The penalty for man's sin has been paid for in Christ. The only reason for God's wrath

is to demonstrate to mankind in general, and to its blind leaders in particular, that sin is wrong, illogical, and results in nothing but misery and death."

Thus, afflicted by the web of evil while under the law, Israel at times struggled to overcome sin. A Savior or Messiah was their only hope, and through their prophets they were promised that a Messiah would come to lead them and the world out of the terrible predicament of evil, sin, and death.

PROMISE OF GOD'S LOVE AND JUSTICE

Knowledge and truth are progressive; Christians clinging to interpretations, doctrine, creeds, and rituals devised during and since the Dark Ages, by looking, can now find that increasing knowledge, truth and change is bringing about fulfillment of the promise God gave to Abraham:

> *"In thee and in thy seed shall all the families of the earth be blessed."*—Genesis 28:14

And the prophecy of Isaiah:

> *"They shall not hurt nor destroy in all my holy mountain: for the earth shall be full of the knowledge of the LORD, as the waters cover the sea."* —Isaiah 11:9

And the wonderful prophesy of Jesus:

> *"Marvel not at this: for the hour is coming, in the which <u>all that are in the graves shall hear his voice, And shall come forth;</u>"* —John 5:28, 29

The apostle Paul expanded further on this subject:

357

> *"For as in Adam all die, even so in Christ shall all be made alive, but every man in his own order: <u>Christ the first-fruits;(the church)</u> afterward <u>they that are Christ's (mankind) at his coming (spiritual presence).</u>"*   —1 Corinthians 15:22–23

It may safely be said that any interpretations or doctrine not in harmony with the above scriptures are to be re-interpreted or abandoned, as such doctrine or interpretations do not reflect the truth of God's Word. For example, the prospect of God's condemnation of evil and its future demise is originally given in Genesis, to Adam and Eve, as enmity between evil and the seed of the woman, which is the Messiah.

The promise was then told to Abraham, then told by the prophets and the Messiah, Jesus the Christ, and lastly, by the apostles, who spread the message during the Gospel Age with a calling out for a Little Flock who will reign with the Lord in the restoration to life for all having desire for peace, righteousness, and justice in Jesus the Christ.

> *"And I will put enmity between thee and the woman, and between thy seed and her seed; it shall bruise thy head, and you shall bruise his heel."* —Genesis 3:15

This picture language or symbolism hides the correct interpretation from unbelievers and sometimes believers. The words "thee," "woman," "seed," "head," "bruise," and "heel" are symbolic and are to be understood that way by believers. A literal interpretation does not make sense. Abraham understood the meaning and was given further revelation, with:

> *"And thy seed shall be as the dust of the earth, and thy seed shall spread abroad to the west, and to the east, and to the*

north, and to the south: and in thee and in thy seed shall
all the families of the earth be blessed."—Genesis 28:14

When Jesus the Christ gave his life as a "ransom for all," God's
plan yielded the first-fruit. Then when he became the first to
be raised from the dead, as spirit, his followers became more
aware that all in the grave would also be raised; that Little
Flock (faithful Christians, his spiritual body, chosen during the
Gospel Age) are resurrected first to reign with him

They have died in Jesus the Christ and therefore are his spiritual
body (symbolically beheaded, as he is their head). They are also
of the first fruits. Next, in reverse generational order (based
upon reason), all mankind are to be resurrected upon earth
for judgment, a trial period, with the opportunity to learn
righteousness and justice, the willing learning of the knowledge
of the Lord as it covers the earth with the prospect of life
eternal. This is told in John:

> *"and shall come forth; they that have done good* (the
> chosen), *unto the resurrection of life; and they that have
> done evil* (rest of mankind), *unto the resurrection of
> judgment."*—John 5:29

The apostle Peter spoke of "times of restitution": approximately
one thousand years of restoring all the willing to harmony
with God, a time when evil activity in every form becomes
unacceptable and eliminated. This prospect is referred to in the
following scriptures:

> *"And out of his mouth goes a sharp sword (truth), that
> with it (truth) he (the spiritual rule of Jesus the Christ)
> should smite the nations: and he shall rule them with a
> rod of iron (shepherd them with a staff of iron, gentle, but*

*firm—Gspd): and he treads the winepress of the fierceness
and wrath of Almighty God."* —Revelation 19:15

Thus, through the spirit of the Lord, there is to be a gradual destruction and elimination of all that is evil.

*"Because He (God) hath appointed a day (the Kingdom),
in the which He (in His spirit through Jesus the Christ
and his Church) will judge the world in righteousness
by [that] man (Jesus the Christ) whom He (God) hath
ordained; [whereof] He (God) hath given assurance unto
all [men], in that He (God) hath raised him (Jesus the
Christ) from the dead."*—Acts 17:31

These promises of God through Jesus the Christ are prophesied in Psalms:

*"Let the heavens (religion) rejoice, and let the earth (society)
be glad; let the sea (restless society) roar, and the fullness
thereof. Let the field (world) be joyful, and all that [is]
therein: then shall all the trees (the faithful) of the wood
(believer's) rejoice before the LORD: for he comes, for he
comes (spiritual presence) to judge the earth (humanity):
he shall judge the world (society) with righteousness, and
the people with his truth."* —Psalms 96:11–13

Notice that God does all that is prophesied in the above verse under the direction of Jesus the Christ, whom He has appointed.

"Let the sea (restless society) *roar, and the fullness
thereof; the world, and they that dwell therein. Let the
floods* (many people) *clap [their] hands* (rejoice in truth)*:
let the hills* (governments) *be joyful together before the
LORD; for he comes to judge the earth* (society)*: with*

righteousness shall he judge the world (societies) *and the people with equity.*"—Psalms 98:7–9

Behold, the LORD (the Messiah, Jesus *"And Enoch also, the seventh from Adam, prophesied of the Christ) comes with ten thousands (all) of his saints (the faithful, the chosen) to execute judgment upon all, and to convince all that are ungodly among them of all their ungodly deeds which they have ungodly committed, and of all their hard [speeches] which ungodly sinners have spoken against him.*"—Jude 1:14–15

And he (truth) *laid hold on the dragon* (evil), *that old serpent* (evil), *which is the devil* (evil), *and Satan* (evil), *and bound* (restrict evil, one link at a time) *him* (it: evil, Serpent, Dragon, Satan, or Devil) (approximately) *a thousand years.*"—Revelation 20:2

"And when the (approximate) *thousand years are expired, Satan (evil, Serpent, Dragon, or Devil) shall be loosed out of his* (its) *prison* (restriction). *And shall go out to deceive the nations* (all people) *which are in the four quarters of the earth, Gog and Magog* (all desiring to undermine Kingdom conditions) *to gather them together to battle* (to replace righteousness and justice with selfishness): *the number of whom [is] as the sand of the sea* (multitudes).*"—Revelation 20:7–8

"And God shall wipe away all tears from their (those who attain life) eyes; and there shall be no more death, neither sorrow, nor crying, neither shall there be any more pain: for the former (evil) things are passed away."—Revelation 21:4

"And there shall in no wise enter into it (eternal life) *any thing that defiles, neither [whatsoever] works abomination, or [makes] a lie* (who seek evil)*: but they which are written in* (accepted according to) *the Lamb's book of life."*—Revelation 21:27

These prophecies point to restored conditions of the excellence of Eden, which, during restitution in the Kingdom, involves enlightenment of God's love, truth, righteousness, justice, mercy, joy, peace, gentleness, and the like. The process of restitution is a much shorter period of time than the process of people multiplying and filling the earth under the reign of evil of about six thousand years.

Paul, in Romans, tells of salvation coming first to the Church or chosen class:

"For if, when we (as unbelievers) *were enemies, we* (as believers) *were reconciled to God by the death of his Son, much more, being reconciled, we shall be saved* (in the first resurrection) *by his life."*—Romans 5:10

In Colossians, Paul writes:

"And you (as unbelievers)*, that were sometime alienated and enemies in [your] mind by wicked works* (not inspired by a Satan)*, yet now hath he reconciled."*—Colossians 1:21

In Luke, Jesus the Christ quotes Isaiah in regard to God's all-inclusive promise:

"As it is written in the book of the words of Easiest (Isaiah) *the prophet, saying, The voice of one crying in the wilderness, Prepare ye the way of the LORD, make*

his paths (teachings) straight. Every valley (needs of society) shall be filled, and every mountain (oppressive government) *and hill* (evil organizations) *shall be brought low; and the crooked* (doctrinal errors) *shall be made straight, and the rough ways* (erring doctrines) *[shall be] made smooth; and all flesh* (people) <u>*shall see the salvation of God*</u> (in the Kingdom, with opportunity for life).*"—Luke 3: 4–6

The above pictorial language describes our present day as of improvement and change as happening throughout the world. The beginning stage of restitution blessings, of learning righteousness, justice, mercy, love, peace, and so on, is on the increase even as those evil, come under judgment as people look for laws to increase justice and righteousness. Some prophetic scriptures show God's plan as progressive, as first applying to the Christian's chosen during the Gospel Age. and then to the world during the Kingdom, Judgment Day, Times of Restitution, and Millennium..

D. Nadal, in the *Bible Study Monthly* of January/February2000, sums up the wonderful prospect of restitution and resurrection promised the world. He wrote:

> "In his letter to the Church at Colosse, Paul takes the restoration one step further when he explains that just as the Son of God was the one through whom all created things were made, just so is it through him that all things shall 'be reconciled to himself.' In the beginning human rebellion had broken the relationship between God and his creation. Man had been given charge of the physical creation on earth and the consequences of his failure had 'dislocated' the rest of the natural world.

Slowly, the results have become apparent to us all. Jesus, by his life and death, has been given the commission to reverse that situation and restore this earth and all that is on it to the wonderful place God originally intended.

Sometimes scriptures are highlighted that seem to speak of the destruction of humanity and its civilization as though it were the end of all things. Firstly, these parts of the Bible are invariably records of parables and visions, neither of which can be interpreted literally.

It must be apparent that to re-make the human race and its home there will be a need to clean up the mess which sin and evil have brought, just as there must be a scheme to re-educate those who have never learned the ways of God. But that does not cancel the original purpose of God expressed in the words of Psalm 145:5–12:

"<u>The Lord is gracious and compassionate, slow to anger and rich in love. The Lord is good to all: He has compassion on all He has made.</u> All You have made will praise You, O Lord, Your saints will extol You. They will tell of the glory of Your kingdom and speak of Your might, so that all men may know of Your mighty acts and the glorious splendor of Your Kingdom."

To help us understand that "God has compassion on all He has made," an article is quoted from the July/August 2000 issue of the magazine, which also points out the reality of God's compassion. It is titled "Bible Teaching on Hell." The article gives reason that belief in a "hell" is built upon a similar background as belief in a Satan. Its author wrote:

"It is important to realize that the purpose of God is not merely the selection of a few good folk to go to heaven and the relegation of all the remainder to 'conscious misery eternal in duration' as the old dogma has it. It is rather the creation of a race of beings that through the sufferings and discipline of the world as it now is, will come to accept the principles of righteousness. These are the laws of God, of the Universe and of all creation and are reached by Jesus Christ's reign in the Golden Age yet to come (It is a fault of humans usually to place prophecy in the future even though its fulfillment can be all around them). Harmony with man's outer environment and his inner harmony with God bring life in full perfection forever. Conversely, failure willingly to accept this offer of sinless life implies that the one concerned wishes to remain sinful, the penalty for which is death. When it is seen that the cessation of existence is the end of the individual who does not renounce sin after a full opportunity has been given and that this is a basic law in God's creation, the concept of Hell as a place of conscious punishment disappears.

It should not be thought that this Hell of fire and brimstone, of devils and lost souls, of torments unspeakable, had its origin in the words of Jesus and the Apostles. The idea is much older. To understand why this teaching became so prominent as a part of Christian theology, it is necessary to go back to the earlier religious faiths that preceded Christianity. The great civilizations which were before Rome: Sumeria, Egypt, Assyria, Babylonia and Persia, had in their religious systems a very definite belief in the existence of malignant gods who had to be propitiated and appeased if hardship in this life was to be avoided.

The intense belief in devils and all kinds of supernatural wickedness that characterized these religions made it easy to imagine a region where the spirits of the dead would be entirely at the mercy of such malevolent powers. Devotees of such faiths were wedded to the forms and ceremonies, which it was believed would avert this dreaded fate. When the teachings of Jesus and His apostles began to be formulated into creeds and confessions of faith, it was difficult to avoid incorporating these old beliefs as explanatory of Jesus and the apostles' words respecting the penalty of sin. It also made the transition to Christianity easier and the priests of that day realized what a potent weapon the Hell could become in their hands."

As the author mentions, the ideas of a hell, devils, lost souls, and torments are much older than Jesus the Christ and the apostles. The beliefs originated in other cultures and carried over into some of the Jewish sects. Likewise, as referred to before in this book, Jesus apparently followed the practice of speaking of evil as a persona, referring to it as Satan or demons or a Devil, since the phenomenon had become part of Jewish custom. For him to attempt to clarify its symbolic nature would bring controversy and distraction from his message of the coming salvation. However, at appropriate times he did emphasize that evil comes from the heart of man, not from an outer evil source.

In Matthew, as mentioned before, Jesus said:

> "For *out of the heart proceed evil thoughts*, murders, adulteries, fornications, thefts, false witness, blasphemies."—Matthew 15:19

And: "*A good man out of the good treasure of his heart brings forth that which is good; and an evil man out of the evil treasure of his heart brings forth that which is evil: for of the abundance of the heart his mouth speaks.*"—
Luke 6:45

These statements of Jesus provide a clearer perspective of the source of evil compared to scriptures using symbolic names for evil or an evil spirit being as the source of evil. This has been confusing to Christians, making it difficult to improve on an erring belief system usually formed in childhood. Years of hearing and reading of a Satan or Devil and verification of his existence by reputable and educated religious leaders are not easily cast aside. This is admitted to by Tom Rademacher; a local newspaper writer of *The Grand Rapids Press*. He did not care to view a movie that treats the Devil in a lighthearted manner and stated:

> "I want to believe that the Prince of Darkness is a figment of some Middle Ages guy's imagination. That he's but a concept, a moral yardstick at most. But I can't. It's the way I was raised, the faith in which I was nurtured. —My own, the Roman Catholic Church, doesn't regard the devil as some 'phantasm at a holdover from scary bedtime stories,' but the real deal. —It's a lot easier on the psyche, of course, to dismiss the devil as a representation of evil, rather than a real catalyst. We explain away the atrocities of this world as being the result of 'fate' or 'destiny.' It's a lot more comforting than closing our eyes to conjure up the image of a real demon who might effect earth's reins."

Yes, "fate" or "destiny" is often used to cover bad decisions and evil acts of humans, but Tom Rademacher's reasoning helps us answer the question of why the average believer does not question traditional doctrine of long-established institutions. Another part of the answer would be that it is not prudent to question centuries-old teachings if one wishes to remain a member of a religious group. Also, to research questions for answers takes time, effort, and exceptional curiosity, for which the average believer has little desire. It is usually more acceptable and less upsetting to follow the path others have created, though it may be confusing because of limited records from past centuries compared to today, but Christians voicing anger, opposition, condemnation, ridicule, and even threats at those who have reason to see doctrine as erring or unacceptable should not blame an evil spirit being called Satan for their anger or evil thoughts.

We live in a day of unending questions that call for and demand reasonable answers, a persistent challenge to present belief systems. Making a comprehensive investigation of available religious resources invites change to one's belief system about the existence of an evil spirit being called Satan and other religious beliefs. Attempting to explain this reality can easily cause turbulence in relationships with those who fear change. But, just as political leadership and civil rights came under intense scrutiny and opposition during the 1960s when many people demanded a political change in attitude towards social needs and refused to obediently accept the bad decisions of politicians, so public questioning of religious beliefs is more common today, especially due to the sex scandals and other evils exposed in the Roman Catholic and some Protestant religious systems. The changes emerging on this earth, such as the fast travel and increasing knowledge the prophet Daniel prophesied of are major indications that we live in the beginning centuries of the restitution blessings of Jesus the Christ's Kingdom:

"But thou, O Daniel, shut up the words, and seal the book, [even] to the time of the end: many shall run to and fro, and knowledge shall be increased."—Daniel 12: 4

An important point of Daniel's prophecy is that he does not write of "the end of time" but of "the time of the end," which is a reference to the end of the reign of evil. God has planned for the days when truth overcomes lies, while righteousness and justice replaces wickedness. Today, increasing knowledge leads to change in every facet of education, medicine, social, commercial, religion, and politics, change that often threatens some people's livelihood or religious beliefs, which is a main reason opposition to change develops and efforts are made to retain present conditions. This is fundamental to understanding why it is taking decades before the blessings of restitution are recognized. The apostle Peter prophesied of change in the book of Acts:

"Whom (Jesus the Christ) the heaven (religion) must receive until the times of restitution of all things, which God hath spoken by the mouth of all his holy prophets since the world began."—Acts 3:21

John's prophecy in Revelation then comes to fruition, but not without resistance from the minds of those who benefit from maintaining things as they are. Believe it or not, some people do not want change if it goes against their income or comfort even if the change will benefit others:

"And I heard a great voice (religious acknowledgment) out of heaven (religion) saying, behold, the tabernacle (family) of God [is] with men, and He (spirit of God through Jesus the Christ) will dwell with them, and they shall be His people, and God Himself shall be with them, [and be] their God."—Revelation 21:3

We can see basic evidence that we are living in the day of increasing knowledge and fast travel that Daniel prophesied of. The *Parade* magazine of March 19, 2000, published a report by the Cato Institute of Washington, DC, which speaks of that reality:

> "The past century (since 1900) change has literally altered lives in this country with greatly improved living conditions and in the process has changed the livelihood of many. New job opportunities have developed along with improved medical aid and financial security that is gradually affecting the whole world.
>
> Toward the end of the twentieth century strong efforts were being made by the USA and other leading nations to communicate and open trade instead of going to war over differences, illustrating the advantage of cooperation and its many benefits. Daily changes have become a part of life. A few changes that have come about in the USA since 1900 are:
>
> Accidental deaths have dropped by 61% despite all the additional cars and airplanes and the millions of people using them.
>
> Manufacturing wages are four times higher.
>
> Household assets are seven times greater.
>
> The workweek is 30% shorter.
>
> Four times as many adults are getting their high school degrees.

Six times as many women have Bachelor's degrees.

The air we breathe is 97% cleaner.

Nearly all American homes (97%) have telephones, electricity and a flush toilet.

More than 70% of Americans have at least one automobile, a VCR, a microwave oven, air conditioning, cable TV, a washer and dryer—all things that many of us tend to take for granted."

Though we complain about the pressures of modern life, we're actually spending twice as much time in leisure activities as our forebears did in 1900.

These changes are just a beginning for the world as it progresses into the Millennium, evidence that the Kingdom of God is developing upon earth. In another article, in *U.S. News & World Report* (January 14, 2002), author Susan J. Blumenthal, M.D., said:

"Americans will live 30 years longer, on average, than they did a century ago. This is due largely to the triumph of public-health interventions: sanitation, health education, improved hygiene and nutrition, clean water and air, measures to reduce infant and maternal mortality, safety regulations, and increased access to health-care. Today, increased attentions in preventing mortal injuries from accidents are improving, along with reducing risk in chronic diseases. Perhaps more than any miracle drug that could be discovered, it is developing and implementing the will in people to reduce health-damaging behaviors and eliminate environmental hazards. This could decrease the 2 million deaths that occur annually in the United States by one half as well as cut healthcare costs. ... Public-health interventions are already being applied to violence, suicide, and accidental injuries. A similar approach is critical for eliminating health disparities due to race, ethnicity, and gender. And public health must address mental illness, diseases that affect 1 out of 5 Americans each year. ... Last year, Americans celebrated scientific discoveries like mapping of the human genome, holding out hope of dramatic new therapies for some diseases."

The Labor paper *UAW Solidarity* of January 2002 is another voice reflecting transition of the Gospel Age to the age of restitution blessings. The paper quotes the words of Franklin Delano Roosevelt:

> The test of our progress is not whether we add more to the abundance of those who have much; it is whether we provide enough for those who have too little.

The article also quotes Irving Bluestone, former vice-president of the International UAW, with the credo of the labor movement:

> "The persistent advancement of individual freedom and social justice everywhere, and the unrelenting struggle against despotism and oppression in all its forms.
>
> The fulfillment of the good life in a compassionate society, secure in employment and decent income, with the unfettered opportunity to exercise the full rights of citizenship.

The commitment to eliminate poverty, hunger and disease, for they embitter and crush the human spirit.

The insistence on equality of opportunity, for bigotry deforms life and cages the soul.

The encouragement of intellectual, spiritual and cultural growth, for ignorance debases life and makes it barren.

The faith to achieve a world at peace with itself, in which bread and roses replace the weapons of war."

Dr. Blumenthal's message, the Cato Institute's conclusion, President Roosevelt's and Irving Bluestone's statements are telling us that knowledge not only brings increasing life span, but is also advancing the quality of life for many people on this earth. We look at progress and change mainly in the USA because it has been founded upon liberty and justice for all. Even then, it has required centuries for new generations to make the changes. The increase of knowledge has exploded this past century and raised opportunities of wealth, improving living conditions, and civil rights. The increase of knowledge, in both religious and secular quarters, indicates that God's purpose through Jesus Christ is bearing fruit through an advancing worldwide respect for human and animal rights. The improving conditions prompted by growing knowledge increases as "the great time of trouble"—a mixture of turmoil, revolution, and reform—are major factors that sweep away longstanding fear, ignorance, suspicion, hatred, superstition, and the like.

The apostle Paul wrote in 1 Thessalonians:

"For when they shall say, peace and safety; then sudden destruction comes upon them, as travail upon a woman with child; and they shall not escape."—1 Thessalonians 5:3

Today, there is an overwhelming demand for peace and safety. Small or civil conflicts and recessions rise up as birth pangs, leaving the world a little smaller and smarter with each one. As mentioned before, demands are increasing to oppose evil in its numerous facets. Often in the process administrations and governments fall or change as people die and destruction takes place; in addition, knowledge increases, and improvements continue. And as knowledge increases, people are learning, evil is addressed, conditions continue to improve, nations learn that war is not the answer, and peace is increasingly demanded worldwide. At the present time, terrorism is a major problem. At times, religious or political leaders, upon attaining power, lead people in hatred and violence towards others to impose their social or religious demands. Ironically, many people support efforts with a conservative label and unwittingly oppose the type action Jesus the Christ said to use, such as to give all you have to the poor and to love your neighbor as yourself.

In contrast, some organizations, through democratic means, join together to oppose harmful or evil policies that claim to support, but really oppose, liberty, rights, and opportunity. The spirit of freedom and justice may appear to fail at times in areas of the world as tyranny achieves temporary power, but such power is limited, for eventually liberty, righteousness, and justice will envelop all nations. The "spirit of the Lord," in Bible prophecy, is descriptive of the attitude and achievement of increasing numbers of people raising the standards of truth, justice, and righteousness for all, which gradually leads nations to overcome corrupt or evil conditions. The prophecies of Joel appear to be past such as the Lord's great army and many terrible things that were to happen. Prophecies were fulfilled during the Gospel Age, the day of the Lord's punishment was strong in the twentieth century.

The apostle Peter's statement in Acts 2:16 implies it was beginning in his day when he said: the prophet Joel prophesied this. Thus, its climax seemed to be apparent in the twentieth century when the growth and fear of communism, with its conquering atheistic power, spread over the earth as an unstoppable great army, as Joel said:

> *"And the LORD shall utter his voice before his army: for his camp [is] very great: for [he is] strong that executes his word: for the day of the LORD [is] great and very terrible; and who can abide it?* ---Joel 2:11

The prophet Zechariah told Zerubbabel, governor of Judah:

> *"Then he answered and spoke unto me, saying, This [is] the word of the LORD unto Zerubbabel, saying, not by might, nor by power, but by my spirit, said the LORD of hosts."*—Zechariah 4:6

Thus, God, through His spirit of righteousness, justice, and truth, is pouring out upon the world restitution blessings even as people increasingly apply God's spirit of truth, righteousness, and justice. It is His spirit that leads people up the highway of holiness that creates the Kingdom of Jesus the Christ, which is being seen in the hearts of many people today as major efforts in many countries rise up to help those in need. The prophet Isaiah prophesied God would allow the spirit of evil, lust, greed, envy, and jealousy to motivate the hearts of many people even into the time of Judgment or unveiling of His Kingdom. Thus, the spirit of evil is heavily prevalent during the Gospel Age, while fading during transition from the Gospel Age into the Kingdom of

Jesus the Christ. The knowledge of the Lord is growing upon earth; the spirit of love, righteousness, justice, and mercy are major motivating forces in country after country, especially in North America, which often illustrates to the rest of the world the virtues of helping one another.

> *"The LORD hath mingled a perverse spirit in the midst thereof (in religion, politics, social or commerce): and they have caused Egypt (symbol of the world) to err in every work thereof, as a drunken [man] staggers in his vomit."*—Isaiah 19:14

Thus, the spirit of God overrules the spirit of evil as people and nations move two steps forward and often one step backward as change is tested, not realizing it is the will of God in righteousness, justice, truth, and love as Isaiah prophesied:

> *"With my soul have I desired thee in the night; yea, with my spirit within me will I seek thee early: for when Thy judgments [are] in the earth, the inhabitants of the world will learn righteousness."*—Isaiah 26:9

> *"So shall they fear* (revere) *the name of the LORD from the west, and his glory from the rising of the sun (the East, spiritual presence). When the enemy* (evil of Atheistic Communism) *shall come in like a flood, the Spirit of the LORD shall lift up a standard* (truth, righteousness, and justice) *against him* (evil, Satan, Devil, Serpent, or Dragon)*."*—Isaiah 59:19

Ezekiel prophesied of Israel leading the world in favor and restoration to God:

> *"And I will give them one heart, and I will put a new spirit within you* (Israel)*; and I will take the stony heart*

out of their (Israel's) *flesh, and will give them* (Israel) *an heart of flesh."*—Ezekiel 11:19'

It is taking time, but it is being fulfilled.

The prophet Joel wrote:

"And it shall come to pass afterward, [that] I <u>will pour out my spirit upon all flesh</u>; and your sons and your daughters shall prophesy, your old men shall dream dreams, your young men shall see visions."—Joel 2:28

This began with the apostles on the day of Pentecost. Today, it looks like the worst of the LORD'S wrath is in the past, and as Peter said in Acts 2:16, the Lord's spirit is affecting many lives.

Zechariah prophesied:

"And it shall come to pass in that day, said the LORD of hosts, [that] I will cut off the names of the idols out of the land, and they shall no more be remembered (desired): *and also I will cause the* (false) *prophets and the unclean* (evil) *spirit to pass out of the land* (in the time of restitution or the Kingdom)."*—Zechariah 13:2

Jesus said:

"But if I cast out devils (evil, Satan, Serpent, or Dragon) by the Spirit of God, then the Kingdom of God is come unto you."—Matthew 12:28

Paul wrote:

> *"For if ye live after the flesh, ye shall die: but if ye through the Spirit do mortify* (humble) *the deeds of the body, ye shall live."*—Romans 8:13

This was written to the Church, but it applies to all mankind.

> *"And then shall that wicked* (evil, Satan, Devil, Serpent, or Dragon) *be revealed, whom the LORD shall consume with the spirit of his mouth* (truth), *and shall destroy with the brightness of his coming* (spiritual presence)." —2 Thessalonians 2:8

Then there's the apostle John's final encouragement, which is rising in many countries:

> *"And the Spirit and the bride* (the Church or the chosen during the Lord's presence) *say, come. And let him* (the repentant) *that hears say, come. And let him that is thirsty* (for truth, righteousness, and justice) *come. And whosoever will, let him take the water* (truth*) of life freely."*—Revelation 22:17

The above prophecies are not referring to a literal "spirit being" initiating thought or action, but refers to the spirit of the Lord, a righteous, just, merciful spirit, which is the attitude and desire of people desiring to practice the principles of God as exemplified and taught by Jesus the Christ and the apostles. The result or product of the spirit of God brings fruitage in harmony with the desires, expectations, and faith of the individual. It is the spirit of righteousness, justice, truth, mercy, and love as manifested by Jesus the Christ, the apostles, and the prophets in doing the will of God.

The spirit of God was the guide of all the writers of the Bible, and we; to understand the Word of God, are to read it in that same spirit of righteousness, justice, love, mercy, etc., with thankful attitude and a willingness to learn and trust with childlike obedience from the heart. These qualities do not imply gullibility or naiveté but an earnest willingness to search Scripture to confirm that what is understood is of the Lord. As the apostle Paul wrote:

> *"Study to show thyself approved unto God, a workman that need not to be ashamed, rightly dividing the word of truth."*—2 Timothy 2:15

We may consider ourselves fairly qualified, but it is not always easy to recognize differing ideas if our mind operates under preconditioned concepts. In other words, what someone says or writes is to be compared to Scripture in the Lord's spirit to determine harmony and reason and if it is in harmony with the principles and love of God. We are to do as Paul wrote, even though it brings change to what was learned in childhood, in order to manifest the spirit of truth our Savior exemplified. Scriptures relating to developing and maintaining a truthful, just, and righteous spirit benefited Christians all during the Gospel Age and, it is my understanding, also guides the repentant during our Lord's Kingdom.

> *"But if the Spirit of Him that raised up Jesus from the dead dwell in you, He that raised up Christ from the dead shall also quicken your mortal bodies by His Spirit that dwells in you."*—Romans 8:11

> *"And such were some of you: but ye are washed (made clean), but ye are sanctified (approved), but ye are justified (made righteous) in the name of the Lord Jesus, and by the Spirit of our God."* —1 Corinthians 6:11

"Who hath also sealed us, and given the earnest of the Spirit in our hearts." —2 Corinthians 1:22

"If we live in the Spirit, let us also walk in the Spirit."— Galatians 5:25

"For the fruit of the Spirit [is] in all goodness and righteousness and truth." —Ephesians 5:9

"Seeing ye have purified your souls (thoughts or minds) in obeying the truth through the Spirit unto unfeigned love of the brethren, [see that ye] love one another with a pure heart fervently (all Christians)."—1 Peter 1:22

"Hereby know ye the Spirit of God: Every spirit that confesses Jesus Christ is come in the flesh is of God." —1 John 4:2

"And he carried me away in the spirit to a great and high mountain (Kingdom of God), and showed me (in a vision) that great city (the Church, body of Christ, first-fruits, little flock, the faithful, saints), the holy Jerusalem (righteous and just government of God), descending out of heaven (truth in religion) from God." —Revelation 21:10

As many of us understand, the spirit of God that brings change is the manifestation of love, patience, truth, care, peace, mercy, and so forth in the hearts of people who hear. It is the spirit that Jesus displayed and that his followers displayed, of prayer, knowledge, and good works. This spirit is to eventually be solidly reflected throughout society, becoming evident through desire and subsequent action of people to follow righteousness and justice. This spirit increases in various ways through physical, mental, and moral efforts to raise living standards for everyone as a result of enlightenment by God's Word.

To Christians waiting and watching for the Lord's return (spiritual presence), the progressive improvements in and of society as a whole are prophetic signs that the Kingdom of God is materializing in troublesome spasms, with an increase of the spirit that Jesus the Christ manifested, which motivates the hearts of many people upon earth The spirit of the Lord grows as people appreciate and apply the principles of righteousness, justice, mercy, and so on. It is many small beginnings that build into numerous organizations worldwide, both religious and secular, that endeavor to operate and serve others in a manner that benefits all those in need, and it is applied in a spirit of trust, truth, righteousness, respect, love, and hope with physical, financial, and medical aid.

This interpretation does not mean trouble or even violence is past. The evils of civil strife, crime, and greed will occur in spasms for quite some time in and between societies, but restitution blessings are increasingly being seen by the quality of care and the love of people for one another, which attracts many up the highway of holiness. Thus, God's Kingdom grows, to eventually lead to eternal life. Through increasing knowledge of what is good and advantageous for others and self, evil will gradually be overcome in all its deceitfulness and destructiveness. This progress over time raises the realization that God's Kingdom is developing through the spirit of Jesus the Christ as material, spiritual, and physical blessings continue to increase over the centuries.

As mentioned before, in answer to his disciples' question as to what would be the sign of his (spiritual) presence, Jesus said;

"For as the lightning (light) comes out of the east, and shines even unto the west; so shall also the coming (spiritual presence) of the Son of man be."—Matthew 24:27

This is closely associated with the statement Jesus made as recorded in Luke:]

"Neither shall they say, Lo here! or lo there! for behold, the Kingdom of God is within you."—Luke 17:21

Jesus was saying that the Kingdom of God would be revealed in all its glory, in gradual fashion, through the hearts and minds of men and women. The Prophet Jeremiah spoke of the coming day when:

...they shall teach no more every man his neighbor, and every man his brother, saying, Know the LORD: for they shall all know Me, from the least of them unto the greatest of them, said the LORD: for I will forgive their iniquity, and I will remember their sin no more. "—Jeremiah 31:34

This does not apply only to the nation of Israel, but also applies to all people desiring peace, truth, and righteousness in all nations upon earth. Many of us remember the apostle Paul provided an abbreviated description of the Kingdom of God upon earth in 1 Corinthians:

"For as in Adam all die, even so in Christ shall all be made alive, but everyman in his own order: Christ the first-fruits (the faithful of the Gospel Age); afterward they (the world) that are Christ's at his coming (spiritual presence). Then [comes] the end (end of thousand years), when he shall have delivered up the kingdom to God, even the Father; when he (his spiritual presence) shall

have put down all rule and all authority and power.
For he (his spirit) must reign, till he hath put all enemies
under his feet. The last enemy [that] shall be destroyed [is]
death (near the end of his Kingdom)." —1 Corinthians
15:22–26

Paul's statement tells us that God's rule, authority and power
through His spirit in Jesus the Christ applies to conditions on
earth. The enemies consist not only of mental and physical
illnesses, but all evil conceived in the minds of men, with the
most-feared enemy of mankind; death inherited from Adam.
As evil (*Satan, Devil, Serpent, or Dragon*) in all its subtle
forms is gradually overcome or eliminated, the memory of the
destructiveness of evil and its terrible consequences will remain
in the memory of all attaining life. The prophecy of Daniel
convincingly points to the change that affects the world:

"And at that time shall Michael stand up (increasing
spirit of liberty, truth, justice, and righteousness, etc.),
the great prince (of truth, righteousness, and justice)
which stands for the children of thy people: and there shall
be a time of trouble (truth, righteousness, and justice
combating evil), *such as never was since there was a*
nation [even] to that same time: and at that time thy
people (the repentant and faithful) *shall be delivered,*
every one that shall be found (who live under the just
and righteous conditions according to principles our
Lord commanded) *written in the book* (God's Word
or the Bible)."*—Daniel 12:1

Christians recognize the name Michael as referring to Jesus the
Christ. His standing up implies his return (spiritual presence),
which is seen in the worldwide changes or commencement of
restitution blessings and improvement of living conditions and
increasing length of life of mankind. The hearts of many people

are revealing that God's spirit of justice and righteousness, mercy, love, compassion, and so forth is escalating through aid, care, and assistance when conflicts, disasters, or troubles occur.

People living today, as compared to past centuries, are beneficiaries of the greatest increase of knowledge and aid ever seen or imagined; this is the day that increases in methods and means for willing hearts to avoid evil while also allowing opportunities to display the life-enhancing qualities of mercy, justice, love, and righteousness. As mentioned, these characteristics are increasingly seen when natural or man-made disasters occur requiring aid and volunteer assistance.

Secular and religious organizations, government agencies, and the media publicly encourage parents in many countries to be role models to their children by being responsible and a blessing to others, thus demonstrating necessary ethics and morals to live by.

Nations are gradually learning to negotiate with expectations of attaining prosperity and peace. Television brings instant news of ethnic and religious differences to be recognized and addressed, as leaders encourage people to learn to respect and accept one another. The Internet provides ample opportunity for people around the world to exchange information across borders; this increasingly aids in promotion of peace and prosperity. Remote cameras are a major invention that helps provide security and control in regard to those who persist in doing evil because, although change is all around, some people will persist in wickedness.

As the roots of the Kingdom of Jesus the Christ spread throughout the earth, due mainly to the great increase of knowledge, relief and opportunity will gradually replace harmful conditions. Again, I repeat, the increasing efforts in the Lord's spirit by concerned people is to encourage justice, righteousness, and liberty that are to overcome all forms of evil *(Satan, Devil, Dragon, or Serpent)* that have afflicted mankind since Adam and Eve. It is during increasing restitution that people have opportunity to go up the highway of holiness, and this may be where those in the spirit of the Lord have the obligation that the Prophet Ezekiel prophesied of, when he said:

> *"When I say unto the wicked, You shall surely die; and you give him not warning, nor speak to warn the wicked from his wicked way, to save his life; the same wicked [man] shall die in his iniquity; but his blood will I require at your hand. Yet if thou warn the wicked, and he turn not from his wickedness, nor from his wicked way, he shall die in his iniquity; but thou hast delivered thy soul.*
> —Ezekiel 3:18,19

Thus, the spiritual, physical turmoil and struggle between good and evil in and among nations is seen as "the Battle of Armageddon" in which the binding of evil, *(Satan, Devil, Serpent, and Dragon)* is the major factor. As mentioned before, the binding of Satan, *(Dragon, Serpent, Dragon, or evil)* is accomplished a link at a time, the links composed of truth, righteousness, justice, love, mercy, etc.

The Battle of Armageddon

The Battle of Armageddon is the battle of righteousness versus evil and produces fiery tribulation at times that affects the whole known world. Peloubet's *Bible Dictionary* renders a definition of Armageddon as the hill or city of Megiddo, the scene of the struggle between good and evil as suggested by the critical conflicts on that battlefield, the Plain of Esdraelon. It tells us the plain was famous for two great victories—that of Barak over the Canaanites and that of Gideon over the Midianites—and for two great disasters—the deaths of Saul and Josiah. Hence, it signifies in Revelation a place of great slaughter, a prophetic scene of final retribution upon all who continue in wickedness:

> *"And he gathered them together into a place called in the Hebrew tongue Armageddon."*—Revelation 16:16

The "place" mentioned by John well applies to a developing condition in which the desire to overcome wickedness rises in the hearts of many people looking for righteousness and justice, which, in a relatively short time (a few centuries) binds the destructiveness of evil still prevalent in society. The apostle

Peter gives an overall description of it as a great time of trouble, a time in which people, both individuals and organizations, institutions, religious systems and nations, promote righteousness and justice and steadily lead people into abandoning the will to do evil and to become a part in a world without end of love, respect, honesty, trust, peace, joy and so forth, far removed over time from the previous reign of evil, Satan, Devil, Serpent, and Dragon.

The following prophesies are quoted to remind the reader of the importance of this transitional time we see about us today. In 2 Peter we read:

> *"But, beloved, be not ignorant of this one thing, that one day [is] with the LORD* <u>*as*</u> *a thousand years, and a thousand years* <u>*as*</u> *one day. The LORD is not slack concerning his promise, as some men count slackness; but is longsuffering to us-ward, not willing that any should perish, but that all should come to repentance. But the day* (thousand years) *of the LORD will come as a thief* (the world not being aware) *in the night (time of ignorance and evil); in the which the heavens* (evil in religion) *shall pass away with a great noise* (intense trouble), *and the elements* (erring doctrines, rules, rituals, creeds, and images) *shall melt with fervent heat* (controversy), *the earth* (evil society) *also and the works* (evil-doing) *that are therein shall be burned up* (destroyed). *[Seeing] then [that]* <u>*all these things shall be dissolved,*</u> *what manner [of persons]* <u>*ought ye to be in [all] holy conversation and*</u> <u>*godliness*</u> (righteousness, justice, mercy, and love). *Looking for and hasting unto the coming of the day of God, wherein the heavens* (religious organizations) *being on fire* (controversy, spiritual cleansing) *shall be dissolved, and the elements* (evil doctrines, rituals, creeds, and customs) *shall melt with fervent heat* (opposition and

controversy). *Nevertheless we, according to his promise, look for new heavens* (truth in religion) *and a new earth* (just society), *wherein dwells righteousness.*"—2 Peter 3:8–13

The prophet Zephaniah prophesied of these days:

"Therefore wait ye upon Me, said the LORD, until the day that I rise up to the prey: for My determination [is] to gather the nations, that I may assemble the kingdoms, to pour upon them Mine indignation, [even] all My fierce anger: for all the earth (societies) shall be devoured (consumed) with the fire (passion) of my jealousy. For then will I turn to the people a pure language (spirit and truth in Jesus the Christ), that they may all call upon the name of the LORD, to serve him with one consent (all in accord in Jesus)." —Zephaniah 3:8–9

We are to remember that the change from under the rule of evil *(Satan, Devil, Serpent, or Dragon)* to the time when the knowledge of the Lord covers the earth requires hundreds of years. Restitution blessings that are physical, spiritual, mental, just, righteous, and truthful grow to encircle the earth amidst trouble and destruction that bring change from numerous evil customs and beliefs. This requires centuries, during which all societies become involved as God's spirit of love, justice, righteousness, and mercy triumphs over evil *(Satan, Devil, Serpent or Dragon)* the end result being the spirit of the Lord reflected from the heart of every willing person attaining life upon earth.

It requires centuries for all the willing to learn of the Lord due to the many errant beliefs that exist and the time it takes for people to learn, the billions of people alive, and the billions that come forth from the grave, generation after generation, all requiring time to learn righteousness and justice under the rule of our Lord's government. We are to remember that, as justice and righteousness grows to cover the earth, there will be people exhibiting a hardness of heart, willingly ignoring the opportunity to learn, believe, and improve their character. Such people become reprobates, unwilling to learn or change and are to die the second death as Isaiah prophesied:

> *"There shall be no more thence an infant of days, nor an old man that hath not filled his days: for the child shall die an hundred years old; but the sinner [being] an hundred years old shall be accursed."*—Isaiah 65:20

The following scriptures also point to this day of the Lord:

> *"For he comes* (spiritual presence), *for he comes to judge the earth: he shall judge the world with righteousness, and the people with his truth."*—Psalms 96:13

> *"With my soul have I desired thee in the night* (times of ignorance and evil)*; yea, with my spirit within me will I seek thee early: for when thy judgments* (truth, righteousness, and justice) *are in the earth, the inhabitants of the world will learn righteousness.* <u>*Let favor be shown to the wicked, yet will he not learn righteousness:* *in the land of uprightness will he deal* unjustly, and will not behold the majesty of the LORD.</u>"—Isaiah 26:9–10

> *"For the earth shall be filled with the knowledge of the glory of the LORD, as the waters cover the sea."*—Habakkuk 2:14

As conditions of liberty, righteousness and justice become more common throughout the world, most people are recognizing, expecting, and demanding in greater unity that leaders in public office, religious organizations, and private industry conduct their responsibilities in a righteous, just, and equitable manner. It is not uncommon today to see efforts to improve substandard conditions because an informed public, in the spirit of justice, necessity, and fairness, demands it. People in most nations are learning and becoming aware of the benefits of peace, justice, love, mercy, truth, righteousness, and kindness in commerce, politics, religion, and social activities; the spirit of benevolence and loving generosity is growing worldwide in increasing measure similar to what was practiced in the early Christian Church, when Christians brought what they owned to share with each other, as told in the book of Acts:

> *"And the multitude of them that believed were of one heart and of one soul: neither said any [of them] that ought of the things which he possessed was his own; but they had all things common. And with great power gave the apostles witness of the resurrection of the Lord Jesus: and great grace was upon them all. Neither was there any among them that lacked: for as many as were possessors of lands or houses sold them, and brought the prices of the things that were sold, And laid [them] down at the apostles' feet: and distribution was made unto every man according as he had need."*—Acts 4:32–35

That early effort failed because the evils of greed, jealousy, fear, and distrust resurfaced, aborting the spirit of love, zeal, trust, and cooperation existing between givers and receivers. It speaks of socialism, the very effort that many of today's politicians and some public commentators speak against. If our mind is against helping our neighbor, we will have to review our attitude or we will not have life.

The account tells how one couple failed because of deceitfulness, doubt, and greed destroyed the refreshing, generous spirit of sharing all things cheerfully. It was a spiritual venture of loving generosity and trust in one another, a liberal and caring spirit of the Lord, that offered a glimpse of the life-enhancing attitude people are to develop in the Kingdom of Jesus the Christ. This is seen in the expectation and desire today that is leading to primary conditions that Christians have long requested when they quoted the Lord's Prayer:

> *"Thy Kingdom come, Thy will be done on earth as it is in heaven."* —Matthew 6:10

Today, countless efforts are being made in the spirit of love, mercy, kindness, justice, and liberty to alleviate suffering and hunger. Such qualities of the spirit are strong indications that the dark clouds of ignorance and evil are being dispersed, as Jesus said in Luke:

> *"The kingdom of God comes not with observation: Neither shall they say, Lo here! Or lo there! For behold, the kingdom of God is within you."*—Luke 17:20–21

The tremendous political, physical, and financial changes in Africa, South America, Asia, and the Middle East are all evidence of increasing restitution blessings. While the evil acted upon from the hearts of some people is brought to public attention. It requires decades for nations to learn war is not the answer. Today, some "Christians" in fear and lack of faith in God's plan continue to support military force as the answer rather than negotiations to settle differences, but increasing knowledge is helping many people to review their values regarding force. Societies expect fairness, righteousness, justice, and mercy to be practiced in all criminal and social situations. The prophet Isaiah told of the end of wars:

"And he shall judge among the nations, and shall rebuke many people: and they shall beat their swords into plowshares, and their spears into pruning hooks: nation shall not lift up sword against nation, neither shall they learn war any more."—Isaiah 2:4

As the world develops into the Kingdom of God through the increase of the Lord's spirit in the hearts of people, we see religious and secular institutions generously giving to the needy, even as erring doctrines as traditional heaven or hell destinations for an immortal soul, the earth destroyed by literal fire, the unsaved lost forever, Jesus the Christ's second coming to be in the flesh, and the necessity to believe in a Triune God in order to have salvation, face questions that bring change as prophesied in both the Old and New Testaments.

The twentieth century brought a crescendo of conflict and trouble after centuries of building up to it. After World War I mistakes were made. As in the past: the winners demanded the losers be punished, which resulted in disaster for all. After World War II, compassion and care was provided through the Marshal Plan to Allies and previous foes, which in turn benefited all nations. Also, the Great Depression of the '30s illustrated the need of government oversight and help in providing financial direction and physical assistance to its citizens and businesses.

Today, there are numerous accounts of government and private aid in response to disasters or need on every continent along with increasing worldwide observance of human rights. This brings attention to nations that lack laws and the need to help those in need for the common good. Yes, there are still too many people practicing deceit, lying, and greed, but the objective of Jesus the Christ's Kingdom is to correct the long-depraved conditions of evil through the spirit of righteousness, justice, love, compassion, mercy, truth, and honesty in the hearts of people as Jesus the Christ encouraged. It is these growing characteristics that gradually overcome the evils of greed, hate, lust, and selfishness and their effects. Thus, the spirit of God is shining more and more unto that "perfect day," as we read in Proverbs:

> *"But the path of the just [is] as the shining light, that shines more and more unto the perfect day* (God's Kingdom on Earth).*"*—Proverbs 4:18

Isaiah wrote of this dawning day, saying:

> *"And he* (spiritual presence of Jesus the Christ) *shall judge among the nations, and shall rebuke many people: and they shall beat their swords into plowshares, and their spears into pruning-hooks: nation shall not lift up sword against nation, neither shall they learn war any more."*—Isaiah 2:4

The prophet Micah echoes Isaiah:

> *"And he (Jesus the Christ's return or presence) shall judge among many people, and rebuke strong nations afar off; and they shall beat their swords into plowshares, and their spears into pruning-hooks:* <u>*nation shall not lift up a sword against nation, neither shall they learn war any more.*</u>*"*—Micah 4:3

The changes are inevitable; every prophet has promised the *Messiah (Jesus the Christ's Kingdom)* would appear in the form of the blessings of God, wherein dwells righteousness, justice, love, compassion, mercy, and peace. As Peter said:

"Yea, and all the prophets from Samuel and those that follow after, as many as have spoken, have likewise foretold of these days."—Acts 3:24

Many Bible prophecies point to the new day. The last one is in Revelation:

"And God (through His spirit) shall wipe away all tears from their eyes; and there shall be no more death, neither sorrow, nor crying, neither shall there be any more pain: for the former things are passed away."—Revelation 21:4

As the world moves through the new millennium, the increasing progress in human relations and the sharing of wealth, love, trust, mercy, encouragement, and peace is to be reflected in due time from every person attaining life. As mentioned before, the improving conditions of restitution will soon be recognized and acclaimed throughout the world. John, in the book of Revelation, speaks of this enlightening day:

"And, behold, I come quickly; and my reward [is] with me, to give every man according as his work shall be."— Revelation 22:12

Another scripture of Revelation expresses a similar message: *"And the seventh angel (last message) sounded; and there were great voices in heaven (truth in religion), saying, the kingdoms (governments) of this world are become (gradually) [the kingdoms] of our LORD, and of his Christ; and He shall reign for ever and ever."* —Revelation 11:15

Some people may find it extremely difficult to abandon traditional teachings of a Satan, Devil, Serpent, or Dragon hovering about, ready to cause a person to do evil. But we are living in the day of enlightenment, and it is only right and just to investigate traditions and doctrine that have been built upon fear and ideas out of harmony with God's objective of peace on earth and goodwill to men. From historical records we can see that Bible prophecies and their fulfillment have often been overlooked, distorted, or misapplied.

In hindsight, with increased understanding of prophetic fulfillment, there are watchmen on the wall who recognize that God's objective upon earth through Jesus the Christ is progressing as planned so that His Kingdom is rising upon the ashes of evil in all its forms, through truth, righteousness, justice, mercy, etc. Some Christians see only troublesome times, but some see the rainbow of the Kingdom even as the clouds of trouble between nations slowly dissipate as nations struggle with internal social problems requiring change.

The sunshine of hope is the beginning of the process that leads the hearts of people to salvation and life eternal through the love of God in Jesus the Christ. Numerous secular and religious organizations, unwarily, are participating in bringing about the Kingdom of God. The organizations are promoting and encouraging righteousness, justice, mercy, respect, kindness, and so forth. Thus, they water the mustard seed (the good news) that started with our Lord and that has grown into a giant tree under which a great mixture of religious and secular organizations find shelter.

While many claim Jesus the Christ as their head, the secular and some religious organizations do not, but they do teach peace, love, mercy, and righteousness and thus share in the symbolic tree that provides shade to all the willing who seek peace and justice. The Kingdom of God does not appear in one hour, one day, one year, or one century; its roots, being the Church or chosen, having developed during the Gospel Age, and having heard the calling out for his name, chosen as faithful, reign with him. The good news of restitution and resurrection is not understood or recognized by many Christians, for they mistakenly look for a physical return instead of spiritual. They also equate all the dead (except extreme wicked) to be in Heaven, while people enjoy Kingdom conditions on earth.

The Prophet Isaiah prophesied:

> *"And in that day shall ye say, Praise the LORD, call upon his name, declare his doings among the people, make mention that his name is exalted."*—Isaiah 12:4

The Prophet Zephaniah wrote

> *"For then will I turn to the people a pure language, that they may all call upon the name of the LORD, to serve him with one consent."*—Zephaniah 3:9

And the apostle Paul wrote to brethren at Rome:

> *"For whosoever shall call upon the name of the Lord shall be saved."* —Romans 10:13

Thus, the call for repentance and learning of righteousness and justice in Jesus the Christ is to increase throughout the Millennium, during which people will become aware that repentance comes first and then learning and practicing righteousness and justice as Jesus gave example, which brings life. Why is this suggested? It is because various prophesy as in the Gospel of Matthew. There, Jesus speaks of both the Gospel and the Millennial Age:

> *"Another parable he put forth unto them, saying, The Kingdom of Heaven is like to a grain of mustard seed* (the Gospel), *which a man* (Jesus the Christ) *took, and sowed in his field* (the World): *which indeed is the least of all seeds: but when it is grown* (during the Gospel Age and restitution), *it is* (becomes) *the greatest among herbs, and becomes a tree* (Kingdom of God), *so that the birds of the air* (claimants of God's will) *come and lodge in the branches* (denominations) *thereof."*—Matthew 13:31–32

The character of God's Kingdom is built upon liberty, justice, righteousness, prosperity, peace, respect, love, mercy, and so on, that reflects from the hearts of countless numbers of people even as the forces of evil through violence, hate, fear, restriction, and extremism of religious and political ideology diminish as truth, righteousness, justice, liberty, and love limits their evil presence throughout the earth. The struggle for righteousness and justice is unstoppable; it often involves the forces of evil destroying other forces of evil, such as the ideology of communism defeating the ideology of fascism, which, in turn, is defeated by the ideology of democracy, which counters greed with attitudes that encourage justice and prosperity for all; thus the Kingdom of our Lord grows. As our Lord said:

> *"And if Satan (evil, Devil, Serpent, or Dragon) casts out Satan* (evil, Devil, Serpent, or Dragon), *he is divided against himself; how then shall his* (evil) *kingdom stand?"*—Matthew 12:26

The worldwide changes going on are initial results of the seventh message indicating the spiritual presence of Jesus the Christ. In Revelation, we read:

"But in the days of the voice of the seventh angel (message of truth, liberty, righteousness, justice, mercy, peace, and the like, are signs of the Lord's presence to establish his Kingdom), when he shall begin to sound, the mystery of God should be finished, as he hath declared to his servants the prophets."—Revelation 10:7

Thus, truth, justice, and righteousness are confronting evil in its many facets, and wherever it takes place and is recognized, doers of evil are punished or bound by the spirit of justice, righteousness, and truth. This involves judgment under troublous times that brings change in nations, which is often recognized by length of time of the nation's leadership.

The question then is, how can this scenario be applied to the day we live in or to the future while there is still much evil being active in the world? The answer would be that, as the first advent of our Lord required specific religious and political conditions to be ripe for him to serve and die according to prophecy and to give his life as a ransom for Adam (which includes all born in Adam), so at his second advent, being of his spirit, the conditions are ripe in political, religious, financial, and social conditions (the four winds) of Matthew:

"And he shall send his angels (messages) *with a great sound of a trumpet, and they shall gather together his elect* (chosen Church) *from the four winds, from one end of heaven* (religion) *to the other."*—Matthew 24:31

Also written in Revelation:

"And after these things I saw four angels (messages) standing on the four corners (supports) of the earth (society), holding (restraining) the four winds (religion, financial, social, and political powers) of the earth (society), that the wind

should not blow (harm) on the earth (society), nor on the sea (troubled people), nor on any tree (the faithful). Revelation 7:1

The gradually changing conditions bring forth God's Kingdom in power and glory with increasing trial and judgment under righteousness, justice, truth, mercy, and love. The "heaven" in the above scripture is interpreted as referring to "religion" because people visualize the spiritual aspect of life with a religious organization or the local church, which they perceive as a spiritual contact between them selves and their Creator.

The apostle John wrote:

"And I heard a loud voice (message) saying in heaven (religion), Now is come (second advent or spiritual presence) salvation, and strength, and the kingdom of our God, and the (spiritual) power of his Christ." —Revelation 12:10

Paul in Acts said:

"Be it known therefore unto you, that the salvation of God (message of Jesus the Christ) is sent unto the Gentiles, and [that] they will hear it."—Acts 28:28

In his letter to the brethren in Rome Paul wrote:

"For I am not ashamed of the gospel of Christ; for it is the power of God unto salvation to every one that believeth; to the Jew first, and also to the Greek (Gentiles)."—Romans 1:16

(For billions of people, the resurrection will be their first opportunity to hear and believe.)

In 1 Thessalonians:

> *"For God hath not appointed us (the chosen and the faithful) to wrath (destruction), but to obtain salvation by our Lord Jesus Christ (at the resurrection)."* —1 Thessalonians 5:9

And in Titus:

> *"For God's mercy has appeared with salvation (through Jesus the Christ) <u>for all men</u>."*—Titus 2:11; Gspd.

In Hebrews, we read:

> *"And being made perfect, he became the author of eternal salvation unto all them that obey him."*—Hebrews 5:9

And in Jude:

> *"Beloved, when I gave all diligence to write unto you of <u>the common salvation</u>," (through Jesus the Christ)* —Jude 1:3

Jesus the Christ said:

> *"I am the way, the truth, and the life: <u>no man comes unto the Father, but by me.</u>"*—John 14:6

Peter is quoted in Acts:

> *"Neither is there salvation in any other: for <u>there is none other name under heaven given among men, whereby we must be saved.</u>"*—Acts 4:12

The above scriptures are clear that, in order to hear that they have a Redeemer and an opportunity for salvation, billions of the dead must be resurrected. Jesus said, "The truth shall make you free." The spirit of truth involves hearing, reasoning, and doing what is good and acceptable in God's sight. Thus, hearing and reasoning in the spirit of truth brings to light the errors of traditional doctrine, which is of men, not of the Lord. For example, traditional teachings such as eternal torment and immortality of the soul developed during dark periods of Jewish and Christian history and were devised through ignorance, fearful imaginations, and restrictive oppression. Why then, upon understanding the glorious truth of the love of God, which offers salvation to all under righteous conditions through Jesus the Christ, would anyone continue to support doctrine and rules that were built under superstition, fear, and traditions of dark (ignorant) periods of history?

The knowledge and truth of God's purpose in Jesus the Christ may be pictured like a stream that swells into a river as it flows towards the sea. It is as a river filled with enlightenment and hope and, according to the picture language of prophecy, grows wider and deeper, a prophetic picture from thousands of years ago by men, filled with the Spirit of God, which Jesus the Christ described to John as a restoration to that which was lost in the Garden of Eden because of Adam's sin.

> *"And he said unto me, It is done. I am Alpha and Omega, the beginning and the end. I will give unto him that is thirsty of the fountain of the water of life freely."*—Revelation 21:6

> *"For the earth shall be filled with the knowledge of the glory of the LORD, as the waters cover the sea."*—Habakkuk 2:14

This fountain of knowledge and truth in Jesus the Christ is to bring life to all who drink of it as the Kingdom of God grows during "the restitution of all things." But, as Peter said of Jesus, that the calling out for his name must take place first during the Gospel Age:

> *"Whom the heaven (religion) <u>must receive until the times of restitution of all things</u>."*—Acts 3:21

The above verse speaks of the end of the Gospel Age.

The apostles understood that the spirit of truth is not a being or persona but the expression and resulting action of the heart of righteousness, justice, integrity, honesty, and fidelity. This spirit of truth flowed from Jesus to the apostles; thus their spiritual eyes were opened to the objective and loving will of God. The apostles' spiritual discernment and zeal brought further revelation as to what Jesus taught. The following scriptures show this, although, in the first verse, the translator uses "he" rather than "it," giving the impression that the spirit of truth is a spirit being.

Jesus the Christ said:

> *"How be it when he* (it)*, the Spirit of truth, is come, he* (it) *will guide you into all truth: for he* (it) *shall not speak of himself* (itself)*; but whatsoever he* (it) *shall hear, [that] shall he* (it) *speak: and he* (spirit of truth) *will show* (reveal to) *you things to come."*—John 16:13

Paul wrote:

> *"But we are bound to give thanks always to God for you, brethren beloved of the Lord, because God hath from the beginning chosen you to salvation through sanctification*

of the Spirit and belief of the truth."—2 Thessalonians 2:13

"We are of God: whoever knows God listens to us; he who is not of God does not listen to us. By this we know the spirit of truth, and the spirit of error." —1 John 4:6; RSV

"By this (love for one another) we know that we abide in him and he in us, because he has given us of his spirit."—1 John 4:13; RSV

*"In this is love perfected with us, that we may have confidence in the Day of Judgment, because as he is **(of the spirit)** so are we in this world."*—1 John 4:17; RSV

As God's Kingdom on earth (Judgment Day, Millennium, Times of Restitution, and the Lord's second coming or spiritual presence) becomes more obvious, the spirit of wickedness or evil (Satan, Devil, Dragon, or Serpent) is increasingly replaced by the spirit of God's love and mercy as Jesus and the apostles promised. This is an understanding of God's Word that is summarized in the Gospel of John:

"For God so loved the world, that he gave his Son, the only begotten, that everyone believing into him may not perish, but obtain Ionian (eternal) life. For God sent not his Son into the world that he (Jesus the Christ) might judge the world; but that the world through him (Jesus the Christ) might be saved. He believing into him is not judged; but he not believing is judged already, because he has not believed unto the name of the only begotten Son of God. And this is the judgment, that the light (truth in Jesus the Christ) has come into the world, and men loved the darkness (ignorance) rather than light (truth), for their

works were evil. For every one that does evil hates the light (truth), and comes not to the light (truth), that his works may not be detected. But he who hears the truth (righteousness and justice) comes to the light (truth), so that his works may be manifested, that they have been done in God."—John 3:16–21, Diaglott

The above Scriptures verify that God's objective has been a calling out for His Name during the Gospel Age, to chose those faithful who follow His son from under evil conditions, while the rest of mankind are given opportunity for life upon earth under the spiritual, righteous reign of Jesus the Christ and his Church, the faithful, chosen from the Gospel Age.

GOD'S LOVING PLAN

There are many scriptures throughout the Bible affirming the love of God through Jesus the Christ for all mankind, but why has God allowed billions of people to live and die without hearing of Jesus the Christ? The answer is that God has prepared the Judgment Day (restitution and resurrection) as a time of opportunity for all people, including those who never heard and the many who heard but did not understand what God's saving grace in Jesus the Christ means. The approximately thousand-year Judgment Day is to give everyone full opportunity to hear under provision of fair judgment with beneficial, merciful, righteous, and just conditions.

The following Scriptures have been mentioned before in this book. Some scripture is used a number of times when it relates to various topics or what was prophesied. For example, in the Revelation of John we are shown a sequential, symbolic picture of the restraint of evil, followed by the end of evil. I will add words to interpret in harmony with the Kingdom of God, under the spiritual direction of His son, Jesus the Christ.

John wrote down the message the Lord gave him:

"And I saw an angel (message) *come down from heaven* (religion), *having the key* (knowledge) *of the bottomless pit* (chasm great depth) *and a great chain* (restraint) *in his hand* (righteousness, justice, truth, etc.). *And he laid hold on the dragon* (evil), *that old serpent* (evil), *which is the devil* (evil), *and Satan* (evil), *and bound him* (restricted evil) (during) *a thousand years.*

And cast him (evil) *into the bottomless pit* (chasm great depth), *and shut (*restricted*) him* (evil*) up, and set a seal* (not desirable) *upon him* (evil), *that he* (evil) *should deceive the nations no more, till the thousand years should be fulfilled: and after that he* (evil) *must be loosed a little season. And I saw thrones* (power), *and they* (the chosen or Church) *sat upon them, and judgment was given unto them: and [I saw] the souls* (the Church) *of them that were beheaded* (Jesus the Christ is their head) *for the witness of Jesus, and for the word of God, and which had not worshipped the beast* (religious system), *neither his* (its) *image* (systems patterned after the beast), *neither had received [his]* (its) *mark* (teachings) *upon their foreheads (minds), or in their hands* (physical or financial support to the systems)*; and they* (the chosen or Church) *lived and reigned with Christ a thousand years.* <u>*But the rest of the dead lived not again until the thousand years were finished.*</u>1 *This [is] the first resurrection* (the chosen from the Gospel Age). *Blessed and holy [is] he* (the chosen or Church) *that hath part in the first resurrection: on such the second death hath no power, but they shall be priests of God and of Christ, and shall reign with him a thousand years. And when the thousand years are expired, Satan* (Devil, Serpent, Dragon, or evil*) shall be loosed out of his* (its) *prison* (chasm).*"* —Revelation 20:1–7

The underlined part of the prophecy (v. 5) that reads "the rest of the dead lived not again until the thousand years are finished" is not in the oldest Greek manuscripts and is considered an interpolation by many scholars; it appears to have been added to support a viewpoint but, instead, creates confusion. The reason for quoting a large amount of the message is that its context presents the plan of God.

Today the world is experiencing the first stage of our Lord's presence in the spirit, for the Bible tells us he gave his flesh for the world; thus he is no longer flesh. The chosen and faithful are also raised in the spirit to be like him—that is, of the spirit. The apostle John tells us that, during the restitution period of approximately a thousand years, which is the Kingdom of God under the spiritual reign of Jesus the Christ and his Church, people will be raised from the dead, and evil (Satan, Devil, Dragon, or Serpent) will be bound or restricted.

The first few centuries of change into the Kingdom brings forth times of war, civil strife, and struggles for truth, justice, and righteousness, a process in the hearts of men that coincides with inventions, prosperity, and recessions. Thus, societies will increasingly learn and prosper in mental and physical health over decades of healing and improvement with many people progressing in truth, righteousness, and justice. The reprobates do not make progress.

It is reasonable that the resurrection of the dead will begin after most people have been progressing up the highway of holiness. It also is reasonable that each generation will be called from the grave in opposite sequence to going into the grave, whereupon, having been resurrected, those with willing hearts will learn of God's love and purpose in Jesus the Christ and endeavor to take their place in a world in which truth, peace, righteousness, and justice rule. It may seem unbelievable to some readers that all the dead will be raised from the grave, but this is the fundamental message of the Bible, the hope and promise of restoration to life to all who have lived because Jesus the Christ gave his life as a ransom for Adam and thus, because Adam disobeyed God before he had children, everyone born is covered by the ransom of the Messiah, Jesus the Christ.

In Acts 3, Peter healed a lame man, which illustrates how through the spirit, the healing and restoration will take place to many people during restitution of all things as conditions warrant. (Acts 3:21).

The world is beginning to experience the first phase, which is the restoring of body and mind to health of those willing who seek righteousness, justice, peace, and health. The scriptures tell us that those who do not care or are not interested in improving life for self and others will not advance in attaining life. As conditions progressively improve, the Scriptures imply that a coming phase will see the resurrection of the dead. The green movement will also become worldwide with people fulfilling the command of our Creator, when he told Adam and Eve in Genesis:

> *"And God blessed them, and God said unto them, Be fruitful, and multiply, <u>and replenish the earth, and subdue it</u>."*—Genesis 1:28

But, it is during the kingdom, that the faithful chosen from the Gospel Age are to reign with the Lord.. John prophesied of this in Revelation:

> *"And I saw thrones (authority), and they sat upon them, and judgment was given unto them: and [I saw] the souls (lives) of them that were beheaded (consecrated, faithful)*

for the witness of Jesus, and for the word of God, (truth).
—Revelation 20:4

"Them that were beheaded" (Jesus is their head) as John speaks of, refers to the Church, those faithful to the truth of Jesus the Christ during the Gospel Age, who reign with him in the Kingdom. They, through the spirit, have shown themselves faithful under the reign of evil and are not subject to the second death. They have made Jesus the Christ their head, serving God in spirit and truth.

At the end of God's Kingdom under Jesus the Christ, having learned under righteous conditions during the (approximately) one thousand years of restitution, people brought to perfection in mind and body (reprobates having been destroyed) will experience a final test. God will again allow evil (Satan, Devil, Serpent, or Dragon) to take root in the hearts of people through temptation, letting lust and selfishness rule as before, but it will be a short period, in which many will fail the advice of the apostle Paul to the Thessalonians to:

"Abstain from all appearance of evil." —1 Thessalonians 5:22

The final test of evil (Satan, Devil, Serpent, or Dragon) is when it is allowed or let loose to reveal any evil in the hearts of those who would desire to institute a previous-type rule, in which the evils of self-centeredness and greed dominate. People who manifest or encourage any form of previous evil activity rather than support the Kingdom of Jesus the Christ during that short trial period are to be destroyed by the second death, while those remaining faithful in righteousness, justice, and love of God through Jesus the Christ will continue to live eternally upon earth without fear, sickness, evil, or death..

They will fully understand the difference between good and evil and thus will never desire evil over paradise conditions upon the new earth (society) through Adam's sin. We are told in Revelation of the destruction of evil (Satan, Devil, Serpent, or Dragon), for John writes:

> *"And the devil (Satan, Serpent, Dragon, or evil) that deceived them (willing wicked) was cast into the lake of fire and brimstone (total destruction), where the beast (religious system) and the false prophet (similar systems) [are], and shall be tormented (sadly remembered) day and night for ever and ever."* —Revelation 20:10

This statement describes, in symbolic terms, that evil (Satan, Devil, Serpent, or Dragon) is eliminated or abolished. Evil will be remembered as a stressful, terrifying, and destructive experience, not ever to be desired or acted upon again. Societies throughout the earth will then be in full harmony with the character of God. The Kingdom of God under Jesus the Christ will bless every willing heart with the reality of paradise conditions upon earth that Jesus told his followers to pray for:

> *"Thy Kingdom come, Thy will be done in earth, as [it is] in Heaven."* —Matthew 6:10

Having experienced evil (Satan, Devil, Serpent, or Dragon) in an evil, stressful, destructive world, people will enjoy the advantageous, peaceful conditions of the Kingdom under the righteous, spiritual rule of Jesus and his Church. All who appreciate life will have learned to love God and one another and no longer allow the temptation of evil (Satan, Devil, Serpent, or Dragon) to have any part in their lives. They will know of evil but will not desire or commit evil. God's statement in the Garden of Eden will then be fulfilled in its entirety:

"And the LORD God said, Behold, the man is become 'as one of us,' to know good and evil (Satan, Devil, Serpent, or Dragon)."—Genesis 3:22

Thus, each person will appreciate his or her responsibility to refrain from evil behavior in word and to live life through truth in Jesus the Christ.

The apostle John wrote:

"Jesus said unto him, I am the way, the truth, and the life: no man comes unto the Father, but by me."—John 14:6

Everyone chosen to serve with the Lord, have faithfully trusted in Jesus the Christ's atoning blood in spirit and truth during the Gospel Age receive a crown of life—immortality—while the rest of mankind, including those not chosen to reign with the Lord, experience judgment at their resurrection during restitution in the Kingdom of Jesus the Christ. In due time, any person not willing to learn and apply the love and righteousness of Jesus the Christ in their lives are destroyed by the second death.

Thus, all the children of Adam, having been born and shaped in sin, will have the opportunity to learn to love God and one another through the grace of God and the merit of Jesus the Christ, their Redeemer. There will be people, unmotivated by the spirit of love and righteousness, who willingly continue to practice evil during the time of restitution and resurrection; they will bring their own destruction with the second death. Four verses in Revelation speak of the second death.

Revelation 2:11 and Revelation 20:14 mention it, but it is the following two verses that refer to who will not and who will be subject to the second death. John, in the spirit, wrote:

> *"Blessed and holy [is] he that hath part in the first resurrection (the chosen or Church): on such the second death hath no power, but they shall be priests of God and of Christ, and shall reign with him a thousand years."*
> —Revelation 20:6

And:

> *"But the fearful* (RSV: cowardly), *and unbelieving, and the abominable, and murderers, and whoremongers, and sorcerers, and idolaters, and all liars, shall have their part in the lake which burns with fire and brimstone* (everlasting destruction)*: which is the second death.* "—Revelation 21:8

God has created the human family with what is considered "free will," the ability to choose between what is often stated as right and wrong or between righteousness and evil. Thus, as the knowledge of the Lord grows during the blessings of restitution and the willing learn righteousness as the Kingdom of God develops in power and glory, evil will continue to have a drawing power to those who have allowed their character (free will) to develop around selfishness and greed, not caring about serving God or fellow man in spirit and truth.

The above verse; Revelation 21:8, is very clear as to who is to be subject to the second death: it is those continuing in evil activity who will be destroyed, because they will have freely chosen to practice evil even as righteousness, justice, mercy, love, and patience are all around them. Their free will allows them to choose the road paved with evil that leads to destruction.

An article that helps us understand man's freedom to choose is titled "Free Will," and appeared in the January/February 2007 issue of the *Herald of Christ's Kingdom*, which quoted

Maimonides (Moses Ben Maimon, 1135–1204, Spanish-born Jewish philosopher and physician), who, in his Mishneh Torah (Laws of Repentance), wrote:

> "Free will is bestowed on every human being. If one desires to turn towards the good way and be righteous, he has the power to do so. If one wishes to turn towards the evil way and be wicked, he is at liberty to do so. ... Man, of himself and by the exercise of his own intelligence and reason, knows what is good and what is evil, and there is none who can prevent him from doing that which is good or that which is evil. Accordingly it follows that it is the sinner who has inflicted injury on himself and he should weep for, and bewail what he has done to his soul (life)—how he has mistreated it.
>
> If God had decreed that a person should be either righteous or wicked, ... or if there were some force inherent in his nature which irresistibly drew him to a particular course, ... how could the Almighty have charged us through the prophets: "Do this and do not do that, improve your ways, do not follow your wicked impulses," when, from the beginning of his existence his destiny had already been decreed, or his innate constitution irresistibly drew him to that from which he could not set himself free. By what right or justice could God punish the wicked or reward the righteous?"

Thus, centuries ago, the concept of every person having 'free will' was questioned, for many people thought there was an evil spirit being that everybody was subject to.

Not too long ago, the ability to learn righteousness was addressed by motivational teacher, trainer, and columnist Zig Zigler, who made a statement that can help anyone to be a better person. He wrote:

> "We can choose what we put into our minds, in most cases, and if we choose to put something that's good, clean, and positive into our minds, doesn't it make sense that our attitude will be better? Your attitude has a big impact—either positive or negative—on every day of your life. If you don't think every day is a good day, just try missing one! After all, today is the day the Lord has made, therefore we will rejoice and be glad in it."

Mr. Zigler's comments point to fundamental requirements for eternal life: it is choosing to have virtuous, positive thoughts that display a thankful heart for God's love through Jesus the Christ's redeeming sacrifice. This attitude is pleasing to God and a blessing to others and essential for everyone expecting to enjoy God's Heavenly Kingdom upon earth instituted under Jesus the Christ and his Church, as informed in the following scriptures:

> *"And the LORD said, I have pardoned according to thy word: But [as]truly [as] I live, all the earth shall be filled with the glory of the LORD."*—Numbers 14:20–21

> *"And the glory of the LORD shall be revealed, and all flesh shall see [it]together: for the mouth of the LORD hath spoken [it]."*—Isaiah 40:5

> *"For the earth shall be filled with the knowledge of the glory of the LORD, as the waters cover the sea."*—Habakkuk 2:14

"And the LORD shall be king over all the earth: in that day shall there be one LORD, and his name one." —Zechariah 14:9 (error of a triune god will be gone)

"Every valley shall be filled, and every mountain (government) and hill (organization) shall be brought low; and the crooked (errors of doctrine) shall be made straight, and the rough ways (traditions, rituals) [shall be] made smooth; and all flesh (willing minds) shall see the salvation of God."—Luke 3:5–6

Most people will not allow evil (Satan, the Devil, Serpent, or Dragon) to govern their minds again, for their knowledge of and experience with evil in the past will be strong, sad memories of Satan *(evil, the Devil, Dragon, or Serpent)*, a stressful life in the past, as the following scriptures testify:

"In that day (during restitution or the Kingdom) the LORD with his sore and great and strong sword (truth in Jesus the Christ) shall punish (destroy) Leviathan the piercing serpent (evil, Satan, the Devil, or Dragon), even Leviathan that crooked serpent (evil, Satan, the Devil, or Dragon); and he (truth) shall slay (destroy, eliminate) the dragon (Satan, the Devil, Serpent, or evil) that [is] in the sea (society)."—Isaiah 27:1

"And the God of peace shall bruise (destroy) *Satan* (Devil, Serpent, Dragon, or evil) *under your feet* (activities) *shortly* (short time compared with eternity).*"* —Romans 16:20

"And he (it, the spirit of God in the hearts of men) *laid hold on the dragon* (evil), *that old serpent* (evil), *which is the devil* (evil), *and Satan* (evil), *and bound* (restrained)

> *him* (evil, Devil, Satan, Serpent, or Dragon) (during) *a thousand years."*—Revelation 20:2

> *"And the devil* (Satan, Serpent, Dragon, or evil) *that deceived them was cast into the lake of fire and brimstone* (eternal destruction), *where the beast* (religious system) *and the false prophet* (similar erring systems) *[are], and shall be tormented* (evil "existence sadly remembered) *day and night for ever and ever..* —Revelation 20:10

> *"And God (through truth in Jesus the Christ) shall wipe away all tears from their eyes; and there shall be no more death, neither sorrow, nor crying, neither shall there be any more pain: for the former things (evil conditions) are passed away."*—Revelation 21:4

The Bible presents God's promise of a new heaven (truth in religion) and a new earth (just society) wherein dwells righteousness, in which evil (Satan, the Devil, Serpent, or Dragon) is no longer desired or practiced. As mentioned before, the words of Peter thrill our hearts with joyful expectation as the Kingdom of our Lord and Savior Jesus the Christ increases as restitution blessings lead willing hearts away from greed and the destructiveness of evil (Satan, the Devil, Serpent, or Dragon).

Peter, looking for that day, wrote:

> *"Repent ye therefore, and be converted, that your sins may be blotted out, when the times of refreshing (restitution) shall come from the presence of the LORD. And he shall send Jesus Christ (spiritual presence), which before was preached unto you, whom the heaven (religion) must receive (preach) until the times of restitution of all things,*

which God hath spoken by the mouth of all his holy prophets since the world began." —Acts 3:19–21

Over a century ago, the author of *"The Divine Plan of the Ages"*, wrote:

> Peter, our Lord, and all the prophets since the world began, declare that the human race is to be restored to that glorious perfection, and is again to have dominion over the earth, as its representative, Adam, had. It is this portion that God has elected to give to the human race. And what a glorious portion! Close your eyes for a moment to the scenes of misery and woe, degradation and sorrow that yet prevail on account of sin, and picture before your mental vision the glory of the perfect earth. Not a stain of sin mars the harmony and peace of a perfect society; not a bitter thought, not an unkind look or word; love, welling up from every heart, meets a kindred response in every other heart, and benevolence marks every act.
>
> There, sickness shall be no more, not an ache nor a pain, nor any evidence of decay—not even the fear of such things. Think of all the pictures of comparative health and beauty of human form and feature that you have ever seen, and know that perfect humanity will be of still surpassing loveliness. The inward purity and mental and moral perfection will stamp and glorify every radiant countenance. Such will earth's society be; and weeping bereaved ones will have their tears all wiped away, when thus they realize the resurrection work complete. —Revelation 21:4

The harmonious, reasonable interpretations of prophecy and truth about evil (Satan, the Devil, Serpent, or Dragon) brought forth in this book will hopefully have its part in destroying Dark-Age doctrines that have held millions in spiritual ignorance and bondage over the centuries. The spiritual presence or return of Jesus the Christ—not his bodily return—is shedding light (truth) on the fact that people are living souls: we do not have a soul; this aspect alone eliminates the fear factor of the eternal torment called hell for the wicked and the ignorant. Death is elimination of life, not transition to another condition. As with any book, the reader must choose what is truth and what is error or evil, as the apostle Paul wrote in Philippians:

> *"Finally, brethren, whatsoever things are true, whatsoever things [are] honest, whatsoever things [are] just, whatsoever things [are] pure, whatsoever things [are] lovely, whatsoever things [are] of good report; if [there be] any virtue, and if [there be] any praise, think on these things."* —Philippians 4:8

The Gospel or Good News is not a message of eternal torment or of an evil spirit being causing or leading people into evil, nor is the Judgment Day a short period of time in which billions of immortal souls are sent to either bliss or blisters. We see instead that the love and knowledge of God through Jesus the Christ is in the process of covering the earth in the present day.

Seeing we are in the beginning stage of the Lord's Kingdom, his spiritual reign upon earth of approximately a thousand years, in which sin and evil (Satan, Devil, Serpent, or Dragon) are examined in the light of truth and judged; slowly but surely evil is eliminated through knowledge of righteousness, justice and etc., so that in due time, the many generations of the dead can be resurrected to share in a fair trial, as prophesied by Isaiah and our Lord:

"There shall be no more thence an infant of days, nor an old man that hath not filled his days: for the child shall die an hundred years old; but the sinner [being] an hundred years old shall be accursed (second death).   "—Isaiah 65:20

"In that day the LORD with his sore and great and strong sword (the truth) *shall punish Leviathan* (evil) *the piercing serpent* (evil), *even Leviathan* (evil) *that crooked serpent* (evil) *and he shall slay the dragon* (evil) *that [is in the sea* (society).*"*—Isaiah 27:1

"Marvel not at this: for the hour is coming, in the which all that are in the graves shall hear his voice and shall come forth; they that have done good (Church or chosen), *unto the resurrection of life* (immortality)*; and they that have done evil* (Satan, Devil, Serpent, or Dragon) (rest of mankind), *unto the resurrection of judgment."*—John 5:28–29

Those continuing in wickedness are to be destroyed, and our Redeemer then turns the new world, wherein dwells righteousness, justice, mercy, and love, over to the Father:

"And when all things shall be subdued unto him, then shall the Son also himself (Jesus the Christ) be subject unto Him (God the Father) that (who) put all things under him (Jesus the Christ), that God may be all in all." —1 Corinthians 15:28

"That in the ages to come he might show the exceeding riches of his grace in [his] kindness toward us through Christ Jesus."—Ephesians 2:7

Thus, Satan Devil, Serpent, Dragon, or evil will no longer exist, except in the memories of past evil days.

"Our Lord said:

> "*So likewise ye, <u>when ye see these things come to pass, know ye that the Kingdom of God is nigh at hand.</u>*"—
> Luke 21:31

Therefore, we understand that the Kingdom of Jesus the Christ is approximately a thousand years or ten centuries of progressive learning and improvement, wherein the dead, in God's due time, are raised to experience a fair trial under the rule of justice and righteousness. The Kingdom of Jesus the Christ is a revelation in progress all around us:

Increasing numbers of people are learning the fundamentals of righteousness and justice even as other people, ignoring law and directives, continue in wickedness and fail to perceive that increasing knowledge within societies are improving living conditions, unmistakable signs that the Kingdom of God is at work. It is the characteristics or spirit of God of righteousness, wisdom, love, and power working in hearts that manifest compassion, mercy, service, and care, which signal the Kingdom is growing through the spiritual presence (return) of Jesus the Christ upon this earth.

Over the years, the desire to do evil, which is historically referred to as Satan, the Devil, Serpent, or Dragon, will fade from the hearts of willing people who learn in the spirit of our Creator of truth, righteousness, justice, love, and mercy that envelops the earth. As Jesus our Lord said: "Seek ye first the Kingdom of God." We do this in faith and love of truth, righteousness, justice, hope, and trust that the Kingdom of Jesus the Christ is to bless all willing hearts upon earth. As God has used men to prophecy in His name, so also, along physical means, the knowledge of improving physical and mental health comes forth from the laboratories of knowledge that enhances and extends life to those willing to apply the knowledge in their lives. Thus, knowledge of God's will and purpose; knowledge of ways to improve and extend quality of life; knowledge in self-discipline; and desire to follow righteousness, justice, love, and mercy are all part in gradually removing desire of lust or evil from the hearts of the willing.

Today, especially in the developed countries, knowledge is all over the news media on how to improve health, physically, mentally, and spiritually, though some of it is questionable as to what is truth or what is beneficial. But, the vision Scriptures give us depicts the transition and function of conditions upon earth with people living under gradually changing conditions in which the Kingdom of Jesus the Christ grows through troubling and stressful, but improving, conditions. Nevertheless, the continuously increasing knowledge replaces evil with righteousness, justice, love, mercy, compassion, and so forth, which continuing for centuries will achieve the goal our Creator is waiting for: His Kingdom upon earth wherein dwells righteousness, as prophesied below:

> *"Who gave himself a ransom for all, <u>to be testified in due time</u>."*—1 Timothy 2:6

> *"<u>Thy kingdom [is] an everlasting kingdom</u>, and thy dominion [endures] throughout all generations."*—Psalms 145:13

> *"<u>The LORD preserves all them that love him: but all the wicked will he destroy</u>."*—Psalm: 145:20

"And then shall that wicked be revealed, whom the Lord shall consume with the spirit of his mouth (truth*), and shall destroy with the brightness of his coming* (spiritual presence)*."*—2 Thessalonians 2:8

"Thy kingdom [is] an everlasting (eternal) *kingdom, and thy dominion [endures] throughout all generations* (forever)*."*—Daniel 7:18

"But the saints (chosen from Gospel Age) of the most High shall take the kingdom, and possess the kingdom for ever, even for ever and ever."—Matthew 4:17

"From that time Jesus began to preach, and to say, repent: for the kingdom of heaven is at hand." —Matthew 13:41:

"The Son of man shall send forth his angels (message or messengers)*, and they shall gather out of his kingdom all things that offend, and them which do iniquity"* —Mark 1:15

"And saying; the time is fulfilled, and the kingdom of God is at hand (in spirit and truth)*: repent ye, and believe the gospel."*—Luke 13:29

"And they (who seek righteousness and justice) shall come from the east, and [from] the west, and from the north, and [from] the south, and shall sit down in the kingdom of God."—1 Corinthians 15:24:

"Then [cometh] the end (of Judgment day, Millennium, Kingdom, Restitution) *when he* (Jesus the Christ) *shall have delivered up the kingdom to God, even the*

Father; when he shall have put down all (evil) *rule and all authority and power.*"—1 Corinthians 15:24

The interpretations and projections made in this book are not meant to be the ultimate in fine-tuning the message of the Gospel or of prophecy, but rather a means to move the reader forward in understanding God's Word in its positive light. A major point emphasized is how the changes upon this earth are ushering in the Kingdom of the Lord, which becomes more apparent as righteousness, justice, love, and mercy increase, even as evil (Satan, Devil, Serpent, or Dragon) manifested by greed, hate, jealousy, fear, and etc. are recognized and decrease in the hearts of people with hearing ears.

The Word of God is vibrant and alive with promises of life upon earth under conditions of peace, kindness, love, righteousness, justice, and mercy, the end result of mankind's deliverance from evils of sin and death, a time when every person born upon earth experiences a fair and just trial in which the willing learn to live in our Lord's Kingdom are given life by manifesting the spirit of God upon this earth This is the good news of the Gospel; thus we are to be thankful to our Creator for His wonderful plan for mankind through Jesus the Christ and his Kingdom, of which there is increasing evidence that the spiritual presence of our Lord has and will bring many more marvelous changes to societies as the Lord's spirit leads the willing up the highway of health and holiness.

As the apostle John wrote in Revelation:

> "*And God (through His spirit) shall wipe away all tears from their eyes; and there shall be no more death, neither sorrow, nor crying, neither shall there be any more pain: for the former things (evil, Satan, Devil, Serpent, or Dragon) are passed away (gone).*" —Revelation 21:4

What a wonderful day that is coming for the world as the power of God through Jesus the Christ and his Church call each generation from the grave to learn righteousness and justice in preparation for life without sin, sickness, or death under paradise conditions with love and peace radiating from every heart. The memories of trials under fear, ignorance, and evil will remind all those attaining life that evil thoughts are not to be manifested in harm to others or self.

With these wonderful prospects from the Bible, we are to look for a great future for us, our loved ones, and everyone willing to learn righteousness, justice, mercy, the spirit of the Lord.

To God be the glory in the name of our Redeemer, Jesus the Christ, for His justice, love, and mercy endures forever.

Sources of information

References

P 37 --------- Rossell Hope Robbins-'Encyclopedia of Witchcraft & Demonology'.

P 44 --------- Mortimer F. Adler, 'The Angels and Us'

P 47 --------- Steve Allen, "The Bible, Religion, & Morality'

P 56 -------- 'Plato', 'Laws'

P 56 --------- Dr. Reville

P 79 --------- The Grand Rapids Press ; "Evil Is in the Mind of the Beholder', Janet McConnaughey.

P 93,94 ------ 'The Bible Study Monthly' 'Tartarus' January/February 1985.

P 123-125 -- 'Harper's Study Bible (p. 1614) 'a footnote'

P 186,266 --- Charles T. Russell, 'The Divine Plan of the Ages' 315, 419

P 189-------- 'Asimov's Guide to the Bible' (Wings Books).

P 209--------- Forbes' 90th anniversary issue of May 7, 2007, title: 'The Inside-Out Web', 'Guts and Glory'.

P 294,250 --- Great Issues in Western Civilization; 'World History at a Glance'; Joseph Reither.

P 251--------- Free Inquiry magazine; October/November 2004, Gregory S. Paul, 'The Great Scandal,

P 258--------- Time magazine, May 6, 2002 issue, 'Criticism on Catholic Church', Andrew Sullivan,

P 268--------- The Art of Creative Thinking' Wilfred Peterson

P 292--------- Parade magazine, March 7, 1993, 'What's Really Going On' Carl Sagan

P 300--------- 'The Herald, News Views' Jan./Feb. 2000, "AD 1000: A World on the Brink of Apocalypse", , Richard Erdoes

P 302--------- 'True Believers': By Flora Lewis

P 303--------- The Washington Post; "Neuroscientists See; Center For Morality in the Brain."

P 304--------- The U.S. News & World Report, Nov. 20, 2000 "Seed of a Sociopath, Violence in the Brain?" By: Josh Fischman,

P 306--------- Bible Study Monthly, Jan./Feb.1998; "Time of Judgment"

P 326--------- Anger, Yours and Mine and What To Do About It" By: Richard Walters,

P 335 -------- 'The Grand Rapids Press' Rick Wilson--, 'Ghosts From the Nursery' By: Robin Karr-Morse

P 336 -------- Satan", published by Cornell University Press

P 340 -------- Coping With Anger" Rosen Publishing Group Inc By: Paul J. Gelinas

P 343 -------- The G.R. Press, Sept. 30, 2000,"Interest in Exorcism Rises in Conjunction with Re-release of Movie," By: Nancy Haught

P 355, 363 --- Bible Study Monthly, Jan./Feb. 2000, "The Saving
    364   Power of God!", July/Aug. 2000 "Restitution & Resurrection" & "Bible Teaching on Hell"; By D. Nadel.

P 367 -------- The Grand Rapids Press. "Devil, the Prince of Darkness." By; Tom Rademacher

P 370 -------- Parade magazine, Mar. 19, 2000; Cato Institute of Washington, DC. "Change since 1900".

P 371 -------- U.S. News & World Report (Jan. 14, 2002) Susan J. Blumenthal, M.D "Longer and Healthier Life."

P 372 -------- Irving Bluestone, International UAW, "Credo of the Labor Movement"

P 415 -------- Herald of Christ's Kingdom, Jan./Feb. 2007, "Free Will" By: Maimonides (Moses Ben Maimon, 1135-1204

P 416 -------- Zig Zigler: Motivational Speaker.

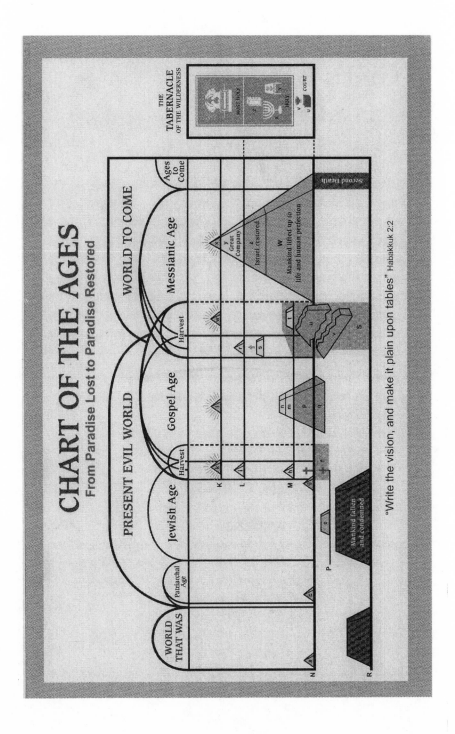

CHART OF THE AGES
From Paradise Lost to Paradise Restored

"Write the vision, and make it plain upon tables" Habakkuk 2:2

Manufactured By: RR Donnelley
Momence, IL USA
September, 2010